Culture, Institution, and Development in China

How does culture shape history, and history shape culture? This book answers this question by bringing readers on a fascinating journey through the evolution of Chinese culture, political and legal institutions, and "national character" of historical and contemporary China. It illustrates how "national character" evolves endogenously along with an institutional environment through the use of economic theories.

Recognizing the unique role of "personality" in violence and social order – important variables that contribute to successful economies, the book provides a meaningful take on "personality" from the "average personality" of a country's people. It analyzes the relationship between culture, institution, and "national character," providing gainful, interesting insights into the monumental transformation of China.

C. Simon Fan is a Professor of Economics at Lingnan University, Hong Kong.

T0371720

Routledge Studies in the Modern World Economy

For a complete list of titles in this series, please visit www.routledge.com.

Culture, Institution, and Development in China

The economics of national character

C. Simon Fan

Routledge
Taylor & Francis Group

LONDON AND NEW YORK

First published 2016
by Routledge

2 Park Square, Milton Park, Abingdon, Oxfordshire OX14 4RN
52 Vanderbilt Avenue, New York, NY 10017

*Routledge is an imprint of the Taylor & Francis Group,
an informa business*

First issued in paperback 2019

Copyright © 2016 C. Simon Fan

The right of C. Simon Fan to be identified as author of this work
has been asserted by him in accordance with sections 77 and 78
of the Copyright, Designs and Patents Act 1988.

All rights reserved. No part of this book may be reprinted or
reproduced or utilised in any form or by any electronic,
mechanical, or other means, now known or hereafter invented,
including photocopying and recording, or in any information
storage or retrieval system, without permission in writing from
the publishers.

Notice:
Product or corporate names may be trademarks or registered
trademarks, and are used only for identification and explanation
without intent to infringe.

British Library Cataloguing in Publication Data
A catalogue record for this book is available from the British Library

Library of Congress Cataloging-in-Publication Data
Names: Fan, C. Simon, author.
Title: Culture, institution, and development in China : the
   economics of national character / by C. Simon Fan.
Description: Abingdon, Oxon ; New York, NY : Routledge,
   2016. | Series: Routledge studies in the modern world
   economy ; 154 | Includes bibliographical references and index.
Identifiers: LCCN 2015039796 | ISBN 9781138185715 (hardback) |
   ISBN 9781315628707 (ebook)
Subjects: LCSH: National characteristics, Chinese. | China—
   Civilization—History. | China—History.
Classification: LCC DS721 .F267 2016 | DDC 951—dc23
LC record available at http://lccn.loc.gov/2015039796

ISBN: 978-1-138-18571-5 (hbk)
ISBN: 978-0-367-37464-8 (pbk)

Typeset in Galliard
by Apex CoVantage, LLC

To Yu, For Her Love

Contents

Tables

Preface

China is an enigma to many outside observers. On one hand, they are impressed at the exuberance of Chinese national pride in Olympic Games, and they are sometimes alarmed by the rising Chinese nationalism, which leads to the theory of "China threat." Also, as illustrated by the famous article about the "Tiger Mother" titled "Why Chinese Mothers Are Superior" in the *Wall Street Journal*, many Chinese parents feel proud that their Confucian culture enables them to enhance their children's educational attainment.

On the other hand, if a foreigner gets to know more about China, he may be puzzled that many Chinese often appear to hate their own culture. Some Chinese books severely criticized the Chinese culture, including *The Ugly Chinaman and the Crisis of Chinese Culture* by Bo-Yang (1985) and *I Don't Want to Be Chinese Again* by Chung (2007). These books are highly popular among Chinese readers. Bo-Yang's book was first published in 1985, and continues to rank among the top 10 bestselling books in Chinese communities even today; Chung's book was first published in November 2007 and has already been printed in 55 editions.

How do the Chinese people exactly judge their own culture? Why do they sometimes hate their own national character? How was the Confucian culture developed? How, if at all, has the Chinese national character evolved over time? This book aims to answer the questions like these and help uncover the myth about China.

Based on the "political Coase theorem," a Nobel Prize–winning contribution in economics, this book's basic tenet is that a "national character" is determined by material fundamentals that may be reflected in social, political, and economic dimensions. No matter whether it is judged today by contemporary standards as ugly or beautiful, cowardly or brave, a national character, defined as the average personality of a people, is an outcome of an optimization process undertaken by the people under a certain historical environment. When these material fundamentals change, a country's national character will change accordingly. The speed with which this change takes place also reflects the fundamental forces governing the initial and subsequent character.

In particular relevance to national character, the emphasis of valor in a culture is a double-edged sword. A strong social tendency to be violent creates more conflicts among people and increases the cost involved in maintaining a stable society. However, when a country faces an ongoing threat of foreign invasion, the toughness of its national character can be a major advantage that guarantees the combative capacity of its army. Thus, there is a tradeoff between these two aspects, and the best choice for a national character differs across the various economic and military environments. The people in ancient China faced severe threats from the nomadic tribes of the Mongolian steppe, which forced China to remain unified. A weak and submissive national character was the best choice for the ancient Chinese to decrease the cost of administering their large country. The Confucian culture developed in such circumstances, a culture that emphasized etiquette, loyalty, filial piety, and education.

The Chinese national character altered drastically during the period of continuous national humiliation from 1840 to 1945, and changed substantially under the communist rule since 1949. The repeated defeats by foreign powers since the Opium War led many Chinese to seek cultural reasons for China's military weakness. In the 1930s, the enormous trauma caused by the horrendous atrocities of the Japanese troops, such as mass-scale rape and murder, turned many Chinese into brave soldiers; the extremely difficult guerilla warfare conducted against the Japanese army made China's national character both brave and bellicose. This personality change and their hatred for the Japanese led the Chinese people to accept the communists, who had the greatest combative capacity, as their leaders.

The People's Republic of China was established on the bases of humiliation and pride. Contemporary Chinese culture in general, and Chinese national character in particular, is closely related to both the recent and ancient histories of China, which may help explain why the rule of the Chinese Communist Party remains stable. However, the social, political, and economic environments that China faces today are fundamentally different from those in ancient times or in World War II. Thus, Chinese people appear to be searching for a new culture that is most suitable to the contemporary environment and brings them more welfare. Developing this new culture is an ongoing process with no definite ending point.

For the past 30 years, China has constantly experienced major changes, not only in economic structures but also in its people's mentality and their perceptions of the rest of the world. China began to pursue an "open door" policy in 1978, when Chinese people were shocked that China was so poor in comparison with the Western world. This observation shattered many Chinese people's belief in communism, and even led some Chinese to have an "inferiority complex," which in turn even led some of them to blame Confucianism as the cause of the national humiliation that China experienced.

In 1988, a documentary film, *River Elegy* (*He-Shang*), was shown on China Central Television and blamed China's backwardness on Confucianism. According to Gifford (2008, p. 165), for example, the film criticizes the symbols of ancient Chinese culture, such as the Yellow River and Great Wall to make the statement that "the Chinese being a wonderful ancient people with a wonderful ancient culture was a big sham, and that the entire population needed to change."

While the film might reflect an "inferiority complex" for Chinese traditional culture and Chinese national character in the 1980s, more recently a "superiority complex" has begun to emerge among a fraction of the Chinese population.

With the continuous fast economic growth, China has become more and more important in the global economy and the politics of international affairs, which fueled the development of strong national pride and nationalism in China in recent years. For example, consider the following commentary from *The Washington Post*:[1]

> China's nationalism today is shaped by its pride in its history as well as its century of humiliation at the hands of the West and Japan. China expert Peter Hays Gries writes: "Chinese nationalists today find pride in stories about the superiority of China's '5000 years' of 'glorious civilization.'" This yearning for lost glory is accompanied by the story of victimization in the past, a narrative central to what being Chinese today means, says Gries.

Albert Einstein pointed out, "the whole of sciences is nothing more than the refinement of everyday thinking." This insightful statement explains well how this book was developed and written, which was based on the long journey of my personal and professional experiences. I was born in the chaotic time of "Cultural Revolution." I was instilled with the communist ideology and was taught in primary school that Confucius was a hypocritical evil man. I went to college in the 1980s, when Chinese intellectuals began to debate fiercely on the choice of the best culture for China, which I experienced vividly and strongly in university campus. I went to Brown University for my PhD study from 1989 to 1994, where I experienced the Western culture. Since 1994, I have taught at Lingnan University, Hong Kong, for over 20 years. The unfettered capitalism in Hong Kong generated possibly the freest media in the world, which constantly and sensationally reports the issues of pride and shame related to the Chinese culture and China. Also, in contrast to Mainland China, the Confucian culture maintains a strong presence in Hong Kong despite one and a half centuries' British colonization. The various cultural environments I experienced allowed me to observe vividly different cultures and mentality.

My main area of research is economics of social behaviors. My first book *Vanity Economics: An Economic Exploration of Sex, Marriage and Family* analyzes the role of "vanity," defined as social status and self-esteem, in social and economic behaviors. It argues that vanity is obtained by having a spouse and children with perceived "high-quality" values, and it demonstrates that vanity plays a crucial role in male–female relationships and intergenerational relationships. When I was about to finish writing this book, it suddenly occurred to me that national pride and nationalism can be regarded as a collective social status; namely, in an abstract theoretical sense, the study of national pride and nationalism also belongs to "vanity economics." This realization prompted me to analyze Chinese nationalism and Chinese history based on economic theories.

A deeper investigation into Chinese nationalism naturally led me to research the underlying Chinese culture. How was the Chinese culture formed and evolved? In thinking over this question, I was much inspired by the Nobel

Prize–winning contribution of Ostrom (1990). The political Coase theorem dictates that individuals tend to choose cultures and social customs that maximize social welfare in the long run. Ostrom (1990) demonstrates this theorem marvelously with numerous case studies, showing that in the management of common resources (e.g., forests, grazing lands), people can often design and implement a social norm that maximizes their welfare. In a similar vein, this book argues that Chinese culture in general, and Chinese national character in particular, was also carefully chosen by ancient Chinese to be most suitable to their unique historical environment.

This book aims to expand the conventional frontier of economics and contributes to the disciplines of history and other social sciences. It adds a dimension to institutional economics, cultural economics, and economics of social behaviors. Moreover, from an economics perspective, this book provides new explanations for a number of historical events and helps resolve many of the puzzles presented by historical and contemporary China. Using basic economic logic, it demonstrates that culture shapes history and history shapes culture.

I am grateful to many people for their generous help and intellectual influences for my writing of this book. First, I owe my intellectual debt to the late Professor Herschel I. Grossman. He taught me the theory of political economics, which aims to explain political and social phenomenon based on the postulation that human nature is largely the same across the people of different races, ethnicity, and culture. According to this doctrine, for example, Japanese and Chinese soldiers behaved differently in the battlefields not because of any genetic difference, but because they faced different constraints and were subject to different incentive mechanisms.

Second, I am fortunate that I had close intellectual interactions with many colleagues of economics and political science, including Brian Bridges, Che-po Chan, Yingying Dong, Hiroyuki Imai, Chen Lin, Greg Whitten, Yiu-chung Wong, Victoria Yeung, Bin Yu, Baohui Zhang, Jie Zhang, and Yifan Zhang. I benefited enormously from numerous lengthy conversations with them on the culture and history of China and Japan. Also, I received valuable comments on my book from several eminent scholars: Richard Davis (historian), Avinash Dixit (economist), Liah Greenfeld (sociologist), Daniel Triesman (economist and political scientist), David Weil (economist), and David Weimer (economist and political scientist).

Finally, I would like to thank the editor of Routledge for this book, Ms. Yongling Lam, who spent much time in revising and polishing this book. Also, I thank Jing He and Xiaoyi Dai for their excellent research assistance.

Note

1 http://www.washingtonpost.com/wp-dyn/content/article/2008/04/28/AR 2008042801122.html

1   Introduction

How does culture shape history – and history shape culture? This book aims to help answer this question by conducting a comprehensive and rigorous analysis of the evolution of the Chinese culture, political and legal institutions, and "national character" throughout historical and contemporary China. By repeatedly applying the political Coase theorem and utilizing other economic theories, it investigates how a "national character" evolves endogenously along with an institutional environment, which is in turn determined by economic, political, and geographical fundamentals.

In a recent influential book, North, Wallis, and Weingast (2009) emphasize the importance of controlling violence to maintaining social order. They argue that successful societies can control violence at a relatively low cost, and that successful economic organizations can operate only in violence-free environments. This book extends North, Wallis, and Weingast (2009) in two ways.

First, it incorporates the role of "personality" into analysis of violence and social order. In a society where people worship bravery and violence, violent actions are often committed frequently between different individuals and groups. However, the individuals in a society that treasures courtesy and kindness usually engage in little violent conflict.

The "personality" described in this book refers to the "average personality" of a country's people, rather than the personality of a particular individual.[1] In the sociology and political science literature, the "average personality" of a country is often referred to as "national character" (e.g., Adorno, Frenkel-Brunswik, Levinson, and Sanford (1950), Barker (1979), Sniderman (1993)).[2] Although "personality" may include multiple dimensions, this book focuses on a people's tendency toward violence, which is the central element of North, Wallis, and Weingast (2009).

Second, this book contends that a people's violent attitude is a double-edged sword for the state. Although it is more costly for a state to manage a people who exhibit more violent tendencies, a bellicose populace is much more effective at defending its country when facing foreign invasion.

In the spirit of the political Coase theorem, which is elaborated in Chapter 7, this book contends that there is an "optimal" personality for a society that maximizes the welfare of its people. Moreover, the exact form of this optimal personality depends on the material fundamentals of the society. For example, the national character of one country can be either "tough" (brave, aggressive, bellicose) or "weak" (timid, submissive, un-militaristic). Both types of character can be optimal choices for countries in different economic, political, and geographical circumstances.

"Institutional economics" has marked a major development in the economics, political science, and history literature in the past few decades, a fact emphasized by the conferment of the Nobel Prize on five intellectual leaders in the field.[3] A large number of studies show that "institutions" matter greatly to economic performance, and they are often determined by economic fundamentals.[4]

North (1991, p. 97) defines "institutions" as follows: "Institutions are the humanly devised constraints that structure political, economic, and social interaction. They consist of both informal constraints (sanctions, taboos, customs, traditions, and codes of conduct), and formal rules (constitutions, laws, property rights). Throughout history, institutions have been devised by human beings to create order and reduce uncertainty in exchange."

According to this definition, this book clearly belongs to the field of "institutional economics." It offers a detailed study of the formation of the archetypical Chinese personality and its evolution in response to the changing economic, political, and military environments in historical and contemporary China. Moreover, it applies economic theories to analyze institutional developments in Chinese history, such as the introduction of the rule of law and the ways that ancient dynasties managed the large country of China.

The book studies the determinants of the Chinese personality in ancient times. China has been a large country in terms of its geographical size and population throughout most of its documented history. This phenomenon is fairly unique in world history. Other large countries such as Russia, the United States, Canada, and Brazil attained their current geographical sizes only in the last 300 years. Continental Europe is similar to China in geographical size, but has almost always been divided into many small countries.

What has influenced China's longevity as a single large country? The historical literature provides an answer to this question. For example, Turchin (2009, pp. 191, 194, 196) observes the following:

> antagonistic interactions between nomadic pastoralists and settled agriculturalists result in an autocatalytic process, which pressures both nomadic and farming polities to scale up polity size, and thus military power. . .
>
> The greatest imperial confederations of nomads in world history (the Xiongnu, the Turks, and the Mongols) arose on the steppe side of the frontier. In other words, the exceptionalism of the East Asian imperiogenesis hotspot was mirrored in the exceptionalism of repeated gigantic imperial confederations in the steppes. Furthermore, there was a striking degree of synchrony between the rise of the steppe imperial confederations and Chinese empires – Xiongnu and Qin/Han, Turks and Sui/Tang, Mongols and Song. . .

A successful raid can be devastating to a farming community. Not only does it lose a large part of the resources needed to survive until the next harvest but the nomads may also kill men of fighting age, and abduct women and children as slaves. Thus, raiding pressure from the steppes imposes a severe selective regime on farming communities. . . The only successful way of resisting nomad pressure is for several local communities to unite into a "meta-community", with a larger defensive force to offset the nomads' military advantage.

Chapters 2 and 3 of this book present economic analyses that complement the history literature in further understanding why China has stayed a single big country and how it could deter powerful horse warriors. China has been a large country throughout most of its documented history due to its unique geographical location. There are vast areas of land at its northern border, including Mongolia and some present-day Chinese provinces. These areas are not suitable for agricultural production, but are ideal places to raise domestic animals such as sheep and cows. The nomadic tribes of China's neighboring countries to the north usually rode horses while raising their sheep and cows. In fact, even today, the Mongols like to call themselves "the race on horseback." The economic theory of "learning by doing" (or "practice makes perfect") means that a worker's productivity in a certain task tends to increase as he performs the same task repeatedly. This idea is generalized at the macro level in economics. Arrow (1962) and Lucas (1993) emphasize that "learning by doing" is an important engine of economic growth.

A nomadic tribe has the advantage over an agricultural community in combat because the action of combat is largely similar to the action of ordinary production for nomads. Even during times of peace, a nomad must ride his horse to raise cattle and fight with wolves and other fierce animals to protect it. Therefore, in ancient times, a nomad who survived into adulthood was usually and "naturally" a good soldier in combat. However, a peasant's production often has little to do with the training to be a professional soldier, particularly in the cavalry. Nomadic tribes were historically much more war-like than agricultural communities.

What could an agricultural community do if its neighbor was a nomadic tribe? People in ancient China found an answer to this question: form a large agricultural country. In contrast, Europe did not face such a grave threat from nomadic tribes for most of its history. This explains why China has long been a large country while Europe has been divided into many countries. A large country can deter the potential attacks of nomadic tribes. If an agrarian country is sufficiently large, it has an edge over a nomadic country in combat for two reasons. First, a large agrarian country can generate substantial revenues, which coupled with its large population enables the government to select high-quality soldiers. In fact, as in the case of ancient China, a large agrarian country could often recruit soldiers from neighboring nomadic tribes when providing them with ample financial rewards. Second, the incentive scheme for soldiers and army officers is usually far better established in a large agrarian country. This scheme depends on both a carrot and a stick. A large agrarian country can provide plenty of bonuses for soldiers who perform well on the battlefield. However, a nomadic country often recruits all of its male citizens when fighting the army of a large agrarian country. In this case, the nomadic country cannot design a credible mechanism for rewarding all of the soldiers who perform well on the battlefield. Furthermore, the discipline shown against soldiers who shirk their combative duty can be very severe in a large agrarian country. Such a penalty mechanism would be hard to implement in a nomadic country, which usually consists of numerous autonomous or semi-automatous tribes.

For example, in the Battle of Mobei that took place near the present-day Mongolian capital of Ulaanbaatar in 119 BC, Chinese troops achieved an overwhelming victory over the powerful nomadic empire of Xiongnu. During the battle, 90,000 Xiongnu soldiers (mostly from cavalries) were killed, and the Chinese army lost only 20,000 cavalry soldiers.

During China's Han Dynasty, Chinese general Chen Tang made a famous statement against the nomadic tribes to the north: "No matter how far away, whoever dares to offend mighty Han will be put to death." This statement was credible only because China was a large country with a strong central government. In his influential book, Diamond (1997) argues that a country's economic development is determined by its geographical location and natural environment. In a somewhat similar vein, this book argues that China's large size has long been determined by its unique geography.

How is the social order of a large country maintained? The first answer is establishing a good rule of law. This book shows that a well-established legal system has been the cornerstone of a united China. In particular, Chapter 4 demonstrates that in the warring period, the Qin state could conquer other states and unite China due to its much better established rule of law. Moreover, it shows that a unique history and the geographical location of the state of Qin gave its king more centralized power than the kings of other states, which made a major legal reform possible in Qin but not in other Chinese states.

In contrast, many European countries had a less-developed rule of law. For example, a significant portion of European conflicts were settled by duels during the period. A duel served as an alternative to other conflicts that were less regulated and larger in scale. Consider the example of a major dispute erupting between two large families or clans. When a dispute could not be resolved in a legal court because the rule of law was not well established, one natural impulse of the families and clans was to resolve the dispute through war. Over time, social norms emerged out of this kind of scenario that resulted in far fewer destructive consequences. If a conflict broke out between two large families, each family was permitted to select a single member, such as its best fighter, and settle it via a duel between the two selected members without harming any other family members.

This book argues that the formation of submissive culture and people's "personality" complements the rule of law in maintaining social order. Conformity is much less costly to enforce when the people involved have a submissive personality. The submissiveness of the ancient Chinese personality was sustained by the Confucian culture. Chapter 8 shows that the imperial exam system (Keju), which was used in selecting government officials based on Confucian literature, served as an effective mechanism of promoting Confucian culture. Keju was based on strict rules that largely guaranteed fairness and eliminated nepotism, racism, and favoritism based on personnel connections or physical appearance from the selection of government officials. Indeed, Douglass North made the keen observation that fairness is a crucial feature of lasting social institutions. That almost every man in ancient China was allowed to participate in the Keju and hence had the chance of becoming a government official with a high income and prestige provided a channel of intergenerational mobility even for the people at the bottom of the society. This "equal opportunity" substantially mitigated the grievances that ancient Chinese people had against income inequality.

Throughout the country's history, Chinese governments and societies have not usually been concerned with race and personal appearance. Cultural unity and a consensus over basic values were maintained through the people's adherence to Confucianism. The nomadic tribes outside China, who did not follow the teachings of Confucian Classics, were initially labeled "barbarians" but considered "Chinese" once they adopted Confucianism (e.g., Chen, 2005). In other words, in ancient times, a person was considered "Chinese" based on culture and personality rather than genetics. The Confucian culture was refined in a system of behavioral code to develop a "servile" personality that helped the ancient Chinese maintain social order in such a large country. Moreover, nationalism was weak because there was only one agrarian country of which the ancient Chinese were aware.

The central theoretical basis of this book is the political Coase theorem, which suggests that people tend to seek optimal choices in all aspects of their lives to maximize the social welfare. However, this implication usually holds true as a long-run trend only. In the short run, people often make mistakes and engage in all kinds of opportunistic behaviors that deviate from the social optimum. This applies well to China's attempts to find optimal ways of maintaining its status as a big country. The Tang Dynasty marked a golden age of Chinese history. However, it was torn apart by the local warlords, to whom the central government delegated too much power. The Song Dynasty resolved this problem by centralizing the military power. However, it did so at the cost of decreasing the military effectiveness of the Song army, which prevented the Dynasty from completely uniting China. The Yuan Dynasty tried to rule China through an alliance with the neighboring states of the Mongol Empire. To forge this alliance, a social hierarchy was created that placed the Mongols at the top, which ultimately led to the revolts of the Han Chinese and the downfall of the Dynasty. The emperors of the Ming Dynasty designed a system that appointed the princes of China's royal families, who served effective roles in monitoring local military generals. However, the extended royal families were provided with a large amount of resources and grew rapidly. The large expenditure of the gigantic royal families ultimately became an unbearable economic burden for the Chinese populace, which led to the downfall of the Ming Dynasty. The Qing Dynasty built by the Manchus replaced the Ming Dynasty. The Manchus were perhaps the best rulers in historical China. They maintained China as a single large country by being benevolent to the people, imposing low taxes, minimizing racial differences, and deterring potential insurrections via a strong alliance with nomadic tribes in Mongolia. Furthermore, the Qing Dynasty forged a strong alliance with Mongolian nomads through both extensive marriages with tribal leaders and military conquests. In fact, the Great Wall was virtually useless in the Qing Dynasty because the Manchus not only forbade the nomads from invading but also placed them under strict control.

The Qing Dynasty unfortunately met with "guns and steel" *à la* Jared Diamond (1997). Following the First Opium War in 1840, the Qing army was repeatedly defeated by Western powers with far superior weaponry. Those defeats convinced the Qing government of the importance of modern technologies and led to China's "Self-Strengthening Movement," a fairly successful endeavor that substantially strengthened the Qing army.

However, the First Sino–Japanese War broke out in 1894 on both land and sea, which again demonstrated the Qing army's weakness. Although the Qing navy was once commonly considered the most powerful fleet in Asia, its army was thoroughly defeated in 1895 by Japan, which did not have arms supremacy. Japan's ground forces and navy achieved overwhelming victories, as illustrated by a comparison of the casualties. During the war, 35,000 Chinese troops were killed or wounded. In sharp contrast, the amount of Japanese casualties numbered fewer than 5,000. Moreover, the Chinese fleet was annihilated by the Japanese navy, which did not lose a single ship. In April 1895, the Qing government realized that the Chinese army was simply no match for the Japanese army, and it sued for peace. The war was ended with the signing of the Treaty of Shimonoseki, by which China ceded Taiwan to Japan in perpetuity and China paid Japan an astronomical war indemnity.

Why was China defeated so completely? This question has puzzled the Chinese people since 1895. In fact, right before the war started, most Western observers perceived that China had a stronger army and would be victorious. The defeat was extremely humiliating to the Chinese people. The difference in weaponry between the two nations did not account for the outcome. Indeed, the main explanation for China's complete defeat among the populace appeared to be that the Chinese had a "national character" that was inferior to that of the Japanese.

This enormous national humiliation has inflicted the minds of the Chinese people for more than a century. Various hypotheses have been advanced to explain the reasons for China's defeat and mitigate this bitter psychological blow. The leading hypothesis is the corruption of the Qing government, which makes Empress Dowager Cixi the major source of blame. It is a familiar story in China that Cixi put a large portion of Chinese fleet funding into the construction of the royal summer palace. However, this explanation is too far-fetched.

The Chinese population was about a half billion at the time. The expenditure for a royal summer palace that was relatively modest in scale was unlikely to account for a major proportion of the total government revenue of such a large country.

By applying economic theories and analyzing Japanese history, this book explains this event from new angles. First, based on the framework of "self-fulfilling" prophecy in the game theory developed by John Nash, it shows that the difference of bravery between Chinese and Japanese soldiers is an important reason for China's defeat. What made the Japanese soldiers braver than the Chinese soldiers? On one hand, the Qing government had a very tight budget at the time due to its enormous expenditure on quelling large-scale domestic rebellions (e.g., the Taiping Rebellion), which led to serious corruption in the army. Consequently, its military discipline and reward system was poorly implemented. Moreover, because most Chinese people had a weak personality and lacked a sense of nationalism at the time, the soldiers fought cowardly and exhibited little military professionalism under the malfunctioning disciplinary system. Chapter 16 shows that in this case, although it was in the best interest of the Chinese soldiers that they all fought together bravely, every soldier expected that other soldiers would be cowards, and hence they competed to run away from battlefields. Indeed, Paine (2003, p. 362) observes that in the First Sino–Japanese War, the Chinese "common soldiers had little incentive to fight."

On the other hand, before the Meiji Restoration in 1868, there were about 250 *de facto* countries, or at least autonomous regions, in Japan. Each country/region had its own private forces that consisted of samurais. The moral code of samurais is "Bushido," which emphasizes loyalty, valor, the mastery of military skills, and honor unto death (e.g., Nitobe, 1900). Honor and pride were most important to a samurai. In fact, most samurais belonged to a low-income class in Japan, and were often poorer than peasants (e.g., Greenfeld, 2001). Samurais mainly received "payment" in the forms of honor and prestige, which were bestowed upon their class on a daily basis. For example, when a samurai passed by, most members of the Japanese society were required to bow to him in a sign of respect. A samurai was legally entitled to strike with his sword at anyone who compromised his honor, such as a farmer or artisan who refused to bow. This right is called "Kiri-sute gomen" in Japanese. The samurai class was outlawed under the Meiji Restoration to strengthen the power of Japan's central government. However, the spirit of samurais remained intact, and was redefined in the form of "Japanese nationalism" in the new era (Greenfeld, 2001). Many individuals of samurai origin quickly joined the Imperial Japanese Army, which substantially enhanced its combative power.

Second, the so called O-ring theory by Kremer (1993) can be applied to provide another explanation of China's defeat in the First Sino–Japanese War. This theory emphasizes that in terms of industrial specialization, the qualities of different intermediate goods are highly complementary in producing the quality of the final consumption good. For example, a computer will not work even if only one out of the thousands of its components fails. Kremer (1993) uses the example of the space shuttle *Challenger* exploding because one of its many components, the O-ring, malfunctioned under very high temperatures.

Kremer's insight can be well applied to a battleship. For example, suppose a battleship has 100 marines. Even if just one marine does not operate well, the artillery fired by the battleship may miss the target. The Japanese marines exhibited much more military professionalism and performed much better in training and combat than the Chinese marines. Thus, a Japanese battleship might have had much greater fighting power than a Chinese battleship even if the two ships were produced by the same British producer and were of the same quality.

The O-ring theory also applies to ground forces. In an army with firearms, coordination between different soldiers was important. Even if an individual Japanese soldier was only slightly better than an individual Chinese soldier in terms of bravery and military professionalism, the Japanese troop would have had greater combative power as a whole.

Soon after China's defeat in the First Sino–Japanese War, some Chinese intellectuals began to ask whether Confucian culture was a major reason for the defeat and the country's being bullied at the hands of foreign powers. The "New Culture Movement" began in China around 1916 and continued through the 1920s. It culminated in the massive demonstration of students and intellectuals in Beijing on May 4, 1919, when many participants strongly denounced the Confucian culture and advocated Chinese nationalism. Against this background, the Chinese Community Party (CCP) was established with the help of the Communist International (Comintern), an international communist organization in Moscow.

In 1937, Japan invaded China and its troops committed horrendous atrocities such as the Rape of Nanjing and the "Three Alls Policy" ("kill all, loot all, and burn all"). Applying various theories of economics and psychology, this book conducts a rigorous analysis of why the Japanese committed hideous war crimes in China and particularly rape on a massive scale. Moreover, it shows that Japanese atrocities in China were the fundamental reason why the United States joined the war against Japan, and that the attack on Pearl Harbor was simply a preemptive strike given the belief of the Japanese generals that the United States would soon inevitably fight against their country.

Japanese atrocities changed China's "national character," which in turn fostered the development of Chinese communist troops and guerillas. For example, some Chinese witnessed Japanese soldiers raping their wives and killing their children. These traumas generated enormous humiliation and hatred, which turned the Chinese from cowards into potentially brave fighters. Indeed, consumed by such tremendous shame and hatred, many Chinese did not hesitate to trade their lives for even a slim chance to seek revenge against Japanese soldiers. Although continuous national humiliations imposed by foreign powers gradually toughened up the Chinese personality from 1840 to 1937, the atrocities of Japanese troops, which far exceeded previous atrocities committed by foreign countries in China in both scale and degree, fundamentally changed that personality.

In parallel to this change, the number of Chinese communist troops grew rapidly. Douglass North argues that social institutions were developed to be conducive to economic growth and the improvement of social welfare. According to this principle, social institutions tend to change along with economic fundamentals. Before the Japanese invasion, most of the Chinese people had rejected communism. One need not study economics to know that the economic system of communism, in which one's payoff is independent of his work effort, provides no incentive to work hard. In fact, even orthodox Marxism argues that socialism should be established on the basis of highly developed capitalism. In other words, communism was not suitable to China at the time, which may explain why the Chinese Red Army was only a small force before 1937.

However, Japan's hideous atrocities changed the Chinese people's mentality. After the Sino–Japanese War, the Chinese were no longer concerned about economic development. Instead, their main concern was to defeat the Japanese invaders. They quickly learned that the only force that could match and beat the Japanese army in terms of bravery and toughness was the Chinese Red Army under the CCP, which was renamed the "Eighth Route Army" of the National Revolutionary Army of the Republic of China after 1937.

In terms of Baumol (1990), Chinese communists were the best "military entrepreneurs." The Chinese communist troops exhibited significant bravery for two reasons. First, they joined the CCP because they believed in the ideology of fighting against oppression and "liberating the entire human race" rather than pursuing personal gains. Indeed, prior to 1937, the CCP was on the verge of annihilation, and the remaining troops were strongly committed to the ideology of communism. Second, the CCP had been a branch of Comintern, largely preventing its leaders from pursuing personal gains. Thus, many young men competed to join the "Eighth Route Army" and its guerillas without demanding any remuneration/financial compensation.

Since then, the Chinese have maintained a bellicose personality, one that was further cultivated when the CCP took over China. For example, China's national anthem is "March of the Volunteers," which starts with the following lyrics: "Arise! All those who don't want to be slaves! Let our flesh and blood forge our new Great Wall!" During the Cultural Revolution, Confucian Classics were denounced as deceptive and anti-revolutionary, and Confucius himself was described as an evil person. The Chinese personality was transformed from servile to tough, with the Chinese people coming to place a high value on valor and national pride. The toughness and bravery of Chinese communist troops can be illustrated by their overwhelming victory in the Chinese Civil War, and China's fearless participation in the Korea War despite the far superior weaponry of its enemy.

However, considering the social, political, and economic environments of the modern world, neither the traditional Confucian culture nor the communist ideology are the best choices for the culture and national character of Chinese people today. The Chinese in Mainland China are virtually "culture-less" after the destruction of Confucianism and several decades of radical communist rule. In terms of the political Coase theorem, the Chinese people are currently searching for a new culture and the best possible "national character" in the new global environment. Although the search continues, it is certain that the personality of a typical Chinese individual will become increasingly "weaker." In the era of advanced military technologies, a soldier's bravery matters little to the outcome of a battle, which removes the material basis for the soldier's personality. Moreover, a "weaker" personality facilitates the establishment of the so-called Socialist Harmonious Society advocated by the current Chinese leaders.

Although this book focuses on China, its basic idea has general applicability. For example, Nisbett and Cohen (1996) show that in the United States, white Southerners have a greater tendency to commit many kinds of violence due to a culture of honor in which a man's reputation is essential to his economic survival. They argue that because the main economic activity in the American South has been the herding of animals that could easily be stolen, the residents there have had a strong incentive to establish a reputation of toughness for their material wellbeing and even for survival.[5]

Iyigun (2008) suggests that the Ottomans' military campaign in Europe led the people in Europe to be more tolerant of others' religious beliefs. In particular, it allowed the Protestant Reformation to survive its infancy and mature. Based on a European dataset covering 1401 to 1700 CE, the author demonstrates a negative correlation between the incidence of military engagements between the Protestant Reformers and the Counter-Reformation forces between the 1520s and 1650s and the Ottomans' military activities in Europe. Although this book analyzes different issues, it is in line with Iyigun's study (2008) in showing that the threat from a formidable nomadic tribe affects the formation of cultures.

Moreover, consider the personality of Jewish people. The "national character" of the European Jews who were to form the core of the State of Israel before its formation could be said to be extremely non-aggressive and un-militaristic, with little exhibition of national interest. Within a generation, this character was turned on its head, much as the Chinese national character was over the course of the mid-20th century. In both cases, active political action was taken intended to change that character.[6] When the Jewish people lived in the countries of "other" people, a non-aggressive and un-militaristic personality enabled them to live more harmoniously with others. However, after the establishment of Israel, they lived in a hostile environment and were vastly outnumbered on battlefields by the enemies of the neighboring countries. Thus, Israeli soldiers had to be extremely brave to have a chance at winning the wars to ensure the survival of their new nation.

The basic theoretical foundation of this book is the political Coase theorem, which dictates that individuals tend to choose cultures and social customs that maximize social welfare in the long run. The Nobel Prize–winning contribution of Ostrom (1990) achieved this goal marvelously, with the Nobel Committee noting that Ostrom's "research brought this topic from the fringe to the forefront of scientific attention . . . by showing how common resources – forests, fisheries, oil fields or grazing lands – can be managed successfully by the people who use them rather than by governments or private companies."[7]

Ostrom (1990, p. 25) states, "As an institutionalist studying empirical phenomena, I presume that individuals try to solve problems as effectively as they can. That assumption imposes a discipline on me. Instead of presuming that some individuals are incompetent, evil, or irrational, and others are omniscient, I presume that individuals have very similar limited capabilities to reason and figure out the structure of complex environments. It is my responsibility as a scientist to ascertain what problems individuals are trying to solve and what factors help or hinder them in these efforts." This book follows Ostrom's spirit by conducting numerous case studies from a different angle, guided by the political Coase theorem.

Notes

1 Some psychology studies have shown that the people in geographically and historically related countries often exhibit similar personality profiles (e.g., Allik and McCrae (2004), Nisbett and Cohen (1996), and Schmitt, Allik, McCrae, and Benet-Martínez (2007)).
2 In this book, "national character" is determined by a nation's social-economic environment and geography (rather than genetics), and is hence a completely neutral term. This book intends to investigate the role of "culture" in history, and narrows it down to one important component of national culture, i.e., the typical personality of the people.
3 These leaders include Douglass North (in 1993), Elinor Ostrom (in 2009), Oliver Williamson (in 2009), Robert Fogel (in 1993), and Ronald Coase (in 1991).
4 For example, see Acemoglu, Johnson, and Robinson (2001), Acemoglu and Robinson (2012), Berkowitz and Clay (2011), Clark (2007), Dixit (2007), Easterly and Levine (1997), Gallup, Sachs, and Mellinger (1999), Garfinkel and Skaperdas (2007, 2012), Ginsburgh and Throsby (2014), Glaeser and Shleifer (2002), Greif (2006), Guiso, Sapienza, and Zingales (2006), Harrison and Huntington (2000), Iyigun (2015), North (1990), North and Thomas (1976), Nunn and Puga (2012), Pomeranz (2000), Rodrik, Subramanian, and Trebbi (2004), Sokoloff and Engerman (2000), Weimer (1995, 1997), Treisman (2007), and Williamson (1985, 1996, 2000).
5 Although this book shares some basic ideas with Nisbett and Cohen (1996), it analyzes the issues in a different context. Furthermore, Nisbett and Cohen (1996) use psychology as their basic analytic framework, and the current book focuses on economics.
6 I am very grateful to David N. Wei for this insightful suggestion.
7 Some economists argue that Ostrom's research is not related to the Coase theorem, which in its strictest terms considers only cases in which property rights are well defined. However, this view is a narrow interpretation of the Coase theorem, which is broadened in the political Coase theorem.

Part I
Geography, nomadic threat, and the size of ancient China

2 Why has China stayed a single big country?

Before this chapter's titular question is addressed, a survey of the related economics and political science literature is presented. In ancient times, the main benefit of being a larger country was greater national security. The advantage of better national defense has been well recognized at least since Plato, who stated that "the number of citizens should be sufficient to defend themselves against the injustice of their neighbors."[1] Political scientists have made similar statements more recently. In explaining the reasons why independent regions choose to form federations, Riker (1964) observes that "(they) are willing to do so because of some form of external military–diplomatic threat or opportunity. Either they desire protection from an external threat or they desire to participate in the potential aggression of the federation." Gilpin similarly (2001) notes that "[t]he few examples of successful federal experiments have been motivated primarily by national security concerns. Indeed, the two most successful federal republics – Switzerland and the United States – were created in response to powerful external security threats."

However, there are costs involved in forming a large country. In ancient times, information flows were slow and communication and transportation costs usually increased considerably with distance. Consequently, the level of administrative efficiency tended to be lower in a larger country. One may argue that government decentralization may solve these problems. However, political decentralization often increases corruption due to the danger of uncoordinated rent seeking as government structures become more complex (e.g., Fan (2006), Shleifer and Vishny (1993)). For example, Fan, Lin, and Treisman (2009) show that corruption is more rampant in countries with larger numbers of administrative tiers and local public employees.

Furthermore, when one area is divided into many small countries, competition arises between those countries, restricting their rulers from engaging in excessive rent seeking. As a result, people tend to live better material lives and enjoy more personal freedom. Moreover, Alesina and Spolaore (1997) emphasize that when a country becomes larger, its population becomes more diverse, which usually implies that there will be more conflicts between different groups of people. The conflicts may arise out of material concerns, such as different preferences for the location of a major infrastructure project. Social customs and religions may alternatively arouse serious ideological conflicts.[2]

In sum, large countries experience a tradeoff between the benefit of national defense and the costs involved in administrating large and diverse populations. In a series of theoretical economic studies, Alesina and Spolaore (1997, 2005a, 2005b, 2006) examine the determinants of the number and sizes of nations in a region. The costs of communication and transportation were very high in ancient times compared with today. Thus, holding national security as a constant, the "optimal" size of a nation in ancient times would have been much smaller than it is today. However, national security varied widely across regions in ancient times, which implies that the optimal country size differs under heterogeneous circumstances.

As explained in the introduction, China was a large country in ancient times due to its unique geographical location. Indeed, China has been one of the largest countries in the world in terms of geographical size and population throughout most of documented human history. In contrast, Europe, which is of similar size to China, has been divided into numerous countries throughout history. Of course, China has not consistently remained a single united country. According to some historians, Chinese history has largely been characterized by "dynastic cycles," meaning that every dynasty experienced a rise and fall.[3] When a dynasty ended, it was usually preceded and sometimes followed by periods of chaos and disorder, which sometimes broke the country up into small regimes.

However, China has mostly been united for the past 2,000 years and shown a strong tendency to be united even during periods of disintegration. Chien (1963, p. 19), possibly the most influential Chinese historian of the last century, clarifies this point:

> Chinese politics was characterized by unification, while the Western political system encompassed multiple countries. Of course, China was not always a unified state, but political unification was the norm in Chinese history and disintegration was unusual. In contrast, political unification was an aspiration in the West and integration was unusual. Furthermore, even when China was in a state of disintegration, its spirit moved towards unification. In contrast, when Europe was temporarily integrated, its essence shifted towards disintegration.

In ancient times, China not only dwarfed its neighboring countries in terms of population size, but also enjoyed a much higher standard of living. This greater economic efficiency chiefly stemmed from production-related differences. While China was an agrarian country, its northern neighbors were nomads. Because the productivity of China's agricultural economy was much greater than that of the nomadic economy, the average income in China, whose main economic activities were farming related, was greater and far more stable than that of its neighboring countries.

However, China was usually on the defensive rather than offensive side when it confronted a foreign country. For example, the nomadic tribes in present-day Mongolia were a constant fear for the ancient Chinese. The fear of foreign invasions was vividly illustrated by the construction of the Great Wall.

The Great Wall is considered one of the Seven Wonders of the World. Those who have the opportunity of visiting it usually marvel at its magnificence and sheer size. The Great Wall comprises a series of fortifications made mainly of stone and brick, and stretches across almost the entire northern border of historical China. It is estimated that the length of the Great Wall reached 8,850 kilometers during the Ming Dynasty. An image is provided to illustrate its length and size. If all of the bricks that form the Wall were laid out around the Equator, they would form a wall five feet high around the central surface of the Earth. Even with today's technology, such an enormous project would cost USD$360 billion, equaling the United States' total highway expenditure for the past 40 years.[4]

In ancient times, construction was much more costly and difficult. The history of the Great Wall began with the fortifications built by various states of the Zhou Dynasty during 771–221 BC. The majority of its construction took place in 220–206 BC by the first Emperor of China, Qin Shi Huang, using forced labor. The Wall was subsequently repaired, added to, and rebuilt by several dynasties. It was important for Chinese national defense until the Qing Dynasty. Numerous emperors in several ancient Chinese dynasties conscripted millions of workers to build, repair, and rebuild the Wall.

It was clearly a concern and fear of invasion from their northern nomadic neighbors that induced the ancient Chinese empires to incur such high material and human costs in constructing the Great Wall. Why were the ancient Chinese so afraid of those nomadic tribes? The question can be answered in one word: horses. The nomadic tribes of China's northern neighboring countries relied on horses to raise their sheep and cows. Even today, the Mongols like to call themselves "the race on horseback."

As discussed in the introduction, because of the natural effect of "learning by doing" in riding horseback, nomads were usually good soldiers in combat. In contrast, a peasant's production had much less to do with his training as a professional soldier, particularly in the cavalry. Thus, a nomadic tribe was usually much more war-like than an agricultural society.

During the Qing Dynasty, there was a kingdom adjacent to China known as Zunghar Khanate, which stretched across a large area located in present-day Northwest China, eastern Kazakhstan, northern Kyrgyzstan, and southern Siberia during the 17th and 18th centuries. Both peasants and nomads lived under its rule. The Zunghar Khanate kings believed that peasants could not live without peace nor nomads without war, a seemingly paradoxical belief that offers a great deal of insight into the period.

It is easy to understand that peasants cannot live without peace. During periods of frequent wars, military forces take farmers' harvests, along with the incentive of peasants to work hard on their farms. By the end of the Han Dynasty (2 AD), the Chinese population was about 58 million (Nishijima, 1986). The Han Dynasty was immediately followed by the Three Kingdoms period, which was characterized by constant wars between different warlords and ultimately between the three kingdoms. The total population in the Three Kingdoms was only about 8 million (Zou, 1992). The transition period from the end of the Han Dynasty to the Three Kingdoms period was only a few decades. However, the constant wars decreased the Chinese population by more than 85 percent, all without the aid of foreign country invasion.

Nomads cannot live without war due to the subsistence constraint of consumption. Nomads live on sheep, cows, and other animals that may suddenly die in large scales due to drastic weather changes and disease. When this occurs, the nomads are unable to survive due to the subsistence constraint of consumption. Consequently, their only survival strategy is to attack neighboring countries. Moreover, because nomads are better at military conflicts than farmers, a country of nomads is often tempted to wage wars against a country of peasants.

The above argument is supported by a number of rigorous empirical studies. Miguel, Satyanath, and Sergenti (2004) present a pioneering empirical study on the impacts of economic shocks on military conflict. Such an econometric study is difficult due to the interactive effects between economic factors and military conflict, which is called the endogeneity problem in economics. They resolved this problem by using rainfall variation as an "instrumental variable" for economic growth. Based on a dataset of 41 African countries from 1981 to 1999, they find that a negative growth shock significantly increased the likelihood of military conflict.

Based on the empirical methodology of Miguel, Satyanath, and Sergenti (2004), Bai and Kung (2011) construct a time-series dataset of rainfall and conflicts in historical China. They show that a reduction of rainfall, which led to a shortage of fodder and consequently the death of some herds of animals, increased nomadic incursions into China proper over a period of about 2,000 years.[5]

Although the northern nomads were mainly motivated to invade an agricultural country for survival, they usually committed horrendous atrocities when they succeeded in their conquests. They robbed the peasants of their rice, wheat, and clothing, and made young women their targets of rape and abduction. As explained in a later chapter, nomads usually lived in a bloodthirsty culture in ancient times, attempting to kill all those who resisted their invasions and showing no mercy toward innocent peasants. The ancient Chinese expression "men's heads were hanged over a horse's head, while women were packed on horseback" vividly portrays the misery of people's lives in ancient China after a nomadic invasion.

The ancient Chinese lived in a unique environment. There were vast areas of land to the country's northern border, which today consist of Mongolia and some Chinese provinces. These lands, which were ideal for raising domestic animals but unsuitable for agricultural production, acted as the lands of numerous nomadic tribes. The land area of Mongolia is 1.56 million square kilometers, ranking 19th in the world, a size more than four times that of Japan (0.378 million square kilometers) and Germany (0.357 million square kilometers). Once the nomadic tribes formed a single country, they had an extremely powerful army that was devastating to their neighbors. In response, the ancient Chinese formed a single large agrarian country as a counterbalance. As noted in the next chapter, this was an effective strategy.

When China became a single big country, the ordinary Chinese became subject to the rule and exploitation of their ruler, the emperor. The political economy literature (e.g., Grossman, 1991, 1999) argues that the ruler often appropriates people's earnings through taxation, and under some circumstances leaves most people to live only at the subsistence level. There is some evidence to support this argument, such as the following story:[6]

> Confucius once passed by the foot of the Tai Mountain. There he saw a woman crying her heart out beside a newly finished grave. The Master stopped and listened. Then he sent Tselu over to inquire of the mourner, saying, "You cry as if you are in great sorrow." "True!" the woman answered. "First my father-in-law was killed by the tiger; then my husband was killed by the tiger; and now my son – he also died at the mouth of the tiger." "Why, then," the Master asked, "didn't you leave the place and go somewhere else?" "But there is no tyrant here!" was the woman's reply. Confucius turned to Tselu and said: "Mark it, my lad! A tyrant is worse than a tiger."

Although some people may live miserably under the rule of a tyrant, most would prefer to live under the stable rule of an emperor than be constantly raided by nomadic tribes. This argument is derived by applying Olson's (1993, 2000) theory of the "stationary" vs. "roving" bandit. Olson conceives of governments as bandits by virtue of their rent-seeking behavior through taxation and/or corruption. However, the degree to which rent is extracted from people may differ substantially depending on the nature of the government. When a ruler foresees ruling a group of people over the long term, he tends to constrain his rent-seeking activities to gain the people's long-term support. Olson calls this type of government a "stationary bandit." In contrast, a "roving bandit" is the type of ruler who expects to have power over a certain group of people for only a short period. Consequently, such a government or authority prefers to extract as much as possible from the people, and even has the incentive to destroy the assets that its troops cannot take away (e.g., houses) and kill people, which may weaken the capacity of those who seek revenge. Indeed, when a nomadic army conquered a city in ancient times, the soldiers commonly killed all of the city's men and raped all of its women.

One study by Acemoglu, Johnson, and Robinson (2001) shows support for Olson's theory. They note that the Europeans who colonized different parts of the world about 200 years ago faced a serious problem: mortality. Due to the dominance of their superior weaponry, the colonizers took little issue with native resistance. However, the new European settlers often lacked the immune capacity to fight against foreign diseases. These diseases did not always lead to death, and mortality rates resulting from illness differed considerably across regions. The Europeans had little clue about how to control diseases in some African regions, resulting in very high mortality rates. For example, 72 percent of the European settlers in an area of Sierra Leone died within one or two years (1792–1793). On one expedition from Gambia to the Niger, 87 percent of

Europeans died within a few months (May–November 1805). Acemoglu, Johnson, and Robinson (2001) emphasize the choice of the British government in 1795 to send British convicts to the island of Lemane in Africa, which was 400 miles up the Gambia River. The plan was aborted because the mortality rates in Africa were considered to be too high even for the convicts. The British government ultimately decided to pay a much higher transportation cost to send the convicts to Australia. The mortality rates were low for European settlers in other colonies including Australia, Canada, New Zealand, and the United States.

The European settlers established institutions that were conducive to economic development in places with low colonizer mortality rates. The United States may be the best example. In fact, the six states in the northeastern corner of the United States that formed the earliest English settlements in North America, including Maine, New Hampshire, Vermont, Massachusetts, Rhode Island, and Connecticut, are still fondly referred to as "New England." Australia is another good example. Most of the early settlers in Australia were convicted British criminals, making most of the people in Australia today their offspring. The British government did not initially take the convicts seriously and failed to define their property rights in the country. However, under the strong demand of the ex-convicts and ex-jailers, the rule of law in Britain began to be implemented in Australia in the later 1840s. In terms of Olson's theory, the British chose to establish a "stationary bandit" type of government. The United States became an important colony for the United Kingdom, and the British government at the time did not expect its later independence. Even today, Australia remains nominally under the rule of the British Crown.

However, the colonial experience was completely different in locations where settlers' mortality rates were high. In such places, colonizers often set up extractive social and political institutions. For example, during the first two decades of the last century, the taxation rates of the French colony of Tunisia in Africa were four times as high as those in metropolitan France. According to one French official in Africa, "the European commandant is not posted to observe nature, . . . He has a mission . . . to impose regulations, to limit individual liberties. . . ., to collect taxes."[7] In this case, the colonizer behaved like a "roving bandit."

The preceding implies that a people's welfare is much higher when its government is a "stationary" rather than "roving" bandit. A roving bandit adopts a basic hit-and-run strategy by stealing and robbing as much as possible and then running away. Even worse, it often commits atrocities such as murder, rape, and arson. In contrast, a stationary bandit has an incentive to help generate peace and economic prosperity, as these ensure it a share of the resultant economic success and social stability. Even when a stationary bandit is a tyrant, he often builds a government that respects private property rights and protects citizens from the harm of foreign invasions (roving bandits). A stationary bandit must gain support from the people to ensure a long-term rule, which induces him to improve their welfare. Thus, he usually tries to improve the quality of the government and spends resources on building infrastructure.

Because it is beneficial for people to be governed by a stationary bandit, they have an incentive to help keep such a government once it is in power. Based on this logic, nomads were the worst enemy of the ancient Chinese. The ancient Chinese would have rather been submissive to the rules and exploitation of their emperors if doing so ensured that they would be protected from the pillage and slaughter of nomadic warriors.

What can an agricultural community do if its neighbor is a nomadic tribe? The ancient Chinese found an answer to this question: a united China. The introduction of this book explains the sharp contrast between China and Europe in terms of the number and size of the countries involved. Throughout most of history, Europe has been divided into many small countries and China has remained one big country. The underlying reason for this was the constant threat that nomads in present-day Mongolia, Inner Mongolia, and Xiangjiang presented to Chinese farmers. Because nomads work and live on horses, they usually have a strong advantage in wars over farmers. Thus, a country of nomads hesitates to invade a country of farmers only when the latter is much larger than the former.

Notes

1 Laws, Book V, translated by Jawett.
2 Chen (2014) provides an empirical test of the theory of Alesina and Spolaore using Chinese data for the past two millennia. He shows that when famines were more frequent, there were fewer nations in China. He interprets this finding as that a larger nation tends to provide public goods at a lower cost per person, which is consistent with the theory of Alesina and Spolaore.
3 See, e.g., Ching (1974) and Wills (1994).
4 http://www.essortment.com/history-great-wall-china-21535.html
5 This finding is confirmed by a more recent study of Chen (2015), who adds that nomadic conquests were more likely to happen when a Chinese dynasty was established earlier and hence was usually weaker.
6 http://www.en84.com/article-2589-1.html
7 Young (1994, p. 101).

3 How can a large agrarian country deter powerful horse warriors?

The previous chapter reveals that the raids and atrocities of nomadic tribes were major concerns for the ancient Chinese, who were induced to unite all of China's regions into a single country. This chapter carefully addresses the credible deterring effects of a large agrarian country on nomadic warriors.

Consider two countries, one agrarian and one nomadic, that are both large in terms of territory size. Although each nomad is a much better fighter than a typical peasant, the agrarian country may easily deter invasions from the nomadic country. The fundamental reason is that agricultural production allows the agrarian country to sustain a much larger population and generate much more fiscal revenues than the nomadic country.

A large agrarian country may build an effective defense mechanism, such as the Great Wall of China. The Great Wall played an important role in protecting ancient China from foreign invasions. It was especially effective in preventing small groups of foreign nomads from raiding and plundering the regions near China's northern borders. Without a major military operation, a small group of cavalry soldiers would have found it extremely difficult to break the defenses of foot soldiers at the top of the gigantic wall. Even if they could have somehow scaled the wall, the nomadic warriors would have had to leave their horses behind. Without their horses, their combative prowess would have been substantially reduced, and the warriors would have posed little threat to a large country such as China. The ancient Chinese were also often gravely concerned about the "shock tactics" of their nomadic neighbors, who often wreaked sudden havoc on the border regions. The Great Wall served as an effective defense system that prevented the horses of the warriors from galloping at full speed against the largely unprepared Chinese army and civilians.

Although the Great Wall served as an effective way of defending against nomadic invasions, it was far from sufficient. If hundreds of thousands of cavalries had launched a major military campaign, a strong fortification alone would not have withheld such a powerful invasion. China relied on a credible large-scale revenge strategy to protect its citizens from being attacked. This revenge was considered "credible" when China's population was far greater in number than that of the attacking nomadic force.

Although a nomadic country performs well in terms of offense, it is often vulnerable in terms of defense. Even today, Mongolia's total population numbers less than 3 million people despite its vast geographic size. The exceedingly large size of a neighboring country is of concern to a nomadic country regardless of its military prowess. Although a nomadic tribe is often efficient in attacking its enemies, it is weak at responding to unexpected attacks launched in return. The population of Mongolia was far lower in ancient times, when production technologies were less efficient and wars were frequent. The people engaged in production in a nomadic country had to live very sparsely to ensure they could provide full pastures for feeding and watering cattle.

However, this pattern of production made nomadic countries very vulnerable to enemy attacks. If a foreign foe sent a 2,000-strong cavalry to launch a surprise attack, the men would meet little resistance no matter where the attack took place because they outnumbered the nomads substantially. Moreover, different from a country whose main economic activities were agricultural and commercial, nomadic countries usually had no fortifications.

In ancient times, agricultural countries did not usually attack nomadic tribes because there was no financial benefit in doing so. Although sheep and cows might have had some value, the cost of transporting them back alive was usually too high, particularly when the enemy could regroup and attack. The cost of transporting dead cattle was also high, and its economic value was low because refrigeration technology was not yet available. Agricultural countries launched large-scale attacks on nomadic countries only when the people in the nomadic countries had to be slaughtered and when the expectation of retaliation was low. These two conditions were met only when the agricultural country was big and strong enough.

Ancient China did launch such attacks against its war-like nomadic neighbors. The most famous story is that of Huo Qubing in the early Han Dynasty. At the beginning of that dynasty, a pastoral nomad country known as Xiongnu was developed to the north of China. Xiongnu raided Chinese territory frequently, inflicting enormous human casualties and financial losses on the Chinese people. Facing this problem, the Chinese emperor Wu Di secretly prepared a strong army for many years in an attempt to annihilate Xiongnu.

Wu Di carefully selected and trained two men who showed military prowess and promoted them to the rank of major general. One of the men, Huo Qubing, demonstrated extraordinary military talent even before he came of age. Huo was proficient in many kinds of combat such as horsemanship, archery, and swordsmanship. One of his well-known strategies involved leading a few thousand cavalries deep into the territory of Xiongnu and killing almost everyone the army encountered. Adopting this strategy created little need for Huo's army to bring any food along. Instead, the soldiers simply slaughtered their enemies' sheep, cows, and horses along the way.

A soldier in Huo's army had to be perfectly healthy. Because Huo's cavalries often traveled 1,000 miles within a few days, a soldier would not have been able to stay with his army if he had even a minor injury or illness. Even if a soldier received a minor injury, he might not be able to ride horses at fast speeds for a long time, which would result in constant bleeding and death. If a soldier had a fever, he usually recovered fully after an appropriate amount of sleep. However, a military strategy might have required the soldiers to move rapidly to another location on horses. In this case, a soldier suffering fever had no other option but to stay behind, and had a low chance of survival due to the threat presented by the revenging Xiongnu warriors. Therefore, Huo's troops had to be healthy, exhibit excellent horsemanship, and show proficiency in other military skills. Amassing a large group of such soldiers required money, which was particularly useful in ancient times when concerns for survival and material wellbeing were paramount and the ideologies of nationalism and ethnicity were weak. If a country had acquired sufficient revenues from taxation, it was able to attract young men with exceptional skills. A country's tax revenue was clearly proportional to its size, which implies that only a larger country would have had the capacity to recruit an army as elite as Huo's.

Realizing the vulnerability of Huo's army, the Xiongnu figured out a strategy: they slaughtered sheep and cows and left them to rot. They then put the rotten animals in every well, spring, and lake in the hopes that the contaminated water would spread infectious diseases to the Chinese soldiers. This strategy was effectively suicidal as the Xiongnu also had to drink the water, and many suffered enormously from the contamination. Given their poor knowledge in medicine, many Xiongnu died from the very diseases they created. However, this form of biological warfare proved a useful weapon against the invading Chinese troops. In particular, Huo Qubing died suddenly at age 24 from a mysterious disease, which according to Chinese historians was very likely contracted from the contaminated water he drank when he and his troops raided Xiongnu.[1]

Under Emperor Wu Di of the Han Dynasty, China annihilated almost the entire race of Xiongnu. The raids of Chinese cavalries, notably those led by Huo Qubing, seriously inflicted damage on Xiongnu tribes. The Xiongnu were ultimately dealt a devastating blow by their complete defeats in several major battles with the Chinese army. One battle was called the Battle of Mobei, which took place in the northern part of the Gobi Desert in January of 119 BC. The battlefield was located in Orkhon Valley in Central Mongolia, about 320 kilometers west from Ulaanbaatar, the current capital of Mongolia. During the Battle of Mobei, the Xiongnu gathered almost their entire available troop, which consisted of over 80,000 cavalries and about 100,000 infantries. On the other side, the Chinese troop consisted of 100,000 cavalries and 200,000 infantries. The battle was a great victory for the Chinese: 90,000 Xiongnu soldiers (mostly cavalries) were killed, and the Chinese army lost only 20,000 cavalries.[2]

The victory was even more impressive from the Chinese perspective for two reasons. First, getting to the site of the battlefield, which was located in the heartland of Xiongnu, proved a very long and difficult journey for the Chinese troops. The troops had to pass through the very wide Gobi Desert, which the Xiongnu hoped would serve as a natural barrier. When the Chinese soldiers arrived at the battlefield, they were utterly exhausted while the Xiongnu soldiers were well rested and prepared. Second, although the Chinese troops outnumbered the Xiongnu army, the difference in the number of soldiers between the two sides was not significant, particularly in terms of the number of cavalries, which served as the main forces.

A nomadic tribe like the Xiongnu tended to have much better soldiers than an agricultural country like China. This leads to a natural question: how did China achieve such a decisive victory in the Battle of Mobei? First, Wu Di of the Han Dynasty was one of the most intelligent emperors in Chinese history. The major battles with Xiongnu had been long anticipated and were well prepared for during his reign. Emperor Wu Di established a system in which soldiers were carefully selected and trained. Furthermore, the material abundance in China enabled Wu Di to select the soldiers of best quality and spend sufficient resources to train them. Moreover, Wu Di had the wise vision to identify two men of military talents, Wei Qing and Huo Qubing, and appoint them as generals in the battles against the Xiongnu. (Although Huo Qubing apparently remained healthy for some time after contracting the plague described earlier, the disease ultimately broke out in full scale and killed him.) Wei Qing and Huo Qubing outsmarted the Xiongnu generals in their command of the troops during the Battle of Mobei.

Furthermore, perhaps most important, the incentive scheme for soldiers and army officers was better established in China than in Xiongnu. In economics, a "free-rider problem" is identified in the interactions of different individuals, and refers to a situation in which the individuals can receive benefits without contributing anything.[3] Wikipedia gives the following examples. "In a labor union, free riding occurs if an employee pays no union dues or agency shop fees, but benefits from union representation. Non-excludable goods such as street-sweeping services may give rise to free riding. For example, imagine an urban street with several property owners along its length. A street-cleaning service would clear the street of litter at a fixed, non-divisible cost, but some owners may refuse to pay, anticipating that the other owners will still pay the cost of the service. If enough owners refuse to pay, the service cannot be hired."[4]

The free-rider problem is particularly serious on the battlefield because one who "free rides" others may have a much lower chance of being injured by the enemy. There are many ways to mitigate and resolve the free-rider problem.[5] Their underlying incentive mechanism is usually a combination of carrots (rewards) and sticks (penalties). This remains true when referring to an army's incentive mechanism.

During the Han Dynasty, China was a large country with a population of about 50 million people cultivating a fertile land. Because the soldiers constituted a very small portion of the entire population, the emperor had sufficient resources to reward the soldiers as long as they performed well in battles. However, in Xiongnu, almost every adult male was a soldier. Because the nomadic country had basically subsisted with little savings and capital accumulation, the King of Xiongnu had little wealth to reward most of the male population for participating in frequent battles. The Xiongnu soldiers and generals were clearly aware of this and thus had much less of an incentive than the Chinese soldiers to risk their lives on the battlefield. Furthermore, the leaders of the different Xiongnu tribes had the incentive to avoid high casualties among the soldiers in their own individual tribes. Thus, the Chinese soldiers fought more bravely on the battlefield and the officers of the Chinese army coordinated themselves much more efficiently, giving the Chinese army a huge advantage over the Xiongnu army in the Battle of Mobei.

In a summary of institutional economics, North (1991) attributes the difference in nations' growth performance throughout history to the mechanisms they used to enforce their legal and social institutions. China's military advantage over its neighboring nomad tribes was also the reward and penalty mechanism it used to encourage its troops to fight bravely in battles.

Li Guang exemplifies the Chinese army's incentive system under the reign of Emperor Wu Di. In the early Han Dynasty, even before Wu Di's reign, Li Guang was an extremely well-known general in both Xiongnu and China. In fact, many Xiongnu soldiers were so fearful and respectful of him that they nicknamed him "the Flying General." He remains a household name in China even today. He was particularly famous for his extraordinary archery skills, which are portrayed in a popular fairytale. One evening, when the moonlight was weak, Li Guang saw a tiger close by. He shot an arrow at the tiger, and his soldiers found that they could not pull the arrow free. The soldiers discovered that the "tiger" was actually a piece of large stone that resembled the beast in a crouching position. Li Guang's strength was such that he could embed an arrow so deeply into stone that no one could remove it. He was extremely popular among his soldiers, and his mere presence boosted the confidence of his men as much as it instilled fear in the Xiongnu soldiers. On many occasions, the Xiongnu warriors were deterred from attacking a location if they knew Li Guang was present.

To many people's surprise and disappointment, Li Guang did not receive a marquisate, an honor that many of his far less famous peers had received. Under Wu Di's reign, it was a strict rule that an army officer's achievements were measured only by the difference between the number of enemies he killed and the casualties inflicted on his own side. Li Guang might have devoted little effort in collecting such hard evidence. Thus, by this measure, Li Guang could not obtain sufficient battle distinctions to receive a marquisate, which was his lifelong dream. During the Battle of Mobei, he and his army unit had the misfortune of becoming lost in the desert and missed the battle. Again according to strict military rule, he would have been summoned to trial in the Chinese martial court. Facing this potential humiliation, Li Guang committed suicide. The strict rules set in place for the Chinese army resulted in tragedy for Li Guang. However, they served as a strong incentive mechanism for Chinese soldiers to fight bravely and intelligently against their enemies.

The defeat of the nomads at the Battle of Mobei in the heartland of Xiongnu was a lethal blow to the nomadic race. In addition to the human causalities, Xiongnu lost a large proportion of its livestock to the Chinese army, which led to famine in Xiongnu. Moreover, the Xiongnu tribes lost the relatively fertile southern grassland on which they raised their cattle, and were driven to a much more hostile living environment in the northern Gobi Desert and Siberia. By the 5th century AD, the Xiongnu had disappeared as a distinct people. Some historians argue that many of the people who remained in Xiongnu after their defeat ultimately migrated to places in central Europe such as Hungary, and that the Huns in Europe were actually people from Xiongnu tribes.[6] (At the end of the 5th century AD, using a military strength that was far superior to that of other Europeans, the Huns quickly conquered a vast area in Europe and established their empire there. Many are familiar with Attila the Hun, who terrorized and ravaged large areas of Europe.)

Military strikes were not the only strategies the ancient Chinese empires used against their nomadic neighbors. Rewards and penalties were both used as incentive mechanisms, and carrots and sticks often accompanied each other in many other strategic relationships. The "carrot" strategy that ancient China used in dealing with its nomadic neighbors was called "He-Qin," which meant establishing a friendly relationship through an alliance by marriage.[7] "He-Qin" usually referred to the marriage between a Chinese princess and the king or crowned prince of a nomadic country.

How did "He-Qin" help bring peace to China in ancient times? First, it made the nomadic kings happy. China's nomadic neighbors typically lived in cold and harsh environments and consequently had coarse skin. The Chinese women who lived in comfortable environments had much smoother skin, and the nomads found them to be much more beautiful. Indeed, both women and material resources were the targets of the nomadic tribes who raided the Chinese territories. However, if the king of a nomadic tribe sought a beautiful wife from China, he would have had much less of an incentive to run the risk of attacking China. Thus, "He-Qin" served as a very useful policy that complemented the policy of military threat to induce the king of a nomadic tribe not to attack China. Although the king could not have controlled all of his soldiers completely, some small groups of individual soldiers would have been much less effective in combat against the Chinese army without his coordination, and their largely unorganized raids and plunders would have been much less of a threat.

Second, "He-Qin" presented China with the option of giving some material resources to a nomadic neighbor in exchange for peace. Indeed, after "He-Qin," China periodically gave gifts of silk, liquor, and rice to the Xiongnu with the pretext of providing the Chinese emperors' daughters in the Mongolian steppe with a better living. War was costly, and the material resources given to a nomadic tribe were relatively trivial. Bargaining with a nomadic tribe over the exchange of food for peace often indicated a loss of dignity for the Chinese empire. However, it was perfectly fine for the Chinese emperor to give his daughter a large dowry for an extravagant wedding, as doing so enhanced the glory of the Chinese royal family. Thus, "He-Qin" served as a perfect disguise for transferring resources to a nomadic tribe to achieve peace, and resulted in a substantial welfare gain for both sides.

Third, as the daughters of Chinese emperors, Chinese princesses were rightfully accompanied by a large number of female servants both at home and away. A group of pretty young women were often selected to serve as maids for the princesses. When those women arrived at the nomadic tribe, they functioned at its discretion. For example, some were divided by a tribe's major generals to serve as the wives or concubines of other members of the ruling class in the "barbarian" country.

Although foreign countries have conquered China on occasion, they have done so only at times when China was disintegrated. The best-known example is the Mongolian invasion that established the Yuan Dynasty. The Mongolians were able to conquer China because it had effectively been divided into two countries: Jin and Song. In fact, the Mongolians took advantage of the hatred of the Song people against Jin, and conquered Jin in 1234 with the assistance of Song. They then went to conquer Europe (e.g., Russia), and finally went back to launch the invasion into Song, which they conquered in 1279. The following figures illustrate the devastation of the Mongolian conquest. When Jin was conquered, its population size decreased from 40 million people to 4 million. When Song was conquered, its population size decreased from 80 million people to 64 million. This indicates that it was in the best interest of the Chinese people to keep China a single large country.

Another important example is the so-called Wu Hu Uprising, during which five barbarian tribes threw China into disorder. The uprising occurred between 304 and 316, with five non-Chinese nomadic tribes or tribal confederacies defeating the army of the Jin Dynasty and capturing its capital city of Luoyang and emperor. China was divided into a large number of regional states in the aftermath. How did it happen?

Although Sima Yan formally founded the Jin Dynasty, his grandfather Sima Yi, who was a general of the state of Wei during the Three Kingdoms period, prepared the way. Sima Yi took advantage of a rare opportunity and seized the throne of Wei in a coup. His sons defeated the other kingdoms and united China again, which led to the establishment of the Jin Dynasty.

As Sima Yi became the *de facto* king by chance and did not plan to become the king or emperor, some Chinese historians argue that the Jin Dynasty was "not well prepared." Although the Sima clan ruled the entire country, the princes were not loyal to the central government. Soon after the establishment of the Jin Dynasty, the "War of the Eight Princes" broke out, devastating the heartlands of China and effectively turning the country into numerous *de facto* states (Graff, 2002).

Recall that the Chinese population during the Three Kingdoms period totaled only 8 million people. Given the continuous major wars fought between that period and the beginning of the Jin Dynasty, the total Chinese population of the Jin Dynasty could not have been much higher than 8 million people. Thus, after the War of the Eight Princes, China was effectively divided into many small countries, each of which had a small population. The nomadic groups finally had the opportunity to conquer China sub-state by sub-state.

Notes

1 Yap (2009).
2 Yap (2009).
3 See, e.g., Baumol (1952).
4 http://en.wikipedia.org/wiki/Free_rider_problem
5 A comprehensive survey related to this issue can be found in Holmstrom and Tirole (1989) and Lazear (1995).
6 See, e.g., Beckwith (2009).
7 See, e.g., Bentley (1993).

4 How did China become a single big country?

China was not always a single big country. From 771 to 221 BC, it was divided into many small *de facto* countries. This period of more than 500 years is known as the Spring and Autumn period (771 to 476 BC) and Warring States period (477 to 221 BC). During the Spring and Autumn period and most of the Warring States period, the small countries in China were symbolically under the common rule of the Zhou Dynasty. However, the kings of the Zhou Dynasty could only effectively control a very small proportion of China centered on the capital city near present-day Luoyang in Henan Province.

The Zhou Dynasty was the longest in Chinese history. It officially lasted from 1046 to 256 BC, although its effective political and military control over China lasted until only 771 BC. The Zhou Dynasty was established by the Ji family, and its first king was Ji Fa, who later became King Wu. Ji Fa formed a large coalition with many intelligent strategists and brave generals, and defeated a much larger army led by King Zhou of Shang at the Battle of Muye, marking the end of the Shang Dynasty and the beginning of the Zhou Dynasty.

The most famous supporter of King Wu of Zhou was Jiang Ziya (or Jiang Taigong), who today is a household name in China, particularly for his wisdom as an old man. Jiang came from humble origins and lived in poverty for most of his life. However, he was very intelligent, and his extensive hardships only enhanced his wisdom. Most remarkably, he had an unshakable faith in his talent. When he was in his 70s, he heard that a noble, Ji Chang (Ji Fa's father), was a man of vision who loved to employ talented people and respected them greatly. Jiang immediately went to the area where Ji Chang lived, and then played a unique strategy of self-promotion. He went fishing every day without using any bait. His bait-less fishing technique became of interest in the area and came to the attention of Ji, who visited the location where Jiang was fishing and asked him about his fishing strategy. Jiang replied, "I am only fishing those who are willing to bait the hook." (In the Chinese language, "hook" carries the innuendo of inducing an individual to do something.)

After Ji Chang died, his son Ji Fa succeeded him to become the leader of the rebels. He achieved great success in defeating the Shang Dynasty and became the new King of China, due in large part to the contributions of Jiang Ziya and other talented men. He was expected to share the fruits of victory with his strategists and generals who made great contributions on the battlefield. Ji Fa, now known as King Wu of the Zhou Dynasty, indeed kept that promise. He awarded his relatives and friends who helped him become the king with five peerage ranks according to their contributions, which in descending order included "gong" (duke), "hou" (marquis), "bo" (count), "zi" (viscount), and "nan" (baron). King Wu also implemented a decentralized system of government in which he effectively divided the whole territory of China into many pieces. The new nobles were awarded with certain amounts of hereditary fiefs according to their ranks. For example, Jiang Ziya was given the title of "grand duke" and was awarded the entire state of Qi, which later became one of the seven states during the Warring States period.

King Wu might have been generous toward his subordinates because he was able to defeat his enemy only with the support of a large coalition. He might have sought to strengthen this coalition by sharing the benefits of the victory and in turn stabilize his newly founded kingdom. Had he not done so, coalition members might have successfully led a major revolt against him for not keeping his promise.

When the Zhou Dynasty was founded in 1046 BC, ancient Chinese were not facing serious threats from the nomadic tribes in the Mongolian steppe. In fact, mounted archery, a form of archery in which a cavalryman armed with a bow shoots arrows while riding on horseback, had not yet been invented.[1] This significantly limited the nomads' advantage in military combat, and may be the reason why the nomads to the north of China divided into numerous tribes and failed to unite, ultimately posing little threat to China. There was no need for China to be a single empire at the time.

Moreover, as discussed in Chapter 2, a decentralized governance structure had some significant advantages in ancient times. First, information flows were slow and transportation costs usually increased considerably with distance. Thus, a more decentralized governance structure created greater administrative efficiency in different regions. This local administrative efficiency might have enhanced the stability of the entire kingdom. Second, under the decentralized structure, there was much competition between different hereditary fiefs. This competition was initially reflected in the attraction of labor migration, but resulted in a much higher level of conflict characterized by explicit threats, wars, land grabbing, and even the annexation of an entire hereditary fief. This competition induced the rulers of every region to increase government efficiency and decrease the rents imposed on the peasants. Hence, again, it might have ultimately enhanced the economic prosperity and political stability of the entire kingdom.

After about a 300-year rule, China under the Zhou Dynasty effectively disintegrated into many countries, due at least in part to the decentralized governance structure of the Zhou Dynasty. In particular, during the late stage of the Zhou Dynasty, the *de facto* states frequently engaged in major wars, which led to considerable human casualties.

At the end of the Zhou Dynasty, China was in its Warring States period, during which it comprised seven countries: Qin, Qi, Chu, Yan, Han, Zhao, and

Wei. At first, these seven states were all relatively powerful states that conquered and absorbed other smaller states. However, Qin eventually became the strongest of the seven, and successfully defeated the other six states to unite China into a single country. The King of Qin at the time, Yingzheng, crowned himself Shi Huangdi, meaning the first emperor of China. In fact, most Chinese today know him as Qin Shi Huang, and few know his original name.

How did Qin reunite China and build a strong central government? Qin became the dominant country due to Shang Yang's reformation. Supported by Duke Xiao of Qin, the *de facto* King of Qin at the time, Shang Yang enacted numerous reforms in Qin according to his "legalist philosophy" or legalism starting in 356 BC. Han Fei Zi best describes the thought of legalism in ancient China in a systematic way (e.g. Fu, 1996). He argues that there are three key components in legalism, including "Fa," "Shu," and "Shi," which are elaborated as follows.

"Fa" means law or principle. To govern a people by the rule of law, their ruler must have a law code that is clear and comprehensive. The law is made public, stating that every citizen will be treated equally before it. It is made known that those who break the law will be punished, and that the degree of punishment will depend on the seriousness of the crime.

"Shu" literally means methods or tactics. A ruler runs a state through his officials, who are the implementers and enforcers of the law. A ruler should be able to manipulate his officials through "Shu." Otherwise, he may be manipulated or controlled by his officials. A tactical ruler should be able to hide his true intentions so that the officials do not know how to please him except by strictly following the law.

"Shi" means legitimacy, power, and charisma. A ruler must be strong to credibly implement laws. It is important that his citizens trust what he says and fear him. Otherwise, the citizens and officials may not take the ruler seriously and hence not take the rule of law seriously.

Legalism and its three key components of "Fa," "Shu," and "Shi" are components of ancient Chinese wisdom, and can be well explained by the modern theory of political economy. First, laws must be clear, consistent, and relatively static over time to ensure that the populace understands and obeys them effectively. Because most people were illiterate in ancient times, there was a significant cost in conveying the details of the laws to the populace. For example, if many people were convicted of crimes simply because they were not aware of the related laws, the implementation of these laws was ineffective and even led to social unrest. Thus, the design of the laws had to account for this "transaction cost" to facilitate their enforcement and enhance the efficiency of the legal system.[2] Second, "Shu" is important for guaranteeing that officials are fair and honest in implementing the laws. If the officials are corrupt, they will pursue their own interests and often not enforce the laws, influencing people to do the same in turn. Third, "Shi" is important for making the legal system credible. Indeed, credibility is key for the successful implementation of any government policy.[3] A strong "Shi" (e.g., a powerful king who follows the law strictly) influences even the most powerful nobles to avoid challenging the legal system.

In line with the philosophy of legalism, Shang Yang implemented his reform and thereby fundamentally transformed the state of Qin. To make the to-be-established rule of law credible, Shang Yang thought up a clever strategy that remains a household story in China even today. First, upon his request, a piece of wood was erected at the south gate of the capital city of Qin. Shang Yang posted an announcement in the city stating that whoever carried the piece of wood to the north gate would receive a reward of 10 taels of gold, an astronomical fortune to most people. The piece of wood was long and conspicuous but not very heavy, and the distance between the two gates was not that considerable. Although a large crowd was attracted by the announcement, nobody accepted the offer, thinking it too good to be true. Shang Yang increased the reward to 50 taels of gold. A member of the crowd then stood to accept the offer, and the crowd watched him carry the wood from the south gate to the north gate. Shang Yang held a public ceremony for the man and awarded him the 50 taels of gold. The crowd was startled and regretted not accepting the offer earlier. The story quickly spread across the state of Qin. It became a popular belief that Shang Yang meant what he said, and this laid the foundation for his credibility and the law that he would soon implement.[4]

Shang Yang then introduced a comprehensive law code into the state of Qin. A vivid example is the Shuihudi Qin bamboo texts, which were excavated in December 1975 from a tomb in China's Hubei Province. The tomb was found to belong to an administrator in the state of Qin. The texts, which comprise over 1,000 bamboo slips, detail the Qin law code.[5] They include 18 types of different laws ranging from agricultural production to military affairs. In particular, the law highlights the protection of land rights. For example, if an individual was found to have moved the signs of the boundary that separated the lands of different owners, he was subject to severe penalty. Fighting among civilians was also strictly prohibited.

Of course, a rudimentary rule of law had existed in all of China's states including Qin before Shang Yang's reform. Shang Yang made the legal system more established. In particular, after his reform, the codes of law were much clearer and more comprehensive, and their enforcements were much stricter regardless of the perpetrator's social status and family background.

Shang Yang also made some important daring reforms.[6] First, he granted most slaves rights of citizenship. However, the new laws stipulated that if a farmer did not work hard enough to meet the quota set by the government, he would be enslaved. Second, the military's aristocracy system was replaced by a meritocracy. Soldiers and officers were rewarded with wealth, promotions, and even slaves according to their contributions and achievements on the battlefield. However, severe penalties were imposed on those who did not follow military orders even slightly, regardless of their family backgrounds. Third, immigration was strongly encouraged. The state of Qin once had large pieces of uncultivated land, which many peasants worked extraordinarily hard to explore and cultivate. Shang Yang induced many men of prime age living in the other six states to come to Qin to work on the unexplored land, granting them low taxes for their early years of migration and the property rights to the land in later years. Moreover, much of the unused land of the Qin nobles was taken away by the government and redistributed to the peasants without land.

The reforms implemented by Shang Yang substantially enhanced the economic power and military strength of the state of Qin. Many peasants worked extraordinarily hard to gain the privilege of land ownership. The many peasants who owned land worked much harder than those without land because the agricultural output was less shared by others. Moreover, soldiers fought much more bravely because a good performance on the battlefield had high returns while shirking their responsibilities resulted in severe penalization. Finally, the uncorrupt system of the Qin army induced many high-quality soldiers and officers to join. Because the state of Qin bordered many nomadic tribes in the north, the army's meritocratic system and the encouragement of the immigration policy allowed the army to absorb many brave and skillful soldiers from the nomadic tribes.

Why did the reforms only happen in the state of Qin? Why did the other six states not implement similar reforms to strengthen their economies and armies? The most important answer is that the kings of the state of Qin were typically much "stronger" than those of the other states. In other words, they were more powerful in controlling the nobles of the state than the other six states. The underlying reason for this was the unique history of the development of the state of Qin.

The kings of the state of Qin were stronger than the kings of the other six states during China's Warring States period due to the results of historical events that occurred during the Zhou Dynasty. In the early years of the Zhou Dynasty, the central government had firm control over China's vast territory. However, over time, it lost its political and military power over hereditary fiefs. In 771 BC, a major domestic dispute erupted within the royal family of the Zhou Dynasty. King You demoted and exiled his queen, deposed the queen's son as the crown prince, and made the son of his favorite concubine the new crown prince. In response, the queen's father, the Marquis of Shen, colluded with a nomadic tribe called the Quanrong to raid the capital city of the Zhou Dynasty, which is near Xian in present-day China. The king was quickly killed and the Quanrong plundered and destroyed the city.

In the aftermath, the Marquis of Shen gathered the troops of some nearby hereditary fiefs to defeat the Quanrong. With the support of a small group of nobles, the marquis declared the original crown prince, the queen's son and his grandson, as the new king known as King Ping. Moreover, as the old capital had been sacked and was still under the threat of the Quanrong tribe, the Marquis of Shen and his supporters decided to found a new capital far away from the old capital and close to present-day Luoyang.

Xian and Luoyang were far apart even by today's standards. Without modern transportation technology, traveling between the two locations involved a long and arduous journey. It was also an extremely dangerous trip for the new king because other nobles were trying to kill him and declare another prince as king.

It was under these circumstances that the Duke Xiang of Qin entered into the picture. In 771 BC, Qin was only an "attached state" (fuyong) of a major state. However, it was a quite important state because it was in the westernmost part of China during the Zhou Dynasty and often engaged in the most intensive fights with the Quanrong tribe. Duke Xiang led the Qin army to escort King Ping from the old capital (near Xian) to the new capital (near Luoyang) and helped install him on his throne. King Ping rewarded Duke Xiang by formally and symbolically elevating the state of Qin from the status of an "attached state" to the status of a vassal state. The new king then made a "conditional award" to Qin: if the state of Qin could defeat Quanrong and expel the nomadic tribe from the large area of land to the west of Qin, which originally belonged to China, then the large piece of land would be given to the state of Qin. Thanks to the effort and sacrifices of several generations, Qin ultimately defeated the Quanrong and took back China's lost land, expanding the map of the state of Qin tremendously.

Due to the frequent military campaigns conducted against the Quanrong, the rulers of Qin had firm control of the army and hence the state. Indeed, even after Qin took back China's lost land from the Quanrong, it was constantly concerned that the Quanrong would launch counterattacks against Qin at any time. Thus, the centralization of power in Qin was essential for Qin to have an effective army that could bear the brunt of a possible attack from the war-like nomadic tribe. Consequently, the Qin nobles put up little resistance to the centralization of power. Had they not done so, the Qin troops would have been inefficiently coordinated by more than one commander-in-chief, and the Quanrong would most likely have defeated the Qin army and plundered and killed everyone in the state of Qin during the invasion, including the nobles. Thus, it was this unique history and the geographical location of the state of Qin that gave its king more centralized power than the kings of other states.

Because a large portion of the land of Qin had recently been taken from the Quanrong, the area was under the direct control of the Qin rulers. These rulers, who were initially called dukes and kings in a later period of the Zhou Dynasty, had effective political and military control of the state and worried little about potential noble insurrections. This made the ruler of Qin much stronger compared with the rulers of the other six states during the period.

Duke Xiao of Qin took the throne of the state of Qin in 361 BC. He joined the army in his early teens, and had a firm grasp of it when he became king. In terms of legalism, the state of Qin had the "Shi" to credibly implement major legal reforms. Duke Xiao also saw that there were more benefits to establishing a good rule of law in Qin than in other states. As described earlier, nomadic tribes occupied a large fraction of its lands. Hence, many of its citizens previously belonged to nomadic tribes, whose culture was much more violent than the Chinese culture. Qin required a comprehensive system of law to effectively discipline violent actions and other socially harmful behavior. Qin's disadvantage could have been turned into an advantage once its citizens followed the rule of law. A large fraction of its citizens were nomads and hence more skillful soldiers. Thus, once a good incentive system was introduced to the army in association with the legal reform, the army of Qin became more powerful than the armies of other states. In sum, the king had more credibility in implementing major legal reforms in the state of Qin than in other states, and the benefit of these reforms was greater. These may be the most important reasons why the reforms made by Shang Yang took place in Qin rather than in any of the other six states.

However, it is usually costly and risky for a ruler to implement a major legal reform, and the reformation in Qin was no exception. The crown prince committed a crime that should have carried a heavy penalty and posed a serious challenge to Shang Yang. A severe penalty could not be imposed on the crown prince, who was set to be the future King of Qin. However, if no one was held responsible for the crime, the rule of law designed and implemented by Shang Yang would have lost much of its credibility. Shang Yang ultimately decided to punish the two teachers of the crown prince. However, the teachers were both powerful figures. Shang Yang ordered one of them, the elder brother of Duke Xiao, to have his nose cut as a penalty.

When a new law is announced, some powerful people do not believe that they will be punished for breaking it. Once they break the law, the ruler faces the difficult choice of whether to punish them. If the ruler is weak, he may have to choose to pardon them, as he may depend on the support of those powerful people to maintain his rule. Even if the ruler is strong, punishing the powerful people may nevertheless weaken the stability of his rule. However, if he is able to stay in power while punishing the powerful people who broke the law, he establishes the credibility of the new law. Therefore, the risk of punishing the powerful people who doubt the credibility of a new law may be the greatest cost of instituting a rule of law in a lawless society.

Moreover, the implementation of a rule of law may hurt groups with vested interests. For example, Shang Yang freed the slaves in the state of Qin, which hurt the interests of their previous masters. He also redistributed some land from the rich to the poor, particularly the newly freed slaves, further antagonizing the large landlords. In fact, most of Shang Yang's reform measures benefited the king and state of Qin as a whole and hurt the interests of the upper class. In addition, the requirement that everyone had to be treated equally by the rule of law substantially lowered the social status of rich people. Therefore, the rich and many powerful government ministers constantly attacked the legal reform, genuinely risking an overthrow of the rule of Duke Xiao in the state of Qin. This might have been the most important reason why Duke Xiao appointed Shang Yang, who came from another state, to implement the reform rather than doing so himself.

Of course, Shang Yang was also an intelligent and determined reformer. To implement such a large-scale dramatic reform, a wise and brave reformer is required to carefully plan and intelligently implement the reform without fear of retaliation. In fact, Shang Yang eventually became the scapegoat for the reform. To appease the nobles who hated the reform, after Duke Xiao's death, the new king of Qin sentenced Shang Yang to death. The style of execution was the worst imaginable to people at the time: he was fastened to five chariots led by cattle and his body was torn to pieces. His entire family was also executed. However, because Shang Yang's reform enormously benefited the king and most of the people in the state of Qin, his reform policies largely continued to be enacted.

Shang Yang is an immortal figure in Chinese history. Due to his reform, the state of Qin enjoyed military superiority over the other six states. Qin ultimately annihilated and annexed the other states and reunited China under the new Qin Dynasty. More important, even after the collapse of the Qin Dynasty, the legal system continued to be well established in China over the following dynasties. The "belief system" or "mindset" that China was ruled by laws extended beyond the state of Qin to the entirety of China and became firmly established among the Chinese people. Powerful nobles did not challenge the law for its own sake, and the Chinese government found the rule of law easy to implement. Although today the rule of law in China is weak relative to that of Western countries, it was far superior to that of European countries throughout most of history.

Finally, let's have a brief comparison of the culture and legal system between Europe and China in ancient times. The ancient European culture may lie somewhere between the ancient Chinese and nomadic cultures. People tended to follow basic laws and social customs, making the social orders generally peaceful in ancient Europe. However, the conflicts between different individuals were not always settled in courts. For example, the "duel" was a common practice in early modern Europe, and continued even into the early 20th century. In the early years, duels were mostly fought with swords. Beginning in the late 18th century and continuing into the 19th century, both pistols and swords were used. The United States had a weak legal system when it was first established, and duels were commonplace there.

Duels have been conducted for emotional reasons or as a way of resolving economic conflicts. When the rule of law was not well established, a duel could be an efficient way of resolving conflicts. A duel served as a better alternative to other forms of conflict that were less regulated and larger in scale. When a major dispute erupted between two large families or clans and could not be resolved by the legal court because the rule of law was not well established, a natural impulse for both families/clans was to resolve the dispute through war. However, such wars were very destructive, and over time a much less destructive option emerged. If a conflict arose between two large families, each family selected a single member, such as its best fighter. The conflict was settled by a duel between the two selected members only, without harm coming to any other members. In terms of economics, the social custom of the "duel" emerged as a way of minimizing the "transaction cost" when the rule of law was not well established.

Notes

1 Karasulas (2004).
2 See Williamson (1979, 1981) for discussions about the importance of "transaction costs" in the design of institutions in general.
3 For example, see Barro and Gordon (1983), Drazen (2000), Grossman and Noh (1990), and Kydland and Prescott (1977).
4 In the economics literature, Greif (1994) studies the importance of cultural beliefs to the formation of socially desirable institutions.
5 See Hulsewé (1985).
6 See, e.g., Li (1977).

5 The threat from the United Nomad Country and the start of the United Chinese Empire

The state of Qin enjoyed military superiority over the other six states largely due to the implementation of Shang Yang's reform policies. Qin ultimately annihilated and annexed the other states and reunited China under the new Qin Dynasty. The first emperor of the Qin Dynasty, Qin Shi Huang, abolished the system of hereditary fiefs and established China's first imperial dynasty. Without landowning lords operating in different regions, China became a much more centralized country, increasing its interregional trade and military security.

A number of administrative reforms were implemented to establish a stable empire. In particular, a centralized administration system replaced the system of hereditary fiefs, and China was divided into four administrative units. The top unit comprised commanderies ("Jun"), which numbered 36 at the beginning and later increased to 40. The next two units were districts ("Xian") and counties ("Xiang"), respectively. The administrative unit at the bottom comprised hundred-family units known as "Li." The identities of the original seven states were completely eliminated. The officials serving in the four administrative units were appointed based on merit rather than hereditary rights.

Moreover, the Qin Dynasty standardized the writings of Chinese characters. Written Chinese is fundamentally different from many other written languages in that it is a logogram as opposed to a phonogram such as written English. During the Warring States period of the Zhou Dynasty, the scripts of the seven states exhibited significant differences. The Qin Dynasty created a standardized script based on the seal script of the state of Qin, and made the newly standardized script the only official script in the whole empire.

There are currently numerous dialects of the Chinese language in different parts of China. When I first arrived to teach in Hong Kong in September 1994, I could not understand Cantonese, the dialect used throughout most of China's Guangdong Province. It is not an exaggeration to say that Cantonese was like a foreign language to me. My experience is typical in China. People often do not understand the dialects in other provinces. However, fortunately, written Chinese is a logogram, and hence people in China can share a written language although their pronunciations of many words are very different.

Why did Qin Shi Huang build an empire that implemented prefectures and counties rather than continue the feudal system adopted in the Zhou Dynasty? Quite surprisingly, this question has never been answered efficiently. Most Chinese believe that the "grandiose" personal character of Qin Shi Huang accounted for the change. Some think that the Qin Dynasty was established upon the ashes of the late Warring States period, when the states often engaged in bloody wars that led to enormous casualties and destruction. Qin Shi Huang might have thought that only an empire could prevent major wars from happening. However, this reasoning does not explain why the clearly advantageous system of hereditary fiefs was widely adopted around the world but not in China. The Zhou Dynasty lasted for more than 1,000 years, making it the longest dynasty in Chinese history. Most of the Zhou Dynasty was characterized by peace and prosperity. Motivated by the feudal system, some states, particularly Qin and Chu, expanded their territories substantially, pushing out China's national boundary considerably in turn.

This book suggests a new answer: Qin Shi Huang moved beyond the feudal system due to concerns over the presence of the nomadic Xiongnu tribe in Mongolia. The ancient Chinese people were not afraid of the nomads themselves. During the Spring and Autumn Period, the Qin state expanded mainly through the continuous conquest and occupation of the lands of non-Chinese nomads, who were segmented and small in number. However, when the Qin Dynasty was established in 221 BC, the nomads in today's Mongolia, Central Asia, and parts of northern China became increasingly integrated. In 209 BC a nomadic empire was formed in this vast region, and all of the nomads referred to themselves as the Xiongnu.[1]

The Xiongnu frequently pillaged the border regions of China even before their unification. Qin Shi Huang turned his attention to the growing threat of the nomadic empire shortly after the unification of China. In 215 BC, he sent 300,000 elite troops to fight the Xiongnu. Under the command of General Meng Tian, the Qin army engaged in a major battle with the Xiongnu army near the Yellow River. The Xiongnu were completely defeated and escaped to the desert areas of Mongolia. The Qin army recaptured large areas of the territory, including most of present-day Inner Mongolia.[2]

However, this brilliant victory did not intoxicate Qin Shi Huang. He was fully aware of the potential combative power of the Xiongnu, and was seriously concerned that they would become much stronger with greater unification. Thus, immediately after the battle, Qin Shi Huang started the large-scale construction of the Great Wall.

Qin Shi Huang also knew very well that his dynasty would always need a strong army to defend against the Xiongnu. This was possible only if China were a united empire. If China were divided into many small states, the tax revenue of each individual state would not support a suitable army. The joint forces among several states usually failed to cooperate efficiently because each state had the tendency to pursue its self-interest by not fighting hard against the common enemy. In fact, even the continuing construction of the Great Wall required China to be a single country. Otherwise, one state would have always wanted the others to pay for a greater share of the expenditure, which would have compromised the construction of the Great Wall.

The Qin Dynasty was a powerful empire that left a significant mark on world history. Nevertheless, it collapsed after a short rule of 15 years because Qin Shi Huang overly exploited Chinese commoners. Peasants were taxed almost to their subsistence level. To make matters worse, "statute labor" or unpaid labor imposed by the state was heavily imposed on most households to facilitate the construction of many massive projects.

The Great Wall was a gigantic project whose construction used up a tremendous amount of human resources. Although it contributed greatly to generations of Chinese people in ancient times, the main concerns of people living in the Qin Dynasty were survival and their own material welfare. An estimated 1 million workers died constructing the Great Wall. A folk tale entitled "Lady Meng Jiang," which was passed from generation to generation for 2,000 years in China, may better illustrate the significance of that number. Wikipedia describes it as follows:

> The story is set during the Qin Dynasty (221BC-206BC). It tells of how Meng Jiangnü's bitter weeping made a section of the Great Wall collapse. Meng Jiangnü's husband Fan Qiliang was caught by imperial officials and sent as Corvee labor to build the Great Wall. Meng Jiangnü heard nothing from him after his departure, so she set out to look for him. Unfortunately, by the time she reached the Great Wall, she discovered that her husband had already died. Hearing the bad news, she cried her heart out. Her howling caused the collapse of a part of the Great Wall. This story indicates that the Great Wall was the result of the hard labour of tens of thousands of Chinese commoners. . .
>
> In memory of Meng Jiangnu, later generations built a temple, called the Temple of Mengjiangnu, at the foot of the Great Wall in which a statue of her is located.

Qin Shi Huang was despotic during his rule, possibly because he thought he had killed all of the other kings and no longer had any rivals. He launched massive building projects that entailed excessively heavy taxation and the drafting of an enormous amount of human labor. Although one may argue that the construction of the Great Wall suited a noble cause for the Chinese people in general, Qin Shi Huang also engaged in other enormous projects such as his Mausoleum, which currently contains the Terracotta Army collection.

The Terracotta Army is an enormous collection of terracotta sculptures depicting the armies of the Qin state. It features an estimated 8,000 life-size soldiers, 130 chariots with 520 horses, and 150 cavalry horses. The soldiers wear vivid facial expressions that may reveal their different personalities. This dazzling project indicates the superb technological capacity and organizational strength of the Qin Empire, which today's Chinese consider a major source of national pride. However, at the time, it necessitated an enormous amount of labor hours.

Qin Shi Huang was considered a tyrant who made people's lives extremely difficult and miserable. The construction of massive projects such as the Great Wall, Mausoleum, and extravagant royal palaces exhausted the empire's financial resources, and many Chinese revolted as a result. After the death of Qin Shi Huang, the new emperor, Qin Er Shi, lacked the political and military skills necessary to control the country, and the Qin Dynasty collapsed quickly.

Qin Shi Huang built the first empire in Chinese history, and it collapsed within a mere 15 years. However, from an economics perspective, it is hard to argue that Qin Shi Huang made any serious mistakes. In economics, an individual makes a rational decision if the expected benefit *ex ante* is greater than the cost. Of course, the *ex post* realization may turn out poorly. For example, many people take planes to travel long distances despite the danger of an air crash. After the unification of China, Qin Shi Huang had to decide whether to build the Great Wall. He knew the expenditure would be tremendous. There was no option to build only a fraction of the Great Wall, as it would have failed to defend his empire against the Xiongnu, who would have destroyed it. Qin Shi Huang's one serious miscalculation was his life expectancy. In fact, he expended an enormous amount of resources in an attempt to achieve immortality. Although he might have expected a long life, he died suddenly at the age of 49,[3] leaving his inexperienced and much less sophisticated son to rule the disgruntled people of a large country. It could be said that Qin Shi Huang's gamble of building the Great Wall failed due to this miscalculation.

After the collapse of Qin, there was a large civil war in China among various groups of rebels. The prevailing group was led by Liu Bang, who thereafter established the Han Dynasty. Learning lessons from the Qin Dynasty, Liu Bang and his offspring, the new emperors of the Han Dynasty, pursued a policy of "benevolent" rule in China. No massive projects were implemented, and even the royal families tried to avoid extravagance as much as they could. Consequently, tax rates were low and statute labor decreased considerably relative to that in the Qin Dynasty. All of these measures encouraged production, economic development, and population growth.

Liu Bang believed that an important reason for the demise of the Qin Dynasty was its complete abolishment of the feudal system. The revolts against the Qin Empire erupted on small scales. For example, the first insurrection led by Cheng Sheng and Wu Guang initially gathered a force of only 900 peasants. However, the local Qin army failed to quell the insurrection, which led the rebel army to quickly increase its number of soldiers to 20,000. After a few months, Cheng Sheng declared himself a king, and only then did the Qin Dynasty feel threatened and send a strong army to fight the rebels. Although Cheng's rebel forces were quelled, their uprising inspired other rebels to follow suit.

Low management efficiency at local areas of the vast Qin Empire was an important reason for the failure to suppress Cheng's rebellion at the very beginning, when it was weak. In such a large country, the central government was able to keep a close eye on only a small area near the capital. In most other areas, the management tasks had to be delegated to local officials.

Two scenarios bear consideration. The first is a scenario in which the political structure of a country is an empire comprising prefectures and counties. In this case, the self-interest of local government officials may differ significantly from the goal of the central government. If a rebellion erupts, the local officials of a county may simply try to drive the rebel force away from their jurisdiction. Even if they have an opportunity to annihilate the rebels, they may find that it is not in their interest to do so. An official may be severely punished if he were to fail in the military operation, and only slightly rewarded for a military victory. This scenario applied to Liu Bang. A large group of Qin soldiers received the news that his rebel force was attacking a county and immediately ran to its rescue. Before the army arrived, it received the news that the county was captured. In fact, Liu's force was weak at the time, and the Qin army would have defeated Liu's rebels even after the county's capture. However, the general of the Qin army decided not to take the risk.

In the second scenario, the political structure of a country is a feudal system in which many princes and nobles are awarded their own fiefs. In this case, if a rebellion were to erupt in a local lord's fief, the lord would do his best to quell the insurrection. He would also try to kill any rebels to demonstrate to the people living under his rule that those who dared to rebel against him would face severe punishment. In fact, he would also be much more careful in managing his fief to guarantee that rebellions would not occur in the first place. Therefore, under the feudal system, each prince does everything possible to maintain the stability of his fief, and when each area of the country is stable, the entire country is stable.

Liu Bang knew about the importance of political centralization and the centralized national power to China's defense against Xiongnu. In fact, he had a personal bitter experience with the powerful army of this nomadic empire. During the final years of the Qin Dynasty, the Qin army was completely occupied with fighting against the rebels. As a result, almost no defense was being provided against the Xiongnu in the border regions. Seizing this opportunity, the Xiongnu took all of the territory to the north of the Great Wall. Moreover, small groups of Xiongnu men frequently raided the border reigns of China, which increasingly threatened Chinese sovereignty in those areas. The Han Dynasty then decided to fight against further incursions from the Xiongnu.

In 200 BC, six years after the establishment of the Han Dynasty, Liu Bang led a large army in combat against the elite Xiongnu forces. In the first few battles, the Xiongnu feigned a quick defeat, and the Han army began to pursue. However, when they reached present-day Datong in Shanxi Province, Liu and his troops discovered that they were surrounded by the Xiongnu army. After a narrow escape seven days later, Liu tried to appease the Xiongnu by offering them a large amount of tributes and marrying some of the daughters of the royal family to their tribal chiefs.[4]

Of course, Liu Bang knew very well that the ultimate deterrence against the Xiongnu incursions was to build a strong army through the political unification of the Han Dynasty. He was also concerned about internal instability, which led him to favor a feudal system. He finally accepted a tradeoff by mixing the imperial and feudal systems. The Han Court took direct control over about one third of the country close to the capital city. The rest of China was delegated to the rule of a number of feudal lords, who were conferred the title of "king." Meanwhile, to mitigate the probability that a regional king would rebel, Liu conspired to kill all of the kings who were initially conferred for their contributions to the founding of the Han Dynasty but were not his close relatives, and then implemented a policy that only those from the Liu clan could be conferred as kings.

This system worked well for some time. Between 180 and 141 BC, China entered into a golden age as measured by the people's welfare, which was mainly determined by general stability and economic prosperity. The Han Court centrally controlled one third of the large empire, which generated enough tax revenue to maintain an army that was usually strong enough to deter potential incursions from the Xiongnu. In comparison with the Qin Dynasty, taxes and other burdens on the people were vastly decreased, which induced people to work hard and led to a substantial increase in production. As the period elapsed under the reign of Emperors Wen and Jing of the Han Dynasty, it was often referred to as the Rule of Wen and Jing. However, even this golden period was not completely peaceful. A major internal war caused by Emperor Wen's attempt to further centralize the government occurred during the third year of his reign. This war is often referred to as the Rebellion of the Seven Kingdoms.

When Emperor Wen took the throne, he immediately found that the Xiongnu were becoming increasingly powerful, and that the Han Dynasty was facing a greater difficulty defending itself against foreign incursions. Establishing a stronger army required more money. The Han government even spent some money to recruit more soldiers of better quality from some of the nomadic tribes. "Nationalism" is really a modern concept that appeared only two or three centuries ago (e.g., Greenfeld, 1992). Most nomads at the time cared little about their national identity. Rather, they united purely for the material gains provided by raiding the farmers in the border regions of China. They often fought with one another, and stole and robbed one another of their livestock and women. Therefore, when they were offered high salaries to join the Han army, many were happy to do so. In fact, the Han Dynasty was often looking for "underdogs" among the nomadic tribes who were bullied by other more powerful tribes as potential soldiers.

The only way for the Han Court to obtain more money was through the collection of taxes via political centralization. In other words, the Han Dynasty felt the urgent need to get rid of the feudal system altogether. Its intention obviously directly contradicted the interests of the kings of the vassal states. The regional lords not only collected their own taxes but also set their own laws and minted their own coins. In fact, the kings of some large states behaved domineeringly, and hardly considered the emperor as their ruler. When Emperor Wen started to implement the policy of decreasing the territory of the vassal states, seven states immediately decided to revolt against him.

The seven vassal states formed a large army that outnumbered the army of the Han Dynasty. However, because the soldiers of the central government were constantly defending against the Xiongnu incursions, they were better trained and more experienced. The generals of the Han army were also wise and well organized. In contrast, the troops of the seven states were often poorly coordinated, and the rebel forces were quickly defeated as a result. After this war, the semi-feudal system created at the beginning of the Han Dynasty was effectively eliminated, and the Han Dynasty became a single empire. Furthermore, the "cultural belief" that China should have a unified empire rather than divided states began to enter into the mindset of the Chinese people.[5]

With the establishment of a stronger army, the Han Dynasty implemented the policy of inducing some Chinese peasants to migrate to the border regions. In the first half-century of the Han Dynasty, the Xiongnu frequently raided its border regions, often bringing destruction to those areas. The Han Dynasty mainly used the "He-Qin" strategy, establishing friendly relations with the Xiongnu via marriage and providing them with large amounts of tributes. However, this strategy at most only decreased the amount of large-scale Xiongnu incursions into the Han territory.

When the nomadic warriors launched an attack, the Han troops often failed to defend against it. Once a border region fell into the hands of the Xiongnu, the civilians there faced all kinds of misery and tragedy. Their food and other properties were robbed, their houses were burned, their loved ones were killed, and their wives and daughters were raped. Over time, most of the Chinese emigrated away from the border regions between the Han Dynasty and Xiongnu.

However, after the Han army became stronger, it was better able to defend the border regions. Given a government subsidy, some poor peasants began to resettle into the border regions. The Han government provided these new settlers with military training so that they could defend themselves against the Xiongnu before the rescuing Han troops could advance.

This migration policy was also beneficial to the Han army for two reasons. First, late food supplies were a concern for Han troops stationed in the border region. For example, a soldier would starve or at least lose his combative power if he had nothing to eat for a week. This concern was greatly decreased when a large number of Chinese peasants settled in the border regions. When a Han troop was in urgent need of food supplies, it could borrow from the Chinese peasants. Second, because the peasants were provided with military training, the Han army could recruit them in imminent situations as needed, such as during sudden attacks by the Xiongnu armies.

Notes

1 See, e.g., Di Cosmo (1999).
2 See, e.g., Beckwith (2009).
3 http://www.princeton.edu/~achaney/tmve/wiki100k/docs/Qin_Shi_Huang.html
4 See, e.g., Yap (2009).
5 See, e.g., Koo (1920).

Part II
The formation of national character in ancient China

6 From the "burning of books and burying of scholars" to the ideology of Confucianism

The Warring States period was a miserable one for the Chinese people due to frequent political chaos and bloody battles. However, it marked a golden age of free thought in the history of China. Numerous schools of thought including Confucianism, Legalism, Taoism, and the School of Names (or the Logicians) were developed during this period and were discussed freely and refined continuously. These thoughts and ideas became parts of the core of the Chinese culture and influenced the entirety of Chinese history.

The rulers in different Chinese states usually allowed and even facilitated such free environments out of concern for their own benefits. First, they became more popular rulers by granting their people more political and personal freedoms. The intense rivalry among different states led to fierce competition over the support of the people under their reigns. In the economics literature, "gift exchange" theory explains the relationship between employers and employees.[1] It argues that an employee's work effort and hence productivity depends on how well he is treated by his employer. A firm often pays its employees a gift of wages in excess of the minimum required in return for a great work effort and productivity from its workers. This logic also applies to the relationship between a king and his people. For example, *ceteris paribus*, people tend to fight for their country and their ruler more passionately on the battlefield if they live happy lives and hence feel more emotionally attached to their country.

One classic example is the Battle of Muye fought between the Shang Dynasty and the rebel forces of Ji Fa and Jiang Ziya. The army of the Shang Dynasty vastly outnumbered the rebel forces. However, the king of the Shang, King Zhou, was a tyrant who levied extremely heavy taxes on the civilians and enslaved many people. When the rebel forces approached, King Zhou provided weapons to about 170,000 slaves and asked them to protect him and the capital city. However, as soon as the battle broke out, these slaves, who had suffered enormously under the king, defected immediately to the rebel army. As a result, King Zhou was killed and the Shang Dynasty collapsed.[2]

Second, again due to the brutal rivalries among different states, the rulers were constantly seeking better ways to govern their states with the hope of building a stronger country with a more powerful army. Indeed, even a strong word like "cutthroat" may be insufficient to describe the degree of competition and hostility among different states during the Warring States period. It was common for a war to result in the casualties of hundreds of thousands of soldiers. A defeat in a major war would have been a disaster for the king of any state. His vassal state would have been annexed by others, and he would have lost everything he had, including his land, property, women, and life in addition to the lives of his clan.

Thus, the rulers encouraged the development of thoughts and ideas that could lead them to establish better methods of government, war, and diplomacy. Talented people often stood out in an environment of free debate and discussion, and the rulers often had a strong urge to identify these people to help them to govern their states. Eminent scholars during this era were not only frequently consulted by the rulers, but also often directly appointed to senior positions in the central government. Shang Yang was such an example.

However, this period of free thought came to an end with the unification of China by the state of Qin. In a dramatic event known as the "burning of books and burying of scholars," Qin Shi Huang eliminated the environment of free thought and intellectual discourse. In 221 BC, State Chancellor Li Si proposed to Qin Shi Huang that the newly unified China should suppress the discourse of political opinion and unify intellectual thought. To achieve this purpose, Li Si suggested burning a broad range of books so that they would not be available to the public. These books included all history books except those written by the Qin historians and the scholarly works of different schools of thought. Qin Shi Huang accepted Li Si's proposal. Imperial orders were issued immediately, declaring that the listed books would be burned for 30 days, and that those who had not burned their books within this period would be arrested as criminals and sentenced to work as slave laborers on the Great Wall. Furthermore, those who discussed Confucian Classics or used ancient examples to ridicule contemporary politics would be executed. One year later, in a more drastic move, Qin Shi Huang ordered that more than 460 scholars be buried alive.[3]

The "burning of books and burying of scholars" remains known to most Chinese today. It has been consistently criticized throughout Chinese history and made Qin Shi Huang into a notorious figure. This book provides a rationale for the act of Qin Shi Huang: The emperor had two reasons for enacting the decree from a political economics perspective. First, the contentions of different schools of thought lost their material foundation for existing after the unification of China. Due to the lack of competition between different *de facto* countries, Qin Shi Huang thought he required less support from the people and therefore deprived them of excess political and personal freedoms. Second, different schools of thoughts often comment on and judge the behavior of rulers. For example, Mencius, who was the most famous Confucian scholar after Confucius himself, once set the following code for the ruler of a state: "To a state, the people are the most important thing, the state comes second, and the ruler is the least important thing." He added that "If a king treats his ministers as brothers, then they will regard the king as a confidant; a king treats his ministers as servants, then they will regard the king as an ordinary person; a king treats his ministers as dirt, then they will regard the king as an enemy." Such sayings served as useful reminders for the kings of different states to treat their people well and hence enhance their economic and military powers during the Warring States period. However, in the unified China, Qin Shi Huang often used extremely brutal measures to quell rebellions. In such a new environment, free speech, which emphasized the significance of the common citizen in the state, would have instigated more rebellions.

According to Mencius, it was acceptable for the people to overthrow and kill a ruler who flagrantly ignored the people's welfare and often resorted to harsh measures to deal with minor conflicts. Mencius used King Zhou of the Shang Dynasty, who had a reputation for extraordinary extravagance and brutality, as an example: "I have merely heard of killing a villain Zhou, but I have not heard of murdering [him as] the ruler."

Mencius's view was reasonable during the Warring States period, when the kings of the seven states competed fiercely and ruthlessly with one another. A king who cared little about his people's welfare would have lacked their support, and his state would have been defeated by other states, leading to not only his downfall from the kinship but also usually his demise and that of his family members. For example, when Qin Shi Huang united China, five kings of the six conquered states were killed. The King of Qi was pardoned from death because the Qi state, the last conquered by Qin, surrendered without a fight.

The fear of possible demise formed a culture in which the kings of the different states during the Warring States period became humble toward intelligent ministers and seriously concerned about their people's welfare. The Confucianism at the time was a particular reflection of this culture. However, the political environment changed considerably after Qin Shi Huang's unification of China. The preceding Zhou Dynasty implemented a decentralized system of government in which a large number of nobles effectively ruled their hereditary fiefs almost independently of the central government. However, the autonomous power of local lords no longer existed in the new era of the strong central government under the Qin Dynasty. Qin Shi Huang literally translates as "the first emperor of Qin," and he was commonly considered to be the first emperor in the history of China.

Qin Shi Huang built China into a highly centralized empire. The new political environment entailed a new Chinese culture. In particular, it required people to be absolutely obedient to the emperor. This was inconsistent with the Confucianism at the time, which during the Warring States period required that a ruler justify his position by acting benevolently toward his people before he could expect reciprocation from the people. As described previously, Mencius stated that a ruler was actually subordinate to the masses of people and the resources of society. Under such a circumstance, Qin Shi Huang might have intended to change the traditional Chinese culture developed during the Zhou Dynasty over more than 700 years, and to establish a new culture by enacting the drastic and conspicuous measure of the "burning of books and burying of scholars."

His actions might have had another cause. Qin Shi Huang implemented a number of very unpopular policies. He imposed heavy taxes and statute labor to launch several massive projects that brought hardship and misery to most Chinese households. He also displeased and angered many nobles and senior generals by building an empire rather than a decentralized political structure. After the unification of China, the nobles and those with important military achievements expected to be awarded with certain amounts of hereditary fiefs. However, to their great disappointment, the emperor decided to abandon the feudal system completely.

With so many people against him and secretly hating him, Qin Shi Huang continued to implement his unpopular policies to make sure that the people feared him. In relation to game theory, he had to guarantee the belief in every individual that everyone else was absolutely obedient to him. Doing so would have made it rational for any single individual to avoid standing up to challenge the emperor and facilitate the stability of his empire. The belief would have therefore been "self-fulfilling." However, if an individual believed that other people would fight against the oppression of the empire, he might have found it optimal to join the rebel forces, which would surely have led to the empire's demise. This belief would also have been self-fulfilling. Qin Shi Huang had to eradicate the second type of belief among his people, and the "burning of books and burying of scholars," which was conspicuous to most people, offered an effective way of achieving this purpose.

In particular, Qin Shi Huang could not allow anyone to challenge his decision and authority in public. This would have altered the necessary "belief," which would have had dire consequences for the Qin Dynasty. However, "scholars" at the time were traditionally more tolerant in expressing their views. (As mentioned earlier, this tradition was encouraged during the Warring States period because it was often an effective way for the kings to identify their most talented people, whom they appointed to govern their states.) Against such a background, some scholars might have effectively become the spokespersons for those against the policies of Qin Shi Huang. Although many nobles were furious at his decision to abandon the feudal system, none dared to challenge the policy openly. One Confucian scholar, Chunyu Yue, stood up at a banquet that Qin Shi Huang set for some well-known intellectuals and argued strongly against the policy, advising the emperor to follow the old tradition.

Most of the scholars might have expressed their opinions honestly rather than out of any political agenda of conspiracy, stubbornly maintaining their scholarly views. However, it cannot be ruled out that some scholars might have been induced or bribed to do so. In any case, Qin Shi Huang decided that this voice must be silenced, and that the only way of doing so was to conspicuously execute outspoken scholars by burying them alive.

Legalism, which requires people to follow the laws strictly or be punished accordingly, became the only ideology endorsed by the Qin Empire. Qin Shi Huang might have been well justified in adopting this ideology, as it ensured that the emperor's authority could never be challenged under any circumstance.

Indeed, in such a large empire, even a good policy would not have pleased everybody. For example, although the construction of the Great Wall benefited the ancient Chinese over the long run, it led to many people's deaths and broke up many families, as vividly illustrated in the story of "Lady Meng Jiang." If the people were permitted to freely judge and openly discuss the emperor's performance, the belief in the emperor's absolute authority would have been undermined, potentially leading to social unrest and rebellion. Therefore, Qin Shi Huang believed that grievances should never be voiced in public as a way of guaranteeing that people would strictly obey the laws and follow his new policies.

Nevertheless, Qin Shi Huang made a serious miscalculation. Although he had hoped to live for a long time, if not forever, he died at the age of 49. After his death, the new emperor was much less skillful at governing the empire, and the Qin Dynasty quickly collapsed.

After a period of civil war, Liu Bang established the Han Dynasty. Liu was born to peasant parents. Due to his relatively low origins, he might have had an inferiority complex that led him to despise Confucian scholars, a generally well-respected class in society. In one display of contempt, Liu took the cap of a scholar, urinated in it, and then placed it back onto the scholar's head.

However, when Liu became the emperor of China, he immediately realized the tremendous value of Confucianism to the governance of his new empire. Confucian scholars also learned a hard lesson from Qin Shi Huang's "burning of books and burying of scholars." Consequently, Confucianism was modified to fit the new environment of a centralized China over time. In particular, a greater emphasis was placed on respect for authority and proper behavior. This made Confucianism a valuable tool for the rule of China. In 195 BC, Liu Bang paid a pilgrim to take him to the hometown of Confucius, and he became the first Chinese emperor to worship the philosopher.

Confucianism was completely revived during the Han Dynasty. Moreover, it became the official ideology of the imperial state of China. Emperor Wu of the Han Dynasty formally announced that China was a Confucian state. It was a strong social norm that rigorously constrained people's behavior. In this way, Confucianism became a kind of religion.

Confucian scholar Dong Zhongshu played a pivotal role in this transformation. He emphasized "three cardinal guides" as being of paramount importance to achieving social stability. The "three cardinal guides" were "ruler guides subject," "father guides son," and "husband guides wife." In particular, the "ruler guides subject" guide was considered unconditional: even if the ruler asked his subject to die, the subject had to accept immediately.

Dong Zhongshu also introduced theology into Confucianism. He proposed a theory about the interaction between heaven and humanity. According to his theory, the emperor was the representative of heaven on earth, and hence the people had to obey him absolutely. Meanwhile, the ruler had to behave benevolently according to the codes of Confucianism to preserve harmony on earth. Emperor Wu of the Han Dynasty immediately perceived the value of "new

Confucianism" to the maintenance of his imperial rule, and hence promoted the ideology considerably across China.

After Confucianism became the official ideology of the Han Dynasty, Confucius became a saint of education and even a semi-god who was often worshipped. The government set up public schools in which regular sacrifices to Confucius were offered. At least one Confucian temple was built in each of the 2,000 counties in the Han Dynasty.[4]

However, it should be noted that Confucianism was never a true religion, and contrasted sharply with other cultures of the world. European countries adopted Christianity, the Arabian world adhered to Islam, and Indian people followed Hinduism. This book provides an explanation for this observation: China faced various transitions that sometimes entailed significant changes in the core values of the culture. Although the major change to Confucianism was not easy, it was much less difficult than enacting a religious change.

Notes

1 See Akerlof (1982) and McDonald and Solow (1981).
2 See, e.g., Wu (1982).
3 See, e.g., Loewe (2006).
4 See, e.g., Kuiper (2011).

7 Economics of the optimal personality in ancient China

The theoretical basis of this chapter is the Coase theorem, named after Nobel laureate Ronald Coase.[1] The theorem states that the market tends to find a way to achieve an optimal allocation of resources, which implies that government intervention is often unnecessary even if conflicts of interest exist among the different agents involved. Wikipedia provides the following description:[2]

> Coase developed his theorem when considering the regulation of radio frequencies. Competing radio stations could use the same frequencies and would therefore interfere with each other's broadcasts. The problem faced by regulators was how to eliminate interference and allocate frequencies to radio stations efficiently. What Coase proposed in 1959 was that as long as property rights in these frequencies were well defined, it ultimately did not matter if adjacent radio stations interfered with each other by broadcasting in the same frequency band. Furthermore, it did not matter to whom the property rights were granted. His reasoning was that the station able to reap the higher economic gain from broadcasting would have an incentive to pay the other station not to interfere. In the absence of transaction costs, both stations would strike a mutually advantageous deal. It would not matter which station had the initial right to broadcast; eventually, the right to broadcast would end up with the party that was able to put it to the most highly valued use. Of course, the parties themselves would care who was granted the rights initially because this allocation would impact their wealth, but the end result of who broadcasts would not change because the parties would trade to the outcome that was overall most efficient. This counterintuitive insight – that the initial imposition of legal entitlement is irrelevant because the parties will eventually reach the same result – is Coase's invariance thesis.

Consider the example of a factory emitting pollution when it engages in production, affecting the livelihood of local residents. From a social welfare perspective, there is usually an optimal level of pollution emission. If the pollution level is too high, local residents will suffer. If the level is too low, the factory will not operate efficiently. How can the amount of pollution emitted be made optimal? One straightforward answer is to direct government intervention to prevent the level of pollution emitted from the plant from exceeding the optimal target. However, the Coase theorem states that even if such a government intervention does not take place, the market can find its own way to solve the problem. According to the social welfare perspective, if the plant were to emit more than the optimal level, local residents could pay the factory to decrease its pollution emissions. This could occur if and only if the "transaction cost" between the factory and local residents were zero or very small.

There is an obvious criticism of the applicability of the Coase theorem: in reality, transaction costs are often high and prevent efficient bargaining from taking place. If local residents were highly emotional over the factory's pollution, they would never consider the idea of paying the factory to decrease its pollution level in the first place.

The Coase theorem is influential in economics because it tends to hold in the long run.[3] People can be emotional in the short run, but over time they tend to find a solution that is in their best interest. Although currently transactions are often extremely costly, over time things can usually be settled in a way that benefits all of the parties involved and maximizes the social welfare. Some empirical studies have supported this theoretical prediction, particularly seminal contributions made by Ostrom (1990, 2010).

In 2009, Ostrom became the first woman to receive the Nobel Prize in Economics. She was cited by the prize-awarding committee "for her analysis of economic governance," with the committee observing that her "research brought this topic from the fringe to the forefront of scientific attention . . . by showing how common resources – forests, fisheries, oil fields or grazing lands – can be managed successfully by the people who use them rather than by governments or private companies."[4]

On June 30, 2012, the *Economist* published an article in memory of Ostrom that nicely and vividly summarizes her work:

> IT SEEMED to Elinor Ostrom that the world contained a large body of common sense. People, left to themselves, would sort out rational ways of surviving and getting along. Although the world's arable land, forests, fresh water and fisheries were all finite, it was possible to share them without depleting them and to care for them without fighting. While others wrote gloomily of the tragedy of the commons, seeing only overfishing and over-farming in a free-for-all of greed, Mrs Ostrom, with her loud laugh and louder tops, cut a cheery and contrarian figure.
>
> Years of fieldwork, by herself and others, had shown her that humans were not trapped and helpless amid diminishing supplies. She had looked at forests in Nepal, irrigation systems in Spain, mountain villages in Switzerland and Japan, fisheries in Maine and Indonesia. She had even, as part of her PhD at the University of California, Los Angeles, studied the water wars and pumping races going on in the 1950s in her own dry backyard.
>
> All these cases had taught her that, over time, human beings tended to draw up sensible rules for the use of common-pool resources. Neighbours set boundaries

and assigned shares, with each individual taking it in turn to use water, or to graze cows on a certain meadow. Common tasks, such as clearing canals or cutting timber, were done together at a certain time. Monitors watched out for rule-breakers, fining or eventually excluding them. The schemes were mutual and reciprocal, and many had worked well for centuries.

The Coase theorem has recently been extended to the fields of political economy and sociology. Based on the same logic, even without government intervention, a community will naturally breed an "optimal" culture and customs. Recent studies extend Coase's insight to analysis of social and political issues.[5] In this context, the political Coase theorem implies that in the absence of transaction costs, people will choose policies that are in line with the society's best interest. By applying this theorem, this book argues that there is an optimal personality for a society that maximizes the welfare of its people. Moreover, by the same logic, the exact form of this optimal personality depends on the society's political, economic, and military circumstances.

An important assumption of the Coase theorem is that the transaction cost must be small. This assumption is often not satisfied in the short run, which implies that a social "institution" such as a social custom or a "national character" may not be optimal in the short run. However, over time, people can find ways of interacting with others to establish the best social institution. This is precisely the essence of the institutional change theory of Douglass North, another Nobel laureate in economics.

What were the optimal social institutions for the ancient Chinese? First, ancient China required a well-established rule of law. The cost of governance would have been too high for such a big country without a sound legal system. The legalism introduced by Shang Yang has been a cornerstone of China's government structures since the Qin Dynasty. For example, in contrast to ancient Europe, duels were not permitted in any Chinese dynasty. Conflicts of interests had to be resolved in a court of law. Indeed, a stable social order was a necessary condition for China to maintain its status as a large country.

However, a good legal system is not always sufficient for maintaining social order, and a culture can substantially complement the rule of law of a large empire such as China. Thus, a culture was developed in China over time that required everyone to obey the authority and be kind to one another, which enhanced the country's social harmony. In an agricultural society surrounded by war-like nomadic tribes, it was in the best interest of the ancient Chinese people to behave humbly toward the government and authority and live harmoniously with one another.

The political Coase theorem argues that the culture and personality of a typical individual in a society are determined by the society's economic and social fundamentals, and that a society's culture is often developed to maximize the welfare of its people. These arguments follow the institutional approach of Douglass North, who is briefly discussed in the introduction. North (1990) demonstrates that from a historical perspective, institutional structures are often modified to be more conducive to economic development as economic and social fundamentals change. This book extends North's work and other related studies by analyzing culture and national character as a single dimension of these institutional structures.

The culture and individual personality (or national character) most suitable for the purpose of maintaining China's status as a big country were captured by the ideology of Confucianism, or more specifically, the brand of neo-Confucianism modified by Dong Zhongshu. In terms of evolutionary theory, neo-Confucianism survived because it was the "cultural gene" that was "fittest" for the survival of the ancient Chinese. In recent years, Dong Zhongshu has been criticized in China for modifying the old brand of Confucianism, and for deviating from some of the original ideas of Confucius to make them more suitable for use by ancient Chinese emperors. However, he might have done so in the best interest of the ancient Chinese.

Chapter 2 introduces Olson's (1993, 2000) theory of the "stationary" versus "roving" bandit, which implies that the ancient Chinese were far better off being ruled by the former rather than the latter. By this logic, stabilizing the rule of a dynasty made the dynasty more like a stationary bandit, which in turn improved the people's welfare. In contrast, if the political system had been highly unstable and the emperors changed frequently, the rulers would have been more like roving bandits. In other words, because it was beneficial for the people to have a stationary bandit government, they had an incentive to keep that government in power.

Why was Confucianism so valuable for the ancient Chinese? The short answer is that it mitigated the conflicts of people during their interactions, which in turn decreased the government's administration costs and hence enabled China to remain a big country. In all human societies, people need to interact with one another frequently. For example, a household usually chooses to live with other households to share the convenience of transportation and other infra-structures. In ancient times, residential proximity often yielded the benefit of mutual protection against robbery and theft. Households usually clustered together either in small (villages) or large (cities) groups. It is in the best inter-est of the people in an agricultural society operating under a "reasonably good" government to live harmoniously.

As long as people interact, they will experience conflict. Their engagement in production and exchange often results in economic conflicts related to the distribution of income and other resources. Even people who participate in social gatherings encounter conflicts related to ego. Every individual demands "respect" from others, and such demands often result in conflicts that may lead to violence. Too much violence breeds an unstable society. Indeed, as North, Wallis, and Weingast (2009) emphasize, a major task for every government is to maintain a stable social order. However, solely relying on the government to maintain social order entails high administration and policing costs that can only be paid via high taxation. The resistance of a higher tax collection can breed violence between police and civilians, creating a vicious cycle between high amounts of violence and high taxes. Thus, the government always strictly pro-hibited civilians from using violence against government officials and the police. However, in many ancient societies and even many developing countries today, violence between civilians is often left unregulated by governments unless seri-ous injury or death results.

How can conflicts and particularly violence be mitigated in a cost-effective way? Once again, the answer is culture. In ancient China, the culture of Confucianism largely originated from the ancient Chinese philosopher Con-fucius (551–479 BC). Confucianism is a Chinese ethical and philosophical system that emphasizes a number of virtues such as humaneness ("Ren"), etiquette ("Li"), loyalty, and filial piety.[6] "Ren" is the first fundamental prin-ciple of Confucianism. Although it is hard to define precisely, it generally means being kind to others. In fact, Confucius established the Golden Rule of "Ren" when one of his students asked him to state the most important principle in life in a single sentence. This Golden Rule, which essentially reflects the ethic of reciprocity, is as follows: "Do unto others as you would have them do unto you."

Moreover, "Ren" not only applies to the economic and social interactions of ordinary people, but also serves as an important guide for emperors and the ruling class. As described in the previous chapter, legalism is a foundation for China to maintain its status as a large country. However, legalism alone is not enough. Although the Qin Dynasty strictly implemented legalism, large-scale insurrections erupted quickly after its establishment, and the dynasty lasted only 15 years (from 221 to 206 BC). Legalism relates to not only the strict imple-mentations of laws, but also the design of those laws. In other words, the ruler must be guided by the right principle when designing a law. According to Confucianism, a ruler must have the virtue of "Ren," requiring him to be humane to his people. Indeed, because a ruler is sovereign, he is often tempted to design laws that benefit him and the ruling class. However, during the Qin Dynasty, the rulers were overthrown by insurrections and revolutions when they did not pay enough attention to people's welfare. An experienced and wise ruler usually knows the intriguing interdependence between his government and the people under his reign.

Xunzi (312–230 BC), a major Confucian philosopher, vividly described the relationship between a ruler and people as follows: a ruler is like a boat, and people are like a river. When their relationship is smooth, the boat can float on the water and sail in the river. However, when their relationship becomes volatile and unstable, the river can sink the boat entirely. There is a similar saying in English: the same knife can cut both the bread and your finger.

Confucian teaching has usually been well received by rulers throughout Chi-nese history. Indeed, as almost every man has a natural tendency to be selfish and egocentric, "Ren" is a constant useful reminder and guide for a ruler in designing and implementing laws and making daily national policy decisions in response to ever-changing natural and social environments. In fact, by the same logic, most emperors in ancient China usually emphasized Confucian teachings to their children and particularly their heirs. These teachings were very important, particularly because a ruler's single inhumane or cruel behavior often did not have a noticeable effect on the country. China was a single large country in ancient times, and no competition existed between the different sovereign kings. If an autocratic ruler acted inhumanely toward his subjects, the resultant effect on the stability of his empire was not usually obvious in the short run. However, in the long run, a habitually inhumane ruler was likely to be ousted.

If a ruler did reign humanely and show concern for his people, he received a very high level of loyalty in return. Loyalty is another virtue that is highly emphasized in Confucianism. Beginning in the Zhou Dynasty, the Chinese emperor was referred to as "Tian-Zi," meaning the "Son of God" or "Mandate of Heaven." Thus, as long as the emperor was considered as humane to the people, Confucianism advocated that the people obey him absolutely.

Of course, most people went their whole lives without seeing an emperor, and their obedience took the form of adhering strictly to the orders of government officials and rule of law. At this point, it is clear that Confucianism highly complements legalism. This might have been the most important reason that it was chosen as the official state ideology of ancient China, which was always strongly promoted by the rulers of every dynasty. Confucianism was also popular among ordinary people because it reflected their best interests. Chapter 2 shows that when faced with threats from war-like nomadic tribes, the ancient Chinese realized that every agricultural society in China had to unite into a single large country. In this context, the emphasis of loyalty to the emperor and obeying the rule of law helped maintain the stability of China as a single large country.

Although obedience to the emperor was sometimes dependent on his virtue, one's utmost respect for his parents was absolute and remains an integral part of Confucianism. Filial piety requires an individual to show respect and provide financial support for his parents rather than rebel. A man's career success is an important aspect of filial piety, as it can allow him to obtain enough material resources to provide for a family. If he is successful, he is able to bring honor and glory to his parents.

Etiquette ("Li") is another important virtue advocated by Confucianism. Under this general principle, the Chinese culture developed a comprehensive system of norms that specify the propriety or politeness that colors everyday life. In particular, *Confucian Analects* provides the following description of "Li" via conversations between Confucius (the Master) and his three students (Yen Yüan, Chung-kung, and Tsze-niû Tsze-niû):[7]

How to attain to perfect virtue: – a conversation with Yen Yüan.

1   Yen Yüan asked about perfect virtue. The Master said, "To subdue one's self and return to propriety, is perfect virtue. If a man can for one day subdue himself and return to propriety, all under heaven will ascribe perfect virtue to him. Is the practice of perfect virtue from a man himself, or is it from others?"

2   Yen Yüan said, "I beg to ask the steps of that process." The Master replied, "Look not at what is contrary to propriety; listen not to what is contrary to propriety; speak not what is contrary to propriety; make no movement which is contrary to propriety." Yen Yüan then said, "Though I am deficient in intelligence and vigor, I will make it my business to practice this lesson."

Wherein perfect virtue is realized: – a conversation with Chung-kung.

Chung-kung asked about perfect virtue. The Master said, "It is, when you go abroad, to behave to every one as if you were receiving a great guest; to employ the people as if you were assisting at a great sacrifice; not to do to others as you would not wish done to yourself; to have no murmuring against you in the country, and none in the family." Chung-kung said, "Though I am deficient in intelligence and vigor, I will make it my business to practice this lesson."

Caution in speaking a characteristic of perfect virtue: – a conversation with Tsze-niû.

1   Sze-mâ Niû asked about perfect virtue.
2   The Master said, "The man of perfect virtue is cautious and slow in his speech."
3   "Cautious and slow in his speech!" said Niu; – "is this what is meant by perfect virtue?" The Master said, "When a man feels the difficulty of doing, can he be other than cautious and slow in speaking?"

It is clear from the preceding quotation that according to strict Confucianism, if one cannot meet the requirements of propriety, then he should neither say nor do anything. In fact, in this case, he is even advised not to see or hear anything. When people behave politely toward one another in a society, fewer conflicts and less violence result. At this point, we can see that the rule of law and etiquette complement each other in encouraging a social harmony. When there is a good rule of law in place, those who resort to violence receive a severe penalty. Consequently, people tend to be friendly toward one another. Furthermore, when people exhibit etiquette and friendship, less violence results and the rule of law is reinforced.

How did the Chinese culture modify people's behavior based on Confucianism? The most important channel was the imperial exam system (Keju), which is discussed in the next chapter. The Keju system was used to select government officials based on Confucian literature, thereby promoting the culture. Another channel was the "reputation effect." Once a society accepted Confucianism as the mainstream culture, the actions of the people in that society were constrained through the reputation effect. In ancient China, people often liked to divide men into two types according to their reputations in the society: "Junzi" and "Xiaoren," which translate as "gentleman" and "petty man," respectively. Of course, these direct translations are not accurate and could be misleading to non-Chinese. More accurate translations reveal that a "Junzi" is a man who is well educated by Confucianism and adheres strictly to its principles in action, and that a "Xiaoren" is a man whose behavior seriously deviates from Confucian principles. More specifically, a "Junzi" is expected to have a high moral standard and level of respect, to take care of his parents, to show courtesy to others, and to be kind and forgiving. In contrast, a "Xiaoren" is extremely selfish and greedy, disregards the wellbeing of others, and is snobbish.

One can be a "Junzi" in the Chinese culture by following a practical and fairly simple method known as the "doctrine of the mean." In simple terms, the doctrine infers that one should never take extreme action.[8] During social interactions and particularly when conflicts of interest arise, one should always try to seek a middle ground for the different parties involved. Furthermore, one should always talk properly and act cautiously by considering the interests and feelings of others. In fact, the ancient Greek philosopher Aristotle put forward a similar proposition (obviously independently), in which he argued that a man's virtue often reflected his ability to find an appropriate middle ground between opposite extreme measures.[9]

The "doctrine of the mean" particularly provides people with two types of practical guidance. First, it dictates that one should not be emotional. When an individual is emotional, he is more likely to take radical actions and may kill others in extreme cases. The "doctrine of the mean" prevents this kind of radical behavior from being exhibited. Second, it constantly reminds an individual to be concerned about others. It is human nature to be selfish, which implies that most people tend to care about themselves much more than they do about others. Thus, the doctrine encourages people to pay more attention to the needs and emotions of others and thereby make the society more harmonious.

In ancient China, those who did not obey the principles of Confucianism might have been labeled as "Xiaoren" and consequently despised by many people in the society. "Xiaoren" took as many different forms as there were various ways to deviate from Confucian principles. However, during periods when the Confucian culture was strong, even those labeled as "Xiaoren" were not prone to using violence against others.

There are some empirical studies that demonstrate rigorously the impact of the Chinese traditional culture of Confucianism in enhancing social stability. For example, Kung and Ma (2014) analyze the causes of peasant rebellion in historical China between 1651 and 1910, and they measure the degree of instrumenting Confucian norms in a county by its Confucian temples and chaste women. They find that holding other things (e.g., crop failure) constant, peasant insurrection was significantly less likely to occur in the counties with stronger Confucian norms.

Notes

1 Coase (1960).
2 http://en.wikipedia.org/wiki/Coase_theorem
3 Ronald Coase received the Nobel Prize in Economics in 1991, and his 1960 article that put forward the Coase theorem has 23,045 citations in Google Scholar,

indicating the academic value of the theorem. In fact, many studies have considered the theorem common sense rather than citing the article directly.

4 Some economists have argued that Ostrom's research is not related to the Coase theorem, the strict version of which considers only cases in which property rights are well defined. However, this view is a narrow interpretation of the theorem. Discussions of the theorem's political application broaden its spirit considerably.

5 See, e.g., Acemoglu (2003), Galiani, Torrens, and Yanguas (2014), Parisi (2003), and Vira (1997).

6 See, e.g., Yao (2000).

7 Translated into English by Legge (1893), http://www.cnculture.net/ebook/jing/sishu/lunyu_en/12.html.

8 See, e.g., Gardner (1998).

9 http://en.wikipedia.org/wiki/Nicomachean_Ethics

8 Meritocracy in ancient China: Keju

Douglass North, a Nobel laureate in economics, keenly observes a crucial feature of the social institutions that sustain: fairness.[1] Even in a time of economic prosperity, if a group of people feel that they are being treated inequitably, they may resent other groups of people and desire to establish an independent country. This idea has been strongly echoed in the history literature. For example, Turchin (2003) argues that the main reason an empire falls apart is that the rich become richer and the poor poorer over time, which leads to jealousy and conflicts and hence undermines the cohesion of the society and its capacity for collective action. In recent decades, many economic studies have been devoted to examining the role of fairness, and have consistently found that fairness is a key determinant of the success of interpersonal cooperation.[2]

An intuitive example of the importance of income equality to happiness is the Tiananmen Square protests of 1989. From 1978 to 1989, the newly implemented economic reform substantially accelerated the growth of the Chinese economy and considerably improved the Chinese people's welfare. One may be tempted to say that the Chinese people should have been overjoyed at the reform, which came after several decades of misery under the rule of the CCP, which did little to change the people's livelihood. Nevertheless, the discontentment of many against the Chinese government rose greatly after the reform, mainly due to the rising income inequality. In particular, many Chinese were furious that those who had close connections with senior government officials became rich due to economic nepotism. This discontent was the major reason for the outbreak of the Tiananmen Square protests in 1989.

In the United States, a country comprising multiple races, the Office of Institutional Equity issued the following notice related to its non-discrimination policy, particularly to all public institutions such as public universities: "The University, as an equal opportunity/affirmative action employer, complies with all applicable federal and state laws regarding nondiscrimination and affirmative action. The University is committed to a policy of equal opportunity for all persons and does not discriminate on the basis of race, color, national origin, age, marital status, sex, sexual orientation, gender identity, gender expression, disability, religion, height, weight, or veteran status in employment, educational programs and activities, and admissions."[3]

This non-discrimination policy was enacted in the United States and many other developed countries only recently. Discrimination against blacks in the United States was overt and prevalent a mere several decades ago. However, throughout most of China's history, the Chinese government has largely prohibited discrimination against a person for reasons of race, religion, or personal appearance. In fact, as discussed in the introduction, race was not an issue at all in ancient China, as at the time it was defined in terms of culture and personality rather than genetics. The use of the term "race" here relates mainly to the contemporary definition.[4]

The best illustration is the system of imperial examinations, known as "Keju" in Chinese. The Keju system was established formally in 605 AD during the Sui Dynasty, but was in fact introduced in rudimentary forms during the Han Dynasty (206–220 AD). The Keju system, which comprised a comprehensive system of centralized examinations, was the major mechanism Chinese emperors used to select government officials until its abolishment in 1905 at the end of the Qing Dynasty.[5] Almost every man was allowed to take part in the Keju system and hence had the chance to become a government official with a high income and prestige. The system provided a channel of intergenerational mobility even for the people at the bottom of society. This "equal opportunity" substantially mitigated the grievances of the Chinese people against income inequality.

Prior to the Keju system, government officials were appointed based on their family backgrounds and the recommendations of aristocrats. However, the aristocrats often acted based on self-interest and personal agendas when making the recommendations. Although it would have been considered improper if an aristocrat were to recommend his children or close relatives to a position, it was easy for the aristocrats to "exchange" recommendations. For example, Aristocrat A would recommend the persons desired by Aristocrat B, and vice versa.

Recognizing this problem, Emperor Wu of the Han Dynasty introduced an imperial examination that helped him select talents for the most important positions in the central government. He asked many local officials to recommend candidates to take part in an examination, which was publicly announced as based on the Confucian Classics. Based on the results of the examination, he personally selected the officials for important positions in his administration. In this selection and promotion process, the candidates with low abilities were usually disqualified by the examination, effectively improving the quality of the government officials and the administrative efficiency of the Chinese empire. However, connections and recommendations remained important, and many talented people could not become government officials if they came from disadvantaged family backgrounds or could not get the necessary recommendations from local officials. Thus, there remained room for major improvement in terms of both fairness and efficiency.

In 605 AD, the Keju system was explicitly instituted in China's Sui Dynasty as a main official channel for recruiting government officials. Most of the bureaucrats had been selected via the Keju system since the Song Dynasty.

Under such a system, any male adult in China could become a bureaucrat regardless of race, height, weight, looks, social origins, or social status by passing the imperial examinations. The examinations were conducted at four ascending levels: local, provincial, national, and palace.

The government entirely determined the structure and contents of the imperial examinations. The Confucian Classics were at the core of all of the examination levels. At the district exams, candidates were tested in terms of their knowledge of Confucianism, calligraphy, and writing ability in certain poetic forms. According to the examination content, performance was assessed objectively to a large extent. In fact, at least in the Ming and Qing Dynasties, the Keju system required one's essay-writing style to take the form of the so-called eight-legged essay ("Ba Gu Wen"), which consisted of eight sections including an opening statement, supporting statements, the main discussion, and an abstract. Meanwhile, each section of the essay served a distinct purpose, and had to follow a number of strict requirements related to aspects such as the number of sentences and words, rhyming, and symmetry.[6]

Although contemporary educators may consider the eight-legged essay pedantic and trite, it served the important purpose of ensuring fairness, as its rigid writing style required careful grading. Different from a math exam, a writing exam usually has no standard answers. If the format of a piece of writing does not follow strict requirements, different examiners' evaluations of the same article may differ significantly. For example, an examiner may strongly prefer prose to poetry. In this case, *ceteris paribus*, the candidates who write prose are more likely to pass the examination than those who write poetry. Therefore, the eight-legged essay emerged as a unified format in civil service examinations, greatly standardizing the grading criteria. This rigid writing format improved the examiners' impartiality and objectivity in identifying potential talent, which was not only beneficial to the ancient Chinese ruler for selecting government official candidates, but also conducive to the social stability and national unity of China.

The national examinations, which were held in China's capital city, added the dimension of testing candidates' capacities to analyze important contemporary issues. Because the emperor directly monitored their administration, their format had to be more flexible. Even so, the government took various measures to ensure that the examinations were conducted as fairly as possible. For example, to avoid favoritism by graders, copyists were often employed to copy the candidates' answers so that the graders could not recognize their signature calligraphy styles.[7] Moreover, each province in China had a quota of the number of candidates it could offer, which was roughly in proportion to its population size.

Corruption in China's ancient dynasties was commonplace, and the emperors did not always take strict measures to eliminate it.[8] Nevertheless, there was zero tolerance toward corruption under the Keju system. The penalty for cheating was extremely high, particularly for those who administered the exam questions and invigilated the exams. For example, in a cheating case discovered in Jiangnan

Province during the Qing Dynasty, 16 principal invigilators were executed immediately and many of the others involved were sentenced to exile in remote areas. The army then escorted several hundred candidates to Beijing to retake the examinations.[9]

The candidates who passed the local-level examination were offered the title "Xiucai," literally meaning "a talented man." They were allowed to participate in the provincial-level examination, which was usually held once every three years. If a "Xiucai" passed this examination, he became a "Juren," literally meaning "a recommended man." The "Juren" were permitted to take part in the exam in China's capital city, usually held in February the following year. A ministry of the central government administered this exam. The candidates who performed well were granted the national degree of "Gongshi," literally meaning "a tribute personnel." Finally, in April of the same year, the "Gongshi" were invited to take the palace-level exam, which the emperor often administrated personally with the assistance of top government officials and major national scholars. Those who performed well on this exam were awarded the title "Jinshi," literally meaning "presented scholar."

Those who passed at least the provincial-level examination (i.e., "Juren") were usually appointed to the government. However, the competition was fierce and the exam success rate was very low. For example, the passing rate in the Tang Dynasty was about 2 percent. Those who passed the examination at a higher level usually received a higher rank. After the Ming Dynasty, one was required to have the title of "Jinshi" to be appointed to the high office in the central government. In each palace-level examination, the "Jinshi" who ranked first, second, and third were honored with the titles "Zhuangyuan" ("exemplar of the state"), "Bangyan" ("eyes positioned alongside," the top-ranked scholar), and "Tanhua" ("selective talent," in reference to the eponymous banquet), respectively, and received immediate respect when they joined the government.

Those who performed well in the Keju system usually obtained a very high social status. For example, Elman (1991, p. 10) makes the following observation: "Despite centuries of repeated criticism and constant efforts at reform, the "examination life," like death and taxes, became one of the fixtures of elite society and popular culture. The examinations represented the focal point through which state interests, family strategies, and individual hopes and aspirations were directed. In the absence of alternative careers of comparable social status and political prestige, the goal of becoming an official took priority. Once set in place and granted full legitimacy, the civil service recruitment system achieved for education a degree of national standardization and local importance unprecedented in the premodern world."

What were the benefits of the Keju system? First, the imperial exams tested general knowledge and skills, such as writing and analytical abilities. To the extent that these skills were valuable for civil services, selecting the candidates who performed well in the Keju system as government officials might have substantially improved bureaucratic efficiency. For example, without modern telecommunications, the correspondences between the governments at different locations in China mainly took the form of written documents. An official with better writing skills could convey his ideas more clearly and pertinently, which decreased the likelihood of misunderstandings. Because the communications between different government levels were frequent and a single misunderstanding could prove costly, an improvement in the writing skills of officials should have greatly improved the effectiveness of the government.

Second, government officials dealt with many complicated issues and hence required a large set of cognitive and non-cognitive skills, many of which were not reflected in their imperial examination performance. However, most skills and particularly cognitive skills are determined by one's mental ability (or IQ). Those who exhibited outstanding performance on the highly competitive imperial examinations usually had very high IQs, which implied that they were likely to have the mental capacity sufficient to master other skills. Therefore, the imperial examinations might have been the best available way to select the most capable government officials in ancient China.

In fact, even in contemporary China, a prerequisite for becoming a civil servant is a university-awarded bachelor's degree.[10] To enter into a Chinese university, one must obtain a good score on the University Entrance Examination, which is standard at the national level. Moreover, after graduating from a university, one must pass another competitive examination specially designed for those who intend to work for the government. Thus, the current system used to select government officials is surprisingly and essentially similar to the Keju system.

Although corruption is rampant in China today, possibly due to the legacy of the Keju system, the University Entrance Examination remains relatively free of corruption. For example, the following recent report argues that meritocracy is emphasized to a much greater extent in China's current university admission system than in the United States:[11]

> Or consider the case of China. There, legions of angry microbloggers endlessly denounce the official corruption and abuse which permeate so much of the economic system. But we almost never hear accusations of favoritism in university admissions, and this impression of strict meritocracy determined by the results of the national Gaokao college entrance examination has been confirmed to me by individuals familiar with that country. Since all the world's written exams may ultimately derive from China's old imperial examination system, which was kept remarkably clean for 1300 years, such practices are hardly surprising. Attending a prestigious college is regarded by ordinary Chinese as their children's greatest hope of rapid upward mobility and is therefore often a focus of enormous family effort; China's ruling elites may rightly fear that a policy of admitting their own dim and lazy heirs to leading schools ahead of the higher-scoring children of the masses might ignite a widespread popular uprising. This perhaps explains why so many sons and daughters of top Chinese leaders attend college in the West: enrolling them at a third-rate Chinese

university would be a tremendous humiliation, while our own corrupt admissions practices get them an easy spot at Harvard or Stanford, sitting side by side with the children of Bill Clinton, Al Gore, and George W. Bush.

Third, the Keju system promoted Confucianism across China. The structure and contents of the imperial examinations were made open and transparent. This uniformity ensured that potential candidates across China learned the exact same core values of the Confucian Classics. The Classics served as the main textbook of the imperial examinations, and the candidates who exhibited excellent performance in the Keju system studied the Classics intensively. In fact, most could not only recite the Classics easily, but also write elegant essays in the spirit of Confucianism. Thus, there was a virtuous interactive effect between Confucianism and the Keju system. To a large extent, the Keju system was strongly related to the Confucian notion of meritocracy. Due to the paramount importance of the Keju system to people's material lives, many people spent years and great effort studying the Confucian Classics. In fact, one ancient poem that tries to persuade young people to study hard remains well known in China today. The poem was written by Emperor Zhenzong (986–1022) during the Song Dynasty, and is translated as follows:[12]

- A rich family need not buy fertile land, since there are thousands of kinds of grains and agricultural products in the BOOK.
- One need not build a big house to live comfortably, since there is a house made of gold in the BOOK.
- A man need not worry that he cannot find a wife, since there is a beautiful woman in the BOOK.
- A man need not worry that he does not have the prestige of being followed by subordinates when walking outside, since there are clusters of horse carriages in the BOOK.
- If a man aims to achieve his lifetime ambition, study hard the Confucian classics sitting in front of the window.

Although many Chinese people are familiar with this poem, they may not know that it was written by an emperor. With the beginning of the Song Dynasty, the location for the final Keju examination was moved to the royal palace, where the emperor administered the exam personally.[13] Therefore, Emperor Zhenzong personally observed candidates from humble backgrounds suddenly become well-respected members of his government and the whole country, which might have inspired him to write the poem.

The poem illustrates that the economic returns reaped from studying Confucian Classics could be enormous and motivated many ambitious young men to study hard.[14] For example, Elman (1991, p. 14) observes the following: "By 1850, approximately two million candidates sat for county examinations, held twice every three years. Of these, only thirty thousand (1.5 percent) achieved licentiate status. Fifteen hundred of the latter (5 percent) passed the triennial provincial examinations, and of these, only three hundred (20 percent) would pass the triennial metropolitan examinations. Each stage eliminated the vast majority of candidates, and the odds for success in all stages of the selection process was one in six thousand (.01 percent)."

This means that far more candidates participated in the Keju examinations than actually passed them. However, all of the candidates were effectively "brainwashed" by Confucianism. Elman (1991, p. 16) further observes that "over 400 thousand characters of textual material had to be memorized to master the examination curriculum of the Four Books and Five Classics." In response, Wakeman (1972, p. 23) notes that "[a] better-than-average apprenticeship for the examinations meant beginning to learn to write characters at the age of five, memorizing the Four Books and the Five Classics by the age of eleven, mastering poetry composition at age twelve, and studying pa-ku {eight-legged} essay style thereafter."

Thus, regardless of whether a candidate could pass the Keju examinations, he was heavily influenced by Confucianism and in turn influenced other members of the society. In fact, many of those who failed to pass the imperial examinations worked as teachers at private schools and passed their ideology on to the next generation. Moreover, many people spent a great deal of time studying Confucian Classics, but ultimately stopped due to poverty or the realization that they were not talented enough to pass the examinations. Although they did not participate in the examinations, they were also dedicated believers in Confucian orthodoxy. Thus, although the main intention of the Chinese government was to select the best talents as bureaucrats, the Keju system also served to promote Confucianism as the core value of the Chinese culture. In other words, the Keju system not only maximized the population basis from which the government could identify and select the educated elite, but also helped maintain a cultural unity across China.

In terms of economics, the Keju examinations had a positive externality effect on the average level of human capital.[15] In an abstract sense, this effect is in line with recent studies of the beneficial brain drain theory, which argues that when a developing country allows a fraction of its educated elites to seek employment overseas, it produces more educated people at home. The theory's logic is that the prospect of working abroad induces more people to acquire an education.[16] The literature explores the cost of this perspective of migration, which includes "educated unemployment" and "over-education." "Educated unemployment" refers to the observation that some workers who fail to arrange employment abroad are less likely to immediately immerse themselves in work in their home country, and remain unemployed to engage in repeated attempts to secure foreign employment. Furthermore, because the possibility of migration induces individuals in a developing country to acquire higher education, when some of these individuals end up remaining in the country, the returns on their education could be less than its costs, resulting in "over-education." However, from a long-run perspective, when the externality effect of human capital is large enough, the higher average level of human capital can prompt the economy to take off, outweighing the short-run costs.[17]

Fourth, the Keju system brought a sense of fairness and justice to the vastly heterogeneous Chinese population. Under the system of imperial examinations, a man had a chance of becoming a government official with a high income level and prestige regardless of his race, color, age, marital status, height, weight, or even minor disability, as long as he performed well on the exams. Family background admittedly might have been a factor that determined one's education opportunities. A poor family might not have been able to provide enough educational resources for children who had ambitions to take the Keju exams. However, Freedman (1966) and Ho (1962) show that even in such cases in ancient China, sometimes a number of families from a clan pooled their money together to fund the educational expenditure required for a single "gifted" child of the clan to take the exams. They did so with the hopes that the child would perform well, become a prestigious government official, and bring much honor to his family and clan. In the Ming and Qing Dynasties, about half of those who passed the Keju exams came from relatively poor families and had fathers who received little education.

To further ensure equitable treatment, a system was adopted in which provincial quotas were roughly proportional to each province's population, meaning that officials were recruited from the whole country. In particular, even those who lived in the disadvantaged peripheral regions of China had an equal opportunity of working for the central government. Consequently, local-level elites across China had a sense of national identity and loyalty that helped maintain the integration of the enormous Chinese state. Moreover, those who passed the exams were appointed as local officials across China and usually not in the provinces from which they hailed, further enhancing the national identity and counterbalancing any potential tendency of regional breakup in the country.

Indeed, racism and other forms of discrimination based on height, weight, and appearance were hardly present throughout most of Chinese history. In addition to the Keju system, the social custom of marriage supported this statement. In traditional China, marriage was blind in the sense that the groom was allowed to see the bride's face for the first time only after the marriage was official. Cheung (1972) provides an economic explanation for this tradition from the perspective of intergenerational conflict. It is human nature for a man to appreciate his spouse's physical appearance. Thus, grooms placed a great deal of emphasis on their bride's looks. However, the bride's looks were not of major concern to the groom's parents. Note that the groom's parents made all of the decisions related to their son's marriage, and tried to impose their wills rather than the groom's in his selection of his bride. To avoid potential conflict between grooms and their parents, a social custom emerged in China that made marriage blind for the grooms. This custom also reflected the core value of the traditional Chinese culture that emphasized internal virtues and downplayed the importance of physical appearance. In fact, this ideology applied to many emperors in addition to ordinary people.

During the Qing Dynasty, an emperor often had many wives and concubines, whom he often selected personally. However, this selection was always made in public, and the emperor was usually accompanied by his mother, as long as she was alive and healthy enough to attend the event. Consequently, an emperor often selected his women based on their internal rather than external beauty. Many photos of emperors' wives and concubines were taken during the late Qing Dynasty and reveal the women to be physically unattractive.

Notes

1 See, e.g., North (1990).
2 See, e.g., Frank (1985, 2011).
3 See, e.g., http://bog.wayne.edu/code/2_28_01.php.
4 One drawback to the system was that the opportunities were given only to men. Women were overtly prohibited from obtaining government jobs in traditional China.
5 For a more detailed description of the Keju system, see, e.g., Elman (2000).
6 See, e.g., Elman (2002) and Suen (2005).
7 It was decided that personal appearance should not be related to exam outcomes. The examiners could not see the candidates' handwriting, let alone their size and physical appearance.
8 See, e.g., Ni and Van (2006).
9 http://zh.wikipedia.org/wiki/%E7%A7%91%E4%B8%BE#.E4.BD.9C.E5. BC.8A
10 This requirement is also common in other countries.
11 http://www.theamericanconservative.com/articles/the-myth-of-american-meritocracy/
12 Suen (2005).
13 Elman (1991).
14 This logic is illustrated in Levitt and Venkatesh's (2000) account of gangsters that was popularized in a best-selling book by Levitt and Dubner (2005). Levitt and Venkatesh (2000) observe that most of the "foot soldiers" in drug gangs receive a very low income that is only slightly above the legal minimum wage. This low wage obviously cannot justify the high risks associated with selling drugs. The authors argue that these drug dealers most probably expect to be "promoted" within their gangs, which would enhance their income significantly. As for the candidates who participated in the Keju system, the reward for "winning the lottery" was more than the pecuniary payment, as the social prestige of being a government official was enormous in ancient China.
15 See, e.g., Acemoglu (1996), Fan and Stark (2008), and Lucas (2001).
16 See, e.g., Mountford (1997), Stark and Wang (2002), and Stark, Helmenstein, and Prskawetz (1997, 1998).
17 See Fan and Stark (2007a, 2007b) and Stark and Fan (2007, 2011).

9 Personality and culture of lawless (nomadic) tribes

Ancient Chinese culture emphasized harmony, politeness, and peaceful coexistence with others. The formation of this non-violent culture and national character required a well-implemented rule of law under the principle of legalism. When this condition was not satisfied, an opposite culture usually emerged. For example, in the opening statements of their book on the culture of "honor," Nisbett and Cohen (1996, p. xv) note: "This is a book of a singular cause of male violence – the perpetrator's sense of threat to one of his most valued possessions, namely, his reputation for strength and toughness. In many of the world's cultures, social status, economic well-being, and life itself are linked to such a reputation. This is true wherever gaining resources, or keeping them, depends on the community's believing that the individual is capable of defending himself against predation."

Nomadic tribes did not adopt a legal system in ancient times. To begin with, there was almost no private property right of land. Because nomads constantly sought green pastures for their cattle in ever-changing natural environments, public land ownership was often their best choice. In other words, a piece of land might have been owned by a nomadic tribe, but not by a single individual.

The government of a nomadic tribe does not remain in a fixed location, as its people are often on the move. Thus, nomads cannot depend on the rule of law when seeking social justice. Indeed, nomadic tribes typically have no police stations, and the people are forced to protect themselves. These circumstances yield an opportunity to obtain resources in an alternative way to engaging in production: by grabbing resources from others.

Many documentary films have shown that in the natural habitats of wild animals, predators (e.g., lions) always target the weakest of their prey (e.g., zebras), such as the sick, injured, and old. This strategy is perfectly rational, as attacking the weakest presents the lowest cost. This logic also applies to a nomadic tribe when one member attempts to use violence or the threat of violence to obtain valuable resources from another member. In particular, holding the fighting capacity of potential victims as a constant, an attacker prefers to pick on the individual who is least determined to resist his attack. For example, if a man has the reputation that he would rather die than be bullied by others, then an attacker will hesitate in trying to rob that man's sheep, believing that he would have to kill the man if his reputation held true. In contrast, a man who has the reputation of being afraid of being injured or killed in a fight is more likely to be robbed, to starve after his assets are taken, and ultimately to die in a brutal environment.

The following example further illustrates this point. Consider two men who are weak and strong, respectively. Each man has five sheep. The strong man can take two possible actions: he can either use force against the weak man or not. If he uses force, he will win the fight regardless of whether the weak man fights back. In this case, he would take three sheep from the weak man. If he does not use force, he will get nothing from the weak man. If the strong man uses force, the weak man has two possible responses: to fight back or not. If he fights back, he will be seriously injured while inflicting only moderate injury on the strong man. If the weak man does not fight back, then he will not be injured. In this example, if the weak man cares about neither the honor of not being bullied nor the humiliation of being bullied, then the strong man will take three sheep from him. However, if the weak man cares greatly about his honor and reputation, then he will fight back when the strong man uses force against him. If the injury that the weak man inflicts on the strong man is serious enough, the strong man may think that the three sheep would not compensate the injury. Therefore, the strong man would not use force against the weak man, leaving the weak man better off.

One may argue that this example is overly simplified. For example, under some circumstances, a strong man may pick on a weak man regardless of whether the weak man fights back. In this case, the weak man's retaliation would result in his own serious injury. However, even with this consideration, it remains in the weak man's interest to fight back. Because his retaliation may give him a reputation of toughness, it may be beneficial for him from a long-run perspective. Otherwise, the strong man would take away all of his assets, and he would starve.

This example shows the importance of reputation in a nomadic tribe. A man must be fearless to survive. If he has any fear, that fear will be discovered over time and exploited by others, leaving him unable to survive in a lawless community. Of course, a woman is not likely to marry a coward who cannot support her and her children. Even if a coward has a wife, she may be taken away by others. Therefore, it can be concluded that in nomadic tribes, bravery and a lack of fear of death are necessary features and personalities for most men. The culture of nomadic tribes has evolved naturally to praise valor and despise cowards.

For example, in their study of the culture of violence in the southern regions of the United States, Nisbett and Cohen (1996, p. xv) state: "The South has long been thought to be more violent than the North. . . Unlike the North, which was settled by farmers from England, Holland, and Germany, the South was settled by herdsmen from the fringes of Britain. Herdsmen the world over tend to be capable of great aggressiveness and violence because of their vulnerability to losing their primary resources, their animals. Also, unlike the North, where population densities have been in general relatively high, the South was a low-population frontier region until well into the nineteenth century. In such regions the state has little power to command compliance with the law, and the citizens have to create their own system of order. The meaning for doing this is the rule of retaliation: If you cross me, I will punish you. To maintain credible power of deterrence, the individual must project a stance of willingness to commit mayhem and to risk wounds and death for himself."

The rule of law is currently well established in developed countries, where the "culture of honor and violence" is usually not well observed. However, prisons constitute one exception. The following passage can be found in an article entitled "Prison Politics," and highlights former inmates' descriptions of the "culture" in United States prisons:[1]

> Prison is the exact opposite of how appropriate society conducts itself. For example, in society you are held accountable for your actions, and if you break its laws or moral code, you are punished. In prison, however, you are rewarded by your peers if you do something inappropriate. For example, if I assault someone, my peers look at me as someone to fear and actually treat me with a type of respect. I say "type of respect," because respect given out of fear is really based on manipulation. . . Prison inmates have a code that says, "Don't tell the guards anything that could get yourself or another inmate in trouble. Always stand up to someone who is trying to hurt you or take your things. Always stay true and don't lie to your partners, but lying to anyone else is okay."

Inmates in American prisons are required not to work, but to remain idle. To eliminate boredom, some inmates like to pick fights and bully others. To avoid being seriously injured, they often choose those who appear to be easily bullied as their victims. All inmates therefore have an incentive to establish a reputation of not being easily bullied. Moreover, they tend to form small groups to avoid being bullied and/or to bully others.

In ancient times, nomadic tribes often engaged in large-scale warfare. As such, a nomadic tribe had a strong incentive to cultivate a culture that worshipped bravery and violence. In such a tribe, those who were considered brave were rewarded with respect, and cowards were treated with contempt. One may argue that a member might have behaved bravely inside the tribe only to behave cowardly once an inter-tribe battle broke out. However, this was unlikely for two reasons. First, one's performance in an inter-tribe battle was often well observed, implying that those who exhibited cowardly behavior during an inter-tribe battle would be penalized in that they would lose their reputation in the community. Second, a man who developed a habit of being brave was usually brave in any battle. In contrast, a man who developed a habit of cowardice was usually a coward in any battle. Once a habit was formed, it tended to be persistent. The following passage elaborates this point.

In *The Seven Habits of Highly Effective People*, which business school MBA students use as a textbook, Stephen R. Covey (1989) states the following:

> Habits are powerful factors in our lives. Because they are consistent, often unconscious patterns, they constantly, daily, express our character and produce our effectiveness or ineffectiveness. As Horace Mann, the great educator, once said, "Habits are like a cable. We weave a strand of it everyday and soon it cannot be broken." I personally do not agree with the last part of his expression. I know they can be broken. Habits can be learned and unlearned. But I also know it isn't a quick fix. It involves a process and a tremendous commitment. Those of us who watched the lunar voyage of Apollo 11 were transfixed as we saw the first men walk on the moon and return to earth. Superlatives such as "fantastic" and "incredible" were inadequate to describe those eventful days. But to get there, those astronauts literally had to break out of the tremendous gravity pull of the earth. More energy was spent in the first few minutes of lift-off, in the first few miles of travel, than was used over the next several days to travel half a million miles. Habits, too, have tremendous gravity pull – more than most people realize or would admit. Breaking deeply imbedded habitual tendencies such as procrastination, impatience, criticalness, or selfishness that violate basic principles of human effectiveness involves more than a little willpower and a few minor changes in our lives. "Lift off" takes a tremendous effort, but once we break out of the gravity pull, our freedom takes on a whole new dimension.

In terms of the economics of conflict, Hirshleifer (2001) shows that in some circumstances human emotions are the only guarantor of threats to and promises of collaboration among individuals. Covey's statement indicates that to make the threat credible, an individual must develop a habit of violence. Furthermore, Fischer (1989, p. 690) notes that the culture of violence in the southern United States was initially cultivated in childhood: "From an early age small boys were taught to think much of their own honor, and to be active in its defense. Honor in this society meant a pride of manhood in masculine courage, physical strength and warrior virtue. Male children were trained to defend their honor without a moment's hesitation." Nisbett and Cohen (1996, p. 2) add the following: "Children themselves rigorously enforced the code of honor. A boy who dodged a stone rather than allow himself to be hit and then respond in kind ran the risk of being ostracized by his fellows."

This analysis is also in line with the political Coase theorem, which argues that a social institution, including the culture and personality of a typical individual in a society, is determined by the society's economic and social fundamentals. In societies where the rule of law is not well established, a culture usually emerges that emphasizes toughness and valor. The government promotes this culture if wars are frequent, providing another explanation for the practice of "duels."

In ancient Europe, if a man felt insulted, he could challenge the man who insulted him to a duel. Such a challenge was rarely refused. If a man were to refuse, his community would have considered him a coward. He would have not only lost his honor but also become a target of bullying. An early chapter of this book explains that duels once served as a way of decreasing the cost of conflict resolution. Moreover, the culture of the "duel" may serve to enhance the toughness of a country's people and generate better soldiers. Even when the rule of law is well established within a country, the balance of the military powers of different countries may maintain the international order. As a way of settling disputes, duels cultivate a social norm that worships honor and violence. Although a small fraction of a country's men perish in duels, they create an environment in which men's personalities become tougher. These men are better able to defend their homelands during foreign invasions. If a country is small, a large fraction of the male population is often recruited to be soldiers when war breaks out. Meanwhile, the government of a small country can usually effectively maintain the social order even when its people exhibit bellicose personalities. A small country may encourage the social custom of the duel when the toughness of its soldiers matters greatly to the outcomes of battles with foreign countries. Duels toughen men's personalities and make them better soldiers. Given Europe's division into many small countries, international conflicts have been frequent, and rulers have encouraged the culture of the duel.

The remainder of this chapter presents a real story about the "culture of honor" to portray it more vividly. The "Wushe Incident" occurred in Taiwan from October 27 to December 1930, during the period of Japanese rule. The incident was carefully documented[2] and served as the basis for a movie entitled *Warrior of Rainbow: Seediq Bale.*

In 1895, Japan defeated China in a major war (elaborated in a later chapter). The two countries signed the Treaty of Shimonoseki (Treaty of Maguan), and Taiwan was ceded to Japan in perpetuity. When Japanese troops went to occupy Taiwan, they met little resistance from the Han Chinese, who were the majority race in China. This lack of resistance was unsurprising given the discussions and analyses provided in the previous chapters. Although fights within China often occurred, people tended to accept a new master as long as there was a clear victor. This strategy improved the welfare of the ancient Chinese. The alternative strategy of tenacious resistance would have divided China into many countries, which would have been ravaged individually by the cavalries from the nomadic tribes to the north. By the same logic, the Chinese in Taiwan had no reason to reject their new Japanese ruler, who was a "stationary bandit" in Olson's (1993) terms.

However, the story was totally different for the indigenous Chinese minority in Taiwan. Before the Japanese rule of Taiwan, the reign of the Qing Dynasty over the indigenous people in Taiwan was mainly symbolic. The aborigines in Taiwan lived a lifestyle that was totally different from that of the Han Chinese. Although the majority of Chinese lived on agriculture and commerce, the indigenous people in Taiwan made their living mainly through hunting and gathering.

There was no essential difference between the Han Chinese in Taiwan and those in Mainland China in terms of lifestyle and style of governance. In particular, private property rights were well defined, and people lived under a well-established rule of law based on the principles of legalism and Confucianism. In contrast, the hunting tribes in Taiwan shared many similarities with the nomadic tribes, except that the hunting tribes had a fixed home in the mountains and each tribe claimed a certain area of the mountains for hunting. Because the tropical weather in Taiwan provided them with hunting opportunities in every season, they did not move around like nomads. However, hunting was usually a more uncertain activity than raising cattle to generate food. Thus, the aborigines in Taiwan supplemented their hunting with gathering in the woods, and survival was a daily concern.

Many indigenous groups in Taiwan had a reputation of valor. For example, several rituals were conducted when a boy was born. First, his mother would place his umbilical cord in a rattan box used for hunting. One week later, an elder of the tribe would give the baby boy a knife as a gift. The mother would hold the boy outside, positioning him toward the road that led to the hunting grounds in the mountains, and pray that he become a brave hunter. When a boy reached the age of 12, he was expected to be equipped with a knife whenever he left the house. In addition to these symbolic rituals, the men received facial tattoos that had to be earned. To receive a facial tattoo, a man had to bring one human head back to his community, one usually belonging to an enemy he killed in combat. The facial tattoo was extremely important to a man because it indicated his social status in the community. Furthermore, in many indigenous groups in Taiwan, a man was not qualified to marry without a facial tattoo.

Why was a man's bravery so important for the Taiwanese aborigines? The first answer is that bravery itself was an important determinant of one's success in hunting animals, particularly those that were large and fierce. However, the most important reason might have related to the unclear property rights of different tribes to hunting places. The indigenous people had no formal rule of law. Individuals had no legally protected private ownership, and the different tribes had no legally specified hunting grounds. However, each tribe had a strong sense of the hunting place left by its ancestors, perhaps because the hunting tribes tended to live in fixed locations. Moreover, different tribes often fought for hunting grounds. The temptation to obtain additional grounds was high, as there was no law against doing so. Of course, the animals were ambivalent to the boundaries of different hunting grounds. If a hunter shot an arrow into an animal, and the injured animal ran onto the grounds of a different tribe, the hunter might have chased the animal onto those grounds, causing a conflict with that tribe.

That men were required to sever a human head to obtain a facial tattoo and thereby marry implies the constant conflicts and fighting between the different tribes. Brave men were valuable assets to their tribes, and cowards were liabilities. Indeed, even in contemporary times, a country's courts-martial can impose a heavy penalty on a soldier on the grounds of cowardice. During World War II, in the Battle of Moscow that took place between October 1941 and January 1942, 8,000 Soviet soldiers and other combat personnel were perceived as cowards and executed.

A hunting tribe does not have a court-martial, and its chief may not have sufficient authority to execute an individual he perceives to be a coward. To solve this problem, the tribe develops a culture that praises bravery and despises cowardice. Moreover, children are educated at a very young age to be brave. The recent Taiwanese historical drama epic film *Warriors of the Rainbow: Seediq Bale* portrays the Wushe Incident fairly realistically. In the film, Mona Rudao, the chief of a village (Mahebu) belonging to an indigenous group (Seediq) in Taiwan, leads his villagers to fight against the Japanese. Many figures in the movie including Mona Rudao and his sons refer to real individuals involved in the Wushe Incident. In the movie, when Mona Rudao was a little boy, his father offered him the following advice: "A true man dies on the battlefield. You will become a true man only after the blood of your enemies has dyed your hands so thoroughly that you cannot wash it off." This statement very much reflects the reality of the culture at the time portrayed.[3]

Although it is shocking to imagine a father imparting this kind of wisdom to his son, most fathers did so within the cultural environment of the time. The cultural implications of the facial tattoo were that if one did not kill others, he would be decapitated. Why was Taiwan's aboriginal culture so bloodthirsty? Perhaps it was due to the prevalent hunting lifestyle. Resources in the mountains were limited, implying that the rate of economic growth was low or zero and even negative when a natural disaster occurred. However, the population often grew rapidly, and when it expanded to a certain level, people did not have enough to eat and sustain their lives. In such cases, people had no choice but to kill others. In this way Taiwan's aboriginal community formed a bloodthirsty culture to control the population growth.

Such a culture may be the most suitable for ensuring the survival and prosperity of a hunting tribe in ordinary times. However, the Japanese occupation of Taiwan did not mark an ordinary time for the Taiwanese aborigines. Different from the Qing Dynasty, the Japanese ruler did not leave the indigenous groups alone. Japan treated Taiwan as an extended territory rather than a colony, and launched the so-called Kominka movement across the entire island. Kominka literally referred to making the people (in Japan's newly acquired territory) subjects of the Japanese emperor, or "Japanization." An important component of the Kominka movement was to replace the original culture in Japan's newly acquired territory with Japanese culture. The teaching of Japanese language rather than the native language was made mandatory in schools, and natives were encouraged to change their names to Japanese names. Moreover, Japan brought capital and technology to Taiwan, leading to industrialization and an improvement in the island's living standards.

The Japanese conquest of Taiwanese aborigines was much more difficult than its conquest of the Taiwanese Chinese. For example, in 1901, the Seediq tribe (the tribe of Mona Rudao) defeated a large Japanese troop of about 670 soldiers, which was unprecedented for the Japanese troops in Taiwan. As a result of this unexpected defeat, in 1902, the Japanese modified their strategy by banning Han Chinese from trading with the Seediq tribe while continuing their military assaults. The joint force of their economic sanctions and military campaign finally yielded victory for the Japanese, who gained control of the Seediq tribe.

After their conquest of the Seediq tribe, the Japanese invested heavily in the tribe's residential area of Wushe. They built schools, hospitals, and other public infrastructure that was comparable with that in Japan in terms of both appearance and quality, and spent substantial amounts of resources on education. By the time of the Wushe Incident, most of the indigenous people were able to speak simple Japanese. This was in sharp contrast with the Taiwanese Chinese, of whom only 25 percent could speak Japanese despite their obedience to the Japanese authority. This means that Japan expended much more educational resources on the indigenous Taiwanese than on the Taiwanese Chinese on average. Moreover, under the strong encouragement of the Japanese government, some Japanese policemen married Seediq women. Some tribal chiefs were invited to visit Japan and shown the details of the country's military strength, such as its machine guns, canons, and warplanes.

However, the culture of the Seediq tribe could not be changed within a short period. In the Seediq culture, a man's dignity was valued higher than his life. As discussed earlier, such a culture made economic sense for the Taiwanese aborigines in ordinary times. Indeed, before the Japanese occupation, a man had to be brave to ensure his own survival and that of his tribe in the brutal combative environment. Such was the culture that led to the Wushe Incident, which was essentially a suicidal action of Mona Rudao, his family, and his entire tribe.

Despite the economic prosperity introduced by Japanese rule, many Seediq men felt a loss of dignity. No one had been overseeing their original economic activities of hunting and gathering. After the Japanese occupation, the men were given jobs as loggers and forced into relationships with managers with whom they often conflicted. In particular, the indigenous people often felt humiliated by their managers' rough attitudes. Some Japanese policemen tried to seduce Seediq women with money, and their misconduct brewed resentment in the tribe.[4]

The tribe's anger toward the Japanese reached its boiling point when the following incident occurred. One day, the tribe held a wedding banquet. Daho Mouna, Mona Rudao's eldest son, saw a Japanese policeman pass by and asked him to drink wine with him in their traditional way. The tradition required two men to hold the same bowl of wine and drink together shoulder to shoulder in an indication of their intimate friendship. Daho Mouna had just helped slaughter a cow and still had its blood on his hands. The Japanese policemen rejected his offer on these grounds. Daho Mouna considered this public rejection a serious humiliation that he could not accept. He took hold of the Japanese policeman to force him into drinking the wine. The policeman fought back, striking Daho Mouna with his stick. More Seediq men joined the fight, and the Japanese policeman was severely beaten. The next day, Mona Rudao brought a flagon of wine to the policeman's house in an attempt to apologize. His apology was rejected, and the policeman told him that he would report the case to the higher authority. Because beating a policeman was a serious crime under Japanese rule that would have severely penalized Daho Mouna, Mona Rudao and his son decided to group the Seediq together to rebel against the Japanese.

Mona Rudao knew that he and his clan would be killed after the rebellion. They simply wanted to kill as many Japanese as possible before that happened. On October 27, 1930, the Seediq converged on a sports meeting held at an elementary school in Wushe with hundreds of Japanese in attendance. They raided the police stations, from which they captured weapons and ammunition, and ultimately stormed the elementary school where they killed 134 Japanese, including women and children.

The Japanese government took harsh military actions to quell the uprising, mobilizing an army with heavy artillery. Moreover, the Japanese army implemented chemical weapons, the first time such weapons were used in Asia. In the end, about 30 percent of the 1,200 Seediq directly involved in the rebellion were killed, and another 25 percent (including Mona Rudao) committed suicide to avoid dishonor. Moreover, the wives of many insurgents hanged themselves.

Mona Rudao had lived under Japanese rule for about 20 years and had visited Japan. He knew from the beginning that the rebellion would result in his death and the demise of his whole tribe. Most of the other members knew it as well. Making sense of this well-planned and organized rebellion requires examining the culture of honor of the indigenous people in Taiwan.

Beating the Japanese policeman would have resulted in a serious penalty for Daho Mouna, who might have had little to lose regardless of whether he rebelled. His father would have been left humiliated by the heavy penalty imposed on his son. However, the penalty would not have affected the other insurgents if they had chosen not to rebel. The uprising can only be explained by the Taiwan aborigines' culture of honor and courage at the time.

The basic tenet of this book is that throughout human history, cultures have mainly been determined by economic fundamentals. In the agrarian country of ancient China, facing threats from the nomadic tribes, the Chinese people realized that it was in their best interest to keep China a single large country to deter invasions and raids. To keep China a single large country, the rule of law had to be rigorously implemented. A culture in line with Confucianism was developed in China that emphasized kindness, courtesy, and social harmony and substantially decreased the cost of mitigating violence and maintaining social order.

The nomadic tribes (and some hunting tribes) were lawless to a large extent. In a lawless society, violence is often used as a means of obtaining material resources and women. A man had to protect his family and assets by himself.

To deter attacks and plundering, the man had to convince others that he would seriously punish or kill those who violated him at any cost, including serious injury or death. A man's dignity would have been seriously offended if others tried to take his possessions by force or bullied him or his family members, whether verbally or physically. Although a man might have appeared irrational when taking such a risk to address a single conflict, from a long-run perspective, it was the most effective way of establishing a reputation that he could not be bullied. A man often claimed to value his honor above his life or his soul above his body.

In sum, this book argues that in ancient times, the culture and individual personality in China was drastically different from those of the country's nomadic neighbors. It would not be an exaggeration to say that the two cultures were opposite. The Chinese culture emphasized social harmony, and one's individual behavior entailed following the law, kindness, etiquette, and the "doctrine of the mean." However, the nomadic culture often worshipped valor, power, and strength, and morally accepted the use of violence to possess another man's resources or women. There was usually no rule of law in a nomadic tribe, only some simple social conventions that had a limited effect on constraining peoples' behavior. In such a lawless environment, a man had to exhibit bravery and toughness to survive and protect his family, which often led him to take radical and risky actions.

Notes

1 http://www.thubtenchodron.org/PrisonDharma/prison_politics.html
2 See, e.g., Roy (2003), Syat, Koh, and Shih (2001), and Tapas (2004).
3 http://www.sight-native.taipei.gov.tw/ct.asp?xItem=1001669&CtNode=17022 &mp=cb01
4 See, e.g., Roy (2003).

Part III

How did the ancient dynasties manage the large country of China?

10 From the Tang Dynasty to the Yuan Dynasty

An early chapter of this book considers the political Coase theorem, which indicates that the economic and social fundamentals of a society determine the culture and personality of a typical individual in that society, and that a society's culture is often developed to maximize the welfare of its people. By the same logic, it can be argued that the geographical and other material factors facing the ancient Chinese determine China's "optimal" country size, which explains why China has tended to remain a large country throughout most of its documented history.

However, this argument remains incomplete. Recall that an important assumption of the Coase theorem in general and the political Coase theorem in particular is that the "transaction costs" are small. This condition is not often satisfied. Although people may find ways to achieve the optimal outcome for most members of a society in the long run, doing so is often impossible in the short run. Moreover, the path to finding the best solutions is often a process of trial and error. These general principles applied well to the ancient Chinese people's search for the optimal social and political institutions to guarantee China's status as a single large country while trying to improve its people's welfare, which was indeed a continuous effort throughout all of the dynasties. This chapter focuses on the efforts made from the Tang Dynasty to the Yuan Dynasty, and finds that they adhered to a famous ancient Chinese proverb: "after a long split, a union will occur; after a long union, a split will occur."

The Tang Dynasty began shortly after the Han Dynasty and covered the period 618–907 AD. It was a golden age of Chinese history that represented a source of pride for the Chinese people. For example, the word "Chinatown" in the United States and other Western countries in Chinese literally means "the street of the Tang people." The Tang Dynasty was largely a period of peace and economic development. Moreover, in its early stages, the Tang Dynasty exerted absolute military dominance over its nomadic neighbors and expanded the Chinese territory, a fact dear to the heart and pride of the contemporary Chinese. After the conquest of several major Turkic nomads, other nomadic tribes living close to China addressed the Emperor Li Shimin as "Tian Kehan," literally meaning "Heavenly" or "Celestial" Khan, which placed him above the leaders of the nomadic tribes (ordinary Khans). Moreover, the political hegemony of the Tang Dynasty led to the spread of the Chinese Confucian culture to the non-nomadic neighboring states, particularly Korea, Japan, and Vietnam.

However, the political structure of the Tang Dynasty exhibited a major deficiency resulting from the so-called Fan-zhen system. A Fan-zhen literally refers to a "defending town" that aimed to serve as a buffer area between the war-like nomadic tribes and China's interior regions, which were strategically located at China's northern border. A Fan-zhen was under the absolute control of a provincial military governor known as the "jiedushi." From a military efficiency perspective, it would have been best to delegate a jiedushi with absolute dictatorship in commanding the army and administering his Fan-zhen. However, the neglected negative consequence was that when a jiedushi was given this much power, his Fan-zhen gradually became his kingdom, allowing him to challenge the authority of the royal court of the Tang Dynasty.[1]

Against this background, the An Lushan Rebellion broke out. An Lushan was originally from a nomadic tribe, and had a Sogdian father and a Turkic mother. As described in an early chapter, "races" were defined by cultural assimilation rather than genetics in ancient China. Thus, An Lushan was not discriminated against because of his family background. Due to his military talents and interpersonal skills in dealing with the senior officials in the Tang court, he rose to prominence in the army and won the favor and trust of the emperor. He ultimately became a jiedushi of three Fan-zhens in northern China. An Lushan took full advantage of the enormous power given to him as a military governor, and developed a strong and loyal army over the course of eight or nine years. In 755 AD, he overtly started his rebellion against the Tang Dynasty.

The An Lushan Rebellion was massive in scale and lasted for seven years. Although the rebellion was finally quelled in 763 AD, its numerous fierce battles led to heavy casualties. The civilian death tolls were heavy as the battles disrupted production, resulting in widespread famine and starvation. Some historians have estimated the total military and civilian casualties at 36 million, about two thirds of the population of the Tang Dynasty or one sixth of the world population at that time.[2]

The rebellion was devastating to the Tang Dynasty from a long-term perspective. After the Tang army killed the rebel leaders, the authority of the central government was considerably weakened rather than strengthened. The Tang government depended on the help of other jiedushi to defeat the formidable rebel forces. As a result, the Fan-zhens and their neighboring areas at China's perimeters became virtually autonomous kingdoms, and the Tang court was unsuccessful in decreasing the powers of the jiedushi, who could pass their titles on hereditarily. In 907 AD, this *de facto* warlord system eventually led to the collapse of the Tang empire, which was replaced by the chaotic period of the Five Dynasties and Ten Kingdoms.

Several political structures took effect during the period. In the north, five short dynasties were established and then quickly succeeded by another. In the south, more than 12 states were created independently and concurrently. The rulers of those dynasties and states were often former jiedushi and engaged in continuous fighting. This period of political upheaval basically ended in 960 AD, when Zhao Kuangyin founded the Song Dynasty.

As soon as Zhao became emperor, his first important agenda was to consolidate his power and command of the army. There is a famous story about how Zhao changed the political structure of the late Tang Dynasty (i.e., the *de facto* warlord system) by playing a simple trick. Zhao invited his major generals to a lavish banquet. After drinking some wine, he thanked the generals for supporting him in establishing a new dynasty, and claimed that he wanted to reward them with large amounts of money and material wealth. Feigning drunkenness, Zhao told the generals that he felt uneasy being the emperor because the generals, including the jiedushi, had been given enough power to plan insurrections against him. The generals immediately understood that Zhao was offering them the opportunity to resign from the army in exchange for an ample reward. They all accepted the deal, not only because the material rewards were tempting, but also because Zhao Kuangyin had firm control of the army at the time. In fact, Zhao had been a jiedushi himself, and had become emperor by staging a coup.

Civilian officials were heavily relied upon as army commanders to strengthen the emperor's control over the military throughout the Song Dynasty. Although the generals and soldiers fought the battles, the Military Council, which was composed of civilian officials, had to approve the troops that a general could command. Somewhat surprisingly, the "royal guards" constituted the main force of the Song army. In ancient times, royal guards were responsible for the protection of an emperor/king and his family, and they were usually small in number. However, for the first half of the Song Dynasty, the so-called royal guards accounted for most of the Song army and were stationed near the capital city, which facilitated the emperors' control of the armed forces.

This new structure considerably mitigated the likelihood of a coup, which led to a period of internal peace and economic prosperity within the realm of the Song Dynasty. However, a negative side effect was that the military effectiveness of the Song army was substantially decreased, which might have been the most important reason why the Song Dynasty was unable to unite China entirely. For example, the royal guards stationed near the capital city were often attracted by the extravagant lifestyles of the rich, which motivated the army officers to engage in corruptive activities (e.g., embezzling the soldiers' salaries). Over time, the soldiers had little desire to fight on battlefields, and the royal guards were weak and unfit for that capacity.

Throughout most of the Song Dynasty, China proper, which excluded present-day Tibet and Xinjiang Province, was divided into four countries: Song, Liao (later Jin), Western Xia, and Dali. Most of the Chinese lived in Song, whose major rival was Liao (later Jin). The Song Dynasty expended substantial effort to recapture the northern territory, which had been a part of previous Chinese dynasties but was under the control and administration of Liao. However, the Song forces were thoroughly defeated by Liao, which was established by a nomadic tribe in what is currently northeast China. Furthermore, after observing the poor performance and military weakness of the Song army, the Liao forces launched frequent campaigns in the border regions of Song, plundering and engaging in other atrocities. Liao's military superiority ultimately convinced Song to sign a treaty in 1005. This treaty was mutually beneficial. Song provided Liao with an annual tribute that while accounting for a substantial fraction of Liao's national income was trivial relative to Song's fiscal revenue. In fact, Song was the richest dynasty in Chinese history in terms of average income, and most of its tribute to Liao took the form of massive goods exports.

However, the treaty was an insult to Song, and in 1115 or so the semi-nomadic Jurchens in northeast China insurrected against Liao. Considering it a rare opportunity to retake its northern territory and negate the Liao tribute treaty, the imperial court of Song decided to form an alliance with the Jurchens. With the help of Song, the Jurchens completely defeated the Liao Dynasty in 1125 and established the Jin Dynasty. Song received nothing in return from Jin, which launched full-scale military campaigns against Song, conquered its capital city at Kaifeng, and captured its emperor and most of the royal families in 1127. This event devastated the Song Dynasty. Song lost almost the entirety of its northern territory and was forced to retreat south of the Yangtze River. Fortunately for Song, the tough nomadic warriors of the Jin Dynasty under-performed in naval warfare. The Yangtze River stopped Jin's further invasion into Song. As a result, China was effectively divided into two major countries almost equal in size.

As China proper was being divided, the Mongol Empire was quickly on the rise. The Jin Dynasty had maintained good control of the nomadic tribes in the Mongolian steppe. However, after ruling northern China for decades, the Jurchen rulers and soldiers became accustomed to their comfortable lives in an agrarian society, and the Jin army's combative power dwindled over time. In the meantime, the Mongolian military genius Genghis Khan emerged. His tribe conquered other nomadic tribes, and by 1206 he had become the sole ruler of the Mongolian steppe.

The Mongol Empire began to conquer the entire world, and every part of China was the priority of its conquest. Its first target was the Western Xia, whose territory included the present-day northwestern Chinese provinces of Ningxia and Gansu, eastern Qinghai, northern Shanxi, northeastern Xinjiang, southwest Inner Mongolia, and the southernmost part of present-day Mongolia. The empire was founded by the nomadic tribe of Tangut in western China. Its population included the Tangut, Han Chinese, Turkic, and Tibetans.

Genghis Khan used the threat of military retaliation to deter the Jin Dynasty from coming to the aid of the Western Xia. After fierce battles that incurred considerable casualties, the Mongol forces conquered the Western Xia in 1227, slaughtering most of its population. According to Man (2004, p. 219), "There is a case to be made that this was the first ever recorded example of attempted genocide. It was certainly very successful ethnocide."

The next target of the Mongol Empire was the Jin Dynasty, an invasion that the Chinese greatly and deliberately facilitated. With General Meng Hong lead-ing the Song army, Song and the Mongols took substantial joint military actions against Jin.[3] Song had a deep hatred for Jin after more than a century's worth of wars and animosity between them. With Song's help, the Mongolians conquered Jin in 1234 and killed about 90 percent of its population.

In 1253, the Mongol Empire invaded and conquered the Kingdom of Dali, which was centered in the present-day Yunnan Province of China. The Mongols went on to conquer the Song Dynasty in 1278, and the Yuan Dynasty was established, finally uniting all of the parts of China.

This series of conquests by the Mongols was unprecedented, and well illustrates that the ancient Chinese could not afford to hate one another and had to maintain a single large country at all costs. Although the conquests marked a dark age in Chinese history, the Chinese were quick to recognize the Mongolian emperors as bearing the "Mandate of Heaven," as they largely adopted the Chinese culture. For example, in 1237, only three years after the Jin conquest, Mongol Emperor Ögedei Khan (the third son of Genghis Khan) announced that the first Keju examination would be held in 1238, and that the contents and structure of the examination would be similar to previous imperial examinations held in China, such as its emphasis on the Confucian Classics. In 1238, 4,030 candidates passed the examination at the national level. In fact, in 1233, one year before the Jin conquest, Ögedei Khan awarded Confucius's 51st-generation descendant Kong Yuanchuo the title of "high honor." (Note that the spelling of Confucius's family name in the Pinyin of modern Chinese is "Kong.")

The actions of the Mongolian ruler were indeed nearly unbelievable considering the following facts. First, the written language of the Mongolians was developed only in 1204 and was very different from Chinese. As such, the Mongolians simply could not compete with the Chinese in the examinations. During the imperial examination of 1238, the Mongolians and Chinese were divided into two separate groups. It was common knowledge at the time that the Chinese candidates would perform much better than the Mongolian candidates. The examination had a significant side effect in that it effectively revealed the inferiority of the Mongols to the Chinese, whom they had just conquered and slaughtered.

Second, Ögedei Khan had been a major conqueror throughout his life. In particular, under his direct leadership and close involvement, the Mongol Empire conquered Jin, Korea, many countries in middle Asia, and many European countries including Poland, Hungry, and Russia. In fact, it is believed that his sudden death in 1241 was the main reason why the Mongols halted their invasions of Austria, Germany, Italy, France, and Spain. Third, most of the conquests were extremely brutal. For example, in 1221, the Mongol army killed virtually all of the males and most of the population of Khwarezm, a country that combined present-day Uzbekistan, Kazakhstan, and Turkmenistan.

Due in large part to his outstanding intelligence, Ögedei Khan was the favorite son of Genghis Khan, and had the wisdom to see the value of Confucianism and Keju to the stability of his reign over China. Although Ögedei allowed his troops to kill and rape on a massive scale in central Asia and Europe, he attempted to rule China in the completely opposite way by following Confucianism.

Previous chapters repeatedly apply Olson's (1993, 2000) theory of the "stationary" versus "roving" bandit. In ancient China, a ruler was usually one or the other. However, Ögedei Khan intended to play both roles. In China, he sought to be a stationary bandit by promoting Confucianism, which emphasized benevolence and kindness. In contrast, he sought to be a roving bandit in some middle Asian countries, allowing his troops to commit horrendous atrocities. This illustrates that the choice between being a stationary and roving bandit was mainly determined by material fundamentals rather than the tastes of the rulers.

Race and personal appearance have not typically been concerns throughout most of China's history. Cultural unity and a consensus on basic values have been maintained through people's adherences to Confucianism. The nomadic tribes outside China, which did not follow the teachings of the Confucian Classics, were simply labeled as "barbarians." Once they became rulers, however, these "barbarians" adopted Confucianism and were encouraged by the culture to become Chinese.

The culture also tempted the Mongol rulers to become Chinese, a fact well illustrated by Ögedei Khan's actions. The temptation appeared to be even greater for Kublai Khan, who established the Yuan Dynasty in 1272 and conquered the Song Dynasty shortly thereafter.

Kublai had a good knowledge of Confucianism even in his early years because his mother hired several Han Chinese teachers to educate him. When he was a prince, he was assigned to rule over Mongol-held territories in China. Kublai frequently sought the advice of Confucian scholars in his administration. For example, he designed a government structure similar in style to those of past Chinese dynasties, and particularly left the local administrative structures unchanged. He also built schools that educated students based on Confucian teachings and revived Chinese social customs. In this way, he gained some popular support from the Chinese when he formally claimed the "Mandate of Heaven" to build the Yuan Dynasty. In fact, Kublai chose the name of this dynasty based on the Yijing, one of the oldest of the Confucian Classics. In the Yijing, Yuan refers to the origin of the universe. Moreover, Kublai often carefully followed the rituals of Confucian propriety in public.

However, Kublai firmly rejected proposals to revive the Keju examinations. This was quite surprising, particularly because Ögedei Khan held the first Keju examinations about 40 years before the Yuan Dynasty was established, during a time of frequent wars. Perhaps more surprisingly, Kublai divided the people of the Yuan society into four classes, including the following in descending order: Mongols, Semu, Northern Chinese, and Southern Chinese. ("Semu" refers to the people in middle Asia and Europe.) This ranking was consistent with the time sequence in which these people joined the Mongolian Empire. Why did Kublai foster this social inequality, which ultimately resulted in the collapse of the Yuan Dynasty? This question has never been fully addressed in the literature, and this book attempts to do so from a political economics perspective.

A careful reading of the Yuan history clearly indicates that the tendency of Kublai's "Sinicization" suddenly reversed after two revolts occurred. The first was the challenge from Kaidu, one of Ögedei's grandsons. Because Kublai was Ögedei's nephew and not a direct descendant, Kaidu refused to submit to Kublai, arguing that he was a more legitimate heir to the Mongol Empire. Furthermore, Kaidu chastised Kublai for becoming Chinese, and often tried to collaborate with other Mongol generals to revolt against the Yuan Dynasty.

When the Yuan Dynasty was established, the Mongol Empire was divided into five *de facto* countries, including the Yuan Dynasty and four others that were large in geographical size. The Yuan Dynasty included much of present-day China and Mongolia, and the other four countries occupied the vast areas of land in middle Asia and Eastern Europe. The other four countries were functionally autonomous, and at most symbolically accepted the emperor of the Yuan Dynasty as the supreme ruler (Great Khan) of the five *de facto* independent countries in the Mongol Empire. Therefore, Kublai was gravely concerned that any further Sinicization would influence the other four countries of the Mongol Empire to join forces to challenge his rule and topple the Yuan Dynasty. As a result, he not only rejected the Keju examinations but also created a social hierarchy that positioned the Mongols at the top, signaling however symbolically that his Yuan Dynasty was a Mongol empire rather than a Chinese empire.

In fact, before Kaidu's revolt, Kublai engaged in a major war with his younger brother Ariq Böke for the throne of the Mongol Empire. The war lasted four years and included numerous fierce battles, the outcomes of which were illustrated by the devastation brought to the Mongolian capital city of Karakorum. Just as in the war against Kaidu's revolt, Kublai's elite forces were Mongolian cavalry. Positioning the Mongols at the highest rank of the social hierarchy was a cheap form of "payment" given to the Mongolian soldiers who risked their lives on the battlefields.

Another major insurrection was a revolt led by Li Tan, a Chinese warlord who had once won favor and trust from Kublai. Although the rebel army was quickly crushed and Li Tan was caught and executed, Kublai felt that his alliance with Chinese warlords was fragile and that his dynasty required the support of Mongol warriors. Thus, positioning the Mongols at the highest rank of the social hierarchy assured their future loyalty to the Yuan Dynasty and indicated a strong alliance with the Mongols in the other four *de facto* countries of the Mongol Empire.

The Confucianism-based Keju exams were also a sign of Sinicization. By the same logic, Kublai decided to reject them in the Yuan Dynasty. Although Ögedei authorized the initial imperial examination in 1237, the Keju system was virtually suspended in the Mongol Empire until 1312. Indeed, most Mongolians were against the Keju system, which not only made them feel inferior but also increased the number of potential candidates to compete with over attractive government positions offering high incomes and prestige. In fact, even after the Keju exams were revived in 1312, they were suspended again from 1336 to 1340, when the emperor was weak and the power of the central government was effectively controlled by Mongolian Chancellor Bayan. Bayan was the commander of the joint central army of the Mongols, Kypchaks, Russians, and Asud, and later became great chancellor of the Yuan Dynasty. In 1340, he was purged in a coup, and the Keju exams were resumed shortly thereafter.

Despite its ultimate adherence to Confucianism as the core value of government, the Yuan Dynasty was short lived. It collapsed in 1368 after less than a 100-year rule in China. An important reason for its demise was that it created racial inequality, which not only aroused resentment from most of the Chinese but also fundamentally contradicted the basic teachings of Confucianism. Once the hierarchy of races was created, it became hard to demolish. The Mongols had already begun considering their position at the top of society as an "entitlement," implying that any attempt of an emperor to demolish it would have led to Mongol insurrections against him. As a result, no emperor of the Yuan Dynasty tried to change the system, no matter how Sinicized he became.

Notes

1 http://paper.people.com.cn/rmlt/html/2007–08/15/content_17149993.htm
2 See, e.g., Pinker (2011).
3 *The History of Song (Song Shi): Meng Hong.*

11 The Ming Dynasty

In 1368, the Yuan Dynasty collapsed and was replaced by the Ming Dynasty. The founder of the Ming Dynasty, Zhu Yuanzhang, came into prominence as a rebel leader. Although Zhu came from a poor family and had received little formal education, he turned out to be an effective administrator. For example, Zhu had the wisdom to know the importance of the rule of law to governance in China. In fact, in 1364, four years before the Ming Dynasty was formally established, Zhu began to contemplate the best rule of law for governing his future empire. As soon as he sat on the throne, he set in motion the construction of the "Da-Ming Lu," the penal law codex of the Ming Dynasty or "Code of the Great Ming."[1]

Zhu Yuanzhang made it a high priority to establish a comprehensive set of law codes that would effectively help him achieve his goals, including maintaining social order, deterring coups and insurrections, increasing government revenues, and enhancing people's welfare and hence the stability of his empire. He worked at refining this law code continuously during his nearly 30-year reign and finished it one year prior to his death.

Although the "Da-Ming Lu" was based on the law codes of previous dynasties, it offered at least two important extensions. First, it emphasized the interactions between Chinese Confucian culture and the rule of law. The implementation of a rule of law entails the enforcement of policemen, judges, and other bureaucrats. However, bureaucratic corruption has always been commonplace. When corruption is rampant, an unpopular law code is difficult to implement. Thus, popularity increases the effectiveness of a law code. The popularity of a law code can be increased by bringing it more into line with the mainstream culture. In ancient China, the mainstream culture was the Confucian culture.

Second, the implementation of a rule of law relies on details. It took a long time to finalize the law code because there were many details to consider. China's social and economic environments after the Mongolian invasions and the subsequent rule of the Yuan Dynasty underwent varying and considerable changes. Thus, an effective law code could not be copied directly from those of previous dynasties. For example, even in the Tang Dynasty, slaves were despised by society and their legal rights were not mentioned in the law code. Consequently, they were often mistreated. Moreover, if a slave was mistreated by someone other than his or her master, it could have initiated a violent conflict between the slave master and the individual who harmed the slave. The Ming Code added detailed clauses related to the protection of slaves and other civilians. Zhu Yuanzhang also noticed that if a law code was either unclear or overly complicated, some officials may abuse the law by deliberately misinterpreting it. To resolve this problem, Zhu mandated that the law code be concise and intelligible in addition to detailed.

Zhu ruthlessly killed those who contributed significantly to the battles against the Mongols of the Yuan Dynasty and other rebels, who had enabled him to become the emperor. The most famous example of these killings involved Hu Weiyong.[2] In 1380, Grand Chancellor of the Ming Dynasty Hu Weiyong was sentenced to death on the charge of treason. His contribution during the war period was not large. He became the grand chancellor based mainly on the strong recommendation of his predecessor, Li Shanchang. Li had been Emperor Zhu's closest comrade during the war, and was commonly considered the greatest contributor to Zhu's ultimate victory against various enemies, which led to the establishment of the Ming Dynasty.

Based on Li Shanchang's support and recommendation, Hu Weiyong immediately became a cabinet member of the central government. Hu arranged a marriage between his niece and Li's nephew, further enhancing his relationship with Li. Hu also had a high level of administrative capacity. Thus, Zhu Yuanzhang quickly appointed him as the chancellor of his administration.

Hu Weiyong became increasingly powerful over time, and his attitudes toward other officials became increasingly arrogant and overbearing. The rewards and penalties administered to an official were often determined by Hu's personal views or self-interests. He sometimes promoted or demoted an official without any justification. Officials found it hard to lodge a complaint against him because any document submitted to the emperor had to pass over Hu's desk first. Hu ultimately became notorious for being an arrogant dictator, and was hated by many officials.

Emperor Zhu became increasing discontented with Hu and decided to depose him. Moreover, Zhu made full use of the opportunity provided by Hu to purge his entire government. He began by accusing Hu of treason based on a very weak piece of evidence that might have been faked with his permission. Hu and his family members were immediately executed. Zhu then launched a large-scale investigation of the officials who had connections and close relationships with Hu. In the end, a large number of officials were convicted for being accomplices of Hu, and were also executed together with their family members. New waves of investigation were launched, and these cases continued for 10 years until 1390. More than 30,000 people were killed, and most had only distant connections with Hu.

In 1393, only three years after the closure of Hu's case, Lan Yu, a legendary general who contributed significantly to the Ming Dynasty, was accused of plotting a coup. The evidence for this accusation was also weak and circumstantial: 10,000 Japanese swords were found in a mandated search of his estates.

The consequence was also catastrophic, as Lan Yu and his family members were immediately executed. About 15,000 people (including many generals and nobles) who Emperor Zhu thought were connected to Lan Yu were also executed shortly thereafter.

Why did Emperor Zhu kill so many officials and generals? The fear of insurrection was surely one reason. Many of the officials and generals were Zhu's subordinates in his rebel army against the Mongols of the Yuan Dynasty, and hence might have continued to harbor a rebellion mentality. It would have been natural for Zhu to think that they had aims to usurp his throne. He was well aware based on the events of previous dynasties that rulers had been ousted and killed by their powerful generals or ministers. Many nobles also had extensive battlefield experience and high amounts of prestige due to their leading roles during the war period, which could have facilitated a rebellion.

Moreover, although those people posed no threat to Zhu, they might have gone on to threaten the successor of his empire after his death. For example, Zhu expressed his concern that his crown prince was too kind, and thus decided not to allow those who had the potential ability to revolt to outlive him. For example, in 1390, he ordered the execution of Li Shanchang, arguing that Li had been fully aware of Hu Weiyong's attempt at treason but never reported him.

Although suspicion of treason and even paranoia were the main reasons for Zhu's massive purge of his government, the killing of officials provided him with other benefits. For example, when the Ming Dynasty was first founded, most of the government officials were either subordinates in his rebel army or were connected to those subordinates. In fact, government appointments were an important way of rewarding subordinates for their contributions on the battlefield. However, these subordinates did not always make the most efficient government bureaucrats, and replacing them with those who performed best on the Keju examinations might have improved the quality of Zhu's administration substantially. Many nobles received very generous "salaries" from the central government that were carried over to their offspring after their deaths. Thus, the elimination of those nobles would have considerably decreased the financial liabilities of the Ming Dynasty.

However, the emperor could not kill officials without a reason or excuse, as it was his intention to rule his empire by the rule of law. Thus, he made clever use of the opportunities presented by the cases of Hu Weiyong and Lan Yu. Although the evidence for their treasonous actions and intentions was weak, Hu and Lan did abuse their power and act very arrogantly, which encouraged the widespread wrath of many officials and ordinary civilians. Thus, the emperor received support from most people to sentence them to death. Treason was an offence punishable by death according to the law, and a planned revolt would have understandably involved a large number of officials and generals.

The next question for Zhu Yuanzhang was how to govern a country of such enormous size as China. He had obviously learned lessons from the Tang

Dynasty, which was torn apart by powerful warlords, and the Song Dynasty, which was devastated by the ineffectiveness of its army. In response, he thought up a strategy that aimed to benefit and involve his offspring at the same time. Zhu had 26 sons, all of whom were appointed to be princes in different areas throughout China. The princes were awarded with large estates and high annual incomes and could participate in military affairs. Zhu had also obviously learned the lessons of the uprisings of the seven princes at the beginning of the Han Dynasty. The princes were not allowed to serve any administrative function, and were usually given only high nominal ranks in the army rather than any real power or control. Zhu might have hoped that this arrangement would serve as an effective deterrent to any potential revolt from any ambitious generals of the Ming army.

Zhu's altruism toward his offspring was natural,[3] and he provided them with the material bases for their luxurious lifestyles. However, doing so suited an additional purpose. The princes had ample resources, and could employ enough personnel to monitor the behavior of the generals stationed in areas close to their fiefs. For example, each prince was usually entitled to a personal army ranging from 3,000 to 19,000 soldiers. The generals were required to pay their utmost respect to the princes, which further facilitated the monitoring. The strategy worked well, as no militarily strong men (that were not from the royal family) revolted during the Ming Dynasty.

However, Zhu Yuanzhang made at least one serious miscalculation in this arrangement that resulted in a major war immediately after his death. A few princes were given the power to gain control of the local Ming troops if they aspired to do so. The potential threat of the princes who were assigned territories in the northern frontier was particularly serious, as they were allowed to possess private troops much larger in number than the upper limit of 19,000 men used to prevent attacks from the Mongolian troops.

Zhu Yuanzhang died in 1398 after ruling the Ming Dynasty for 30 years. When the new emperor Zhu Yunwen ascended the throne, he decided to decrease the power of the princes by curtailing the number of private soldiers they were entitled to have. He did so partly because the Ming Dynasty entered a period of relative peace that no longer justified the possession of such large armies. However, Prince Zhu Di, who was stationed in Beijing, possessed a powerful army and staged an insurrection in 1399. After three years of war, Zhu Di's troops captured the capital city of Nanjing and killed the emperor.

After becoming the new emperor, Zhu Di continued Zhu Yunwen's policy of weakening the power of the princes, and managed to relocate the princes who were initially assigned to the territories at the northern border of China, which had a strong military presence. In a related policy, he moved the capital from the south (Nanjing) to the north (Beijing), a move that proved wise. Having been stationed in Beijing for a long time, Zhu Di observed that the Ming Dynasty would have to station its best troops at the northern border against resurgent Mongol threats. Beijing was close to the would-be invasion routes of the nomadic tribes, and therefore to the Chinese troops with the most combative power. Thus, the emperors were better able to control the best troops of the Ming Dynasty by moving the capital to Beijing.

With the exception of the turmoil of Zhu Di's revolt, the early period of the Ming Dynasty was generally characterized by peace and economic prosperity. Reischauer, Fairbank, and Craig (1960) describe the Ming Dynasty as "one of the greatest eras of orderly government and social stability in human history." This great era reached its zenith in terms of economic prosperity and military might at the beginning of the dynasty, as vividly indicated by the seven enormous explorative voyages led by Zheng He between 1405 and 1433.[4] These expeditions started near present-day Shanghai, passing through the Indian Ocean and reaching Arabia and even as far as the coast of Africa. The gigantic size of the fleet was a glorious demonstration of the national strength of China during the Ming Dynasty. For example, the fleet of the first voyage started in 1405 consisted of 317 ships with about 28,000 crewmen on board.

However, the Ming Dynasty ultimately collapsed in 1644 after a 276-year rule. The history literature has offered a number of explanations for its demise. Some emperors delegated too much power to court eunuchs, who abused that power. The most famous eunuch in Chinese history is Wei Zhongxian (1568–1627) of the Ming Dynasty. Wei and his team of eunuchs virtually dominated the administration between 1620 and 1627. They persecuted and killed many government officials who disobeyed them, which demoralized the civil servants and significantly decreased the government's administrative efficiency.[5]

Another main explanation is the widespread famines caused by weather changes. In the early 17th century, the climate in northern China suddenly became very dry and cold, making the growing season for agricultural products much shorter and decreasing the agricultural output substantially (Spence, 1999).

However, the most fundamental reason for the collapse of the Ming Dynasty is pure and simple: the extended royal family was too large and continued to grow at a rapid rate. This explanation is elaborated as follows, and a more detailed (but somewhat different) explanation may be found on the Internet.[6]

At the beginning of the Ming Dynasty, a population census estimated the total population in China at slightly more than 60 million people in 1393. The population size by the end of the Ming Dynasty was not so clear. Brook (1998), Ebrey (1999), and Fairbank and Goldman (2006) estimate the total at 160 million, 175 million, and 200 million people, respectively. A reasonable estimate is that the population increased three times over.

In contrast, the population of the royal family increased astronomically. The first emperor of the Ming Dynasty, Zhu Yuanzhang, ruled China for 30 years. When he died in 1398, he had 26 sons and 16 daughters, or 42 children in total.[7] By the end of the Ming Dynasty, his offspring numbered more than 200,000.[8] In other words, from the time of his death to the end of the Ming Dynasty, Zhu's offspring increased about 4,762 times over. The average number of Chinese people who supported Zhu and his children at the beginning of the Ming Dynasty can be calculated as follows:

60 million/(1 + 42) = 1.4 million.

The average number of Chinese people who supported Zhu's offspring by the end the Ming Dynasty can be calculated as follows:

180 million/0.2 million = 900.

Thus, from the beginning to the end of the Ming Dynasty, the financial burden for the Chinese people increased 1,556 times over (1.4 million / 900). By the end of the Ming Dynasty, an average of 900 Chinese people had to pay tax to support one royal family member. This was in addition to the tax paid on other expenditures, such as the military expenditures required for the increasing number of soldiers fighting against domestic insurgents and the Manchurians in the northeast. The end result was widespread famine, and the Ming Dynasty crumbled.

As described earlier, Zhu Yuanzhang was extremely brutal and ruthless in killing the officials and nobles who contributed significantly to building his empire. However, Zhu designed a system that was extremely generous in providing for the welfare of his offspring. In fact, one may reasonably argue that Zhu was able to design a system of distribution that strongly favored his offspring precisely because he massacred those nobles.

For example, a prince's salary was seven times that of the highest-ranking official. Each royal offspring began receiving an income from the government at the age of 10, ensuring that he would lead a luxurious life without engaging in any occupation.[9] With the number of royal offspring increasing quickly, the government began to realize in the middle of the Ming Dynasty that China's financial revenue was not enough to meet the payrolls of the royal family. For example, at the end of the Ming Dynasty, the total fiscal revenue in Shanxi Province was about 1.52 million stones of rice per year. However, the salary payment made to the royal family members living in Shanxi was 3.12 million stones of rice per year.[10] The other provinces were often in similar situations, and the government officials had to live on the incomes from engaging in corruption.[11]

More important, as the number of princes increased, an increasing amount of land was given to the members of the royal family to build palaces. Some of the land was also rented to peasants. The national per capita possession of land had been declining since the middle of the Ming Dynasty, and the royal ownership of land had been rapidly expanding. For example, the extended royal family possessed half of the land in Henan Province. Moreover, the royal family always selected the most fertile lands in the best locations.

As demonstrated by Malthus's (1798) classical population theory, population growth was mainly determined by income and wealth until about 200 years ago. A richer man usually had more children, and in the case of China more wives. Furthermore, the infant mortality rate was lower for a richer household. Therefore, the population growth of the royal family was much faster than the national average during the Ming Dynasty.

The members of the royal families lived across China during the Ming Dynasty. Many behaved like bullies in the areas in which they lived. Although the members were nominally under the same rule of law, few government officials dared to prosecute or punish them when they committed crimes. Consequently, they often flagrantly disregarded the rule of law, and even interfered in local government affairs and treated local officials as their private servants. They also treated ordinary civilians as inferiors. For example, it was common for the royal family members to force beautiful young women to be their wives or concubines.

The unbearable financial burdens and bullying introduced by the enormous royal family ultimately resulted in large-scale peasant insurrections by the end of the Ming Dynasty. There were a large number of rebel groups, and they all hated the royal family members to the extreme. When the peasant rebels took a county or city, the first thing they did was kill all of the members of the royal family in the area. Many stories reveal the ways in which the rebels tortured the princes of senior rank to death. Indeed, it is no exaggeration to say that the peasants hated the royal families more than they hated foreign invaders.

After the Manchurian conquest of China during the Qing Dynasty, the Qing army's priority became to kill the offspring of the royal family of the Ming Dynasty. This was not due to its hatred of the Ming royal family, but because it intended to eradicate the hope of some Chinese to revive the Ming Dynasty. As a result, almost all of Zhu Yuanzhang's male offspring were killed.[12]

The Ming Dynasty was doomed to collapse from the beginning, when Zhu Yuanzhang designed a system that guaranteed that his offspring would have a much higher standard of living than ordinary people. Its collapse also explains the collapsing of other dynasties in China. In most dynasties, the offspring of a royal family were much richer than the ordinary citizens. This argument adds to the theory of the "dynastic cycle" in the Chinese history literature,[13] which argues that every dynasty experienced a cycle of rises and falls.

Much of this book demonstrates the benefits of forming a single large country. However, the fall of the Ming Dynasty demonstrates the downside: the emperor is sometimes unconstrained in his rent-seeking behavior. Measuring the degree of rulers' rent-seeking behavior in historical times is a difficult task. This book suggests a new way of doing so that focuses on the population growth of the extended royal family. This method is based on the classical population theory developed by Malthus (1798), who argued that income and fertility were closely positively correlated in historical times. The Malthusian theory has consistently been confirmed in recent empirical studies. In the case of the Ming Dynasty, the royal family produced too many children, which essentially bankrupted the Chinese economy.

Zhu Yuanzhang's ruthless killing of numerous officials and generals who made important contributions to the establishment of the Ming Dynasty further exemplifies the actions of an unconstrained emperor. In contrast, during the

Warring States period of the Zhou Dynasty, the ruler of a state often treated his capable ministers extremely well.[14] Zhu Yuanzhang behaved so differently from the ancient Chinese kings because he had no rivals from competing neighboring countries.

An earlier chapter explained why China was the only major ancient civilization that did not have a religion. The benefits that the ancient Chinese reaped by adhering to a philosophy of Confucianism rather than a religion are discussed further in the next chapter. However, religions do have one major benefit: they put an effective constraint on the behavior of sovereign rulers. For example, Christianity stipulates that a man can have only one wife, regardless of his social status and position in the government. This clause would have effectively controlled the population growth of the royal family, and may explain why many Western countries adopt the religion of Christianity. In the Ottoman Empire, emperors had many wives. However, when a new emperor came to the throne, he would immediately kill all of his brothers. This chapter provides a rationale for this social custom.

The Chinese fortunately discovered that non-ethnic Chinese rulers exhibited constrained behavior. The next chapter discusses the Qing Dynasty, and considers why the Manchus turned out to be much better rulers in China. Because the Manchus were constantly aware of potential insurrections from the Chinese people, they were very constrained in their rent-seeking behavior. This was reflected in the population growth rate of their royal family, which was only about twice the rate in China as a whole.

Notes

1 See, e.g., Jiang (1997).
2 See, e.g., Ebrey (1999).
3 See, e.g., Becker (1991) and Fan (2014).
4 See, e.g., Levathes (1996).
5 See, e.g., Dardess (2002).
6 http://cul.cn.yahoo.com/ypen/20111227/783614_1.html; https://plus.google.com/111967417062761314875/posts/ND2dJ1kEnDV#111967417062761314875/posts/ND2dJ1kEnDV
7 http://en.wikipedia.org/wiki/Hongwu_Emperor
8 See, e.g., Dang Nian Ming Yue (2006).
9 Record of the *History of Ming*: http://zh.wikipedia.org/wiki/%E6%98%8E%E6%9C%9D%E7%9A%87%E5%AE%A4.
10 http://cul.cn.yahoo.com/ypen/20111227/783614_1.html
11 See, e.g., Ni and Van (2006).
12 Indeed, an Internet search indicates that only one person has claimed to have evidence to prove that he or she is the offspring of Zhu Yuanzhang. Note that in China's current cultural environment, people have a large incentive to claim that they are the descendants of a royal family from ancient times.
13 See, e.g., Ching (1974) and Wills (1994).
14 For example, I describe such stories carefully in another book related to ancient and contemporary Chinese nationalism (Fan, 2014).

12 The Qing Dynasty

After the collapse of the Ming Dynasty, the Qing Dynasty was established. Ethnical minority groups including the Jurchens and Manchus ruled the Qing Dynasty, which has often been rated as the best in Chinese history in terms of the people's welfare.

Nurhaci founded the Manchu state in northeast China. The Jurchens were under Chinese rule for most of the Ming Dynasty. They lived in northeast China, which included large areas of fertile land. However, northeast China also had long cold winters during which crops could not grow. During the winter, the Jurchens had to live mainly on hunting and gathering, and therefore shared the nomadic tribe culture that honored bravery, strength, and fighting skills such as horsemanship and archery. However, different from pure nomadic tribes, many Jurchens engaged in agrarian production and had close contacts with the Chinese. Thus, they were also highly influenced by the Chinese culture.

The basic principle for the Chinese rule over the Jurchens was "divide and rule" through a system of commanderies. A commandery was established for a tribal military unit, and hundreds of commanderies were conferred. The Ming army, which was stationed in northeast China and far stronger than the Jurchen forces, kept a close watch on the Jurchen tribes. If it observed one tribe beginning to dominate others, the Chinese army would side with the other tribes in battle. For most of the Ming Dynasty, this system worked very well in preventing the Jurchens' collective rebellions. The Ming Dynasty also made effective use of the Jurchen forces in its battles against the Mongols.

The commander-in-chief of the Ming army in northeast China had a major fissure with the Ming Dynasty at its end, and intended to use Nurhachi to achieve his ambition of becoming the king of Korea. However, Nurhachi used him instead, strengthened his tribe, and ultimately united all of the Jurchen tribes. Nurhachi formally rebelled against the Ming Dynasty, and established his own kingdom in northeast China.

After Nurhachi's death, his children engaged in fierce competition for the throne. During the political struggle, Nurhachi's grand consort (or *de facto* queen) Lady Abahai was forced to commit suicide to be buried together with Nurhachi. This plot was carried out because Lady Abahai's sons Dorgon and

Dodo were in important military positions. Nurhachi's eighth son Huang Taiji ultimately became the new king.

However, Dorgon and Dodo were only 14 and 12 years old, respectively, when Nurhachi died in 1626. (It is indeed amazing that they had substantial military powers at such tender ages.) In contrast, Huang Taiji was 34 years old and had extensive experience on the battlefield and in internal politics. Thus, Huang Taiji was able to obtain the support of most generals and nobles. They were reluctant to select a 14-year-old boy as the leader of the newly established kingdom, which was constantly under the threat of the Ming Dynasty. Because Dorgon and Dodo could have become very powerful, Huang Taiji felt that their mother had to be killed immediately. Huang Taiji might have feared that with the help of Lady Abahai's wisdom and prestige as the former queen, the increasing military prowess and experience of Dorgon and Dodo would challenge his throne.

In 1635, Huang Taiji renamed Jurchen as Manchu. The Manchus were defined as people in northeast China (i.e., Manchuria) who were neither Chinese nor Mongols. In fact, some of the Chinese who spoke the Jurchen language well chose to be Manchu by changing their names, which was usually allowed. In 1636, Huang Taiji named his empire "Qing." By the end of the Ming Dynasty, less than one sixth of the people in Qing were Jurchens, and most of the people in the Jurchen/Manchu kingdom were ethnically Chinese.[1]

In September 1643, Huang Taiji suffered a stroke and died suddenly. Not long before his death, he gave the two elite army units to his eldest son Hooge. However, Dorgon and Dodo were both in their prime age at that time. Moreover, they had accrued substantial military achievements, and Dorgon was by consensus the general who made the most important contributions to Qing and was the most influential general in the army. Although Hooge had a more legitimate claim to his father's throne, Dorgon believed that Huang Taiji initially took the throne through a conspiracy that included forcing his mother to commit suicide. A bitter rivalry ensued between Hooge and Dorgon, and they were on the verge of engaging their armies in a major battle. A compromise was reached that put Huang Taiji's five-year-old son Fulin (i.e., Hooge's brother and Dorgon's nephew) on the throne. From that point on, Fulin was known as Emperor Shunzhi. The throne was passed on to Huang Taiji's offspring, but Dorgon became the *de facto* emperor of Qing. The transition ultimately had a peaceful ending, and Dorgon continued most of Huang Taiji's legacies, including his racial policy, which was kind to Chinese. At the same time, the Ming Dynasty was crumbling, which provided the new Qing kingdom with a golden opportunity to capture China as a whole. When the Ming Dynasty collapsed, the commander-in-chief of the most elite Ming army, Wu Sangui, chose to surrender to the Qing Dynasty. Consequently, their joint forces conquered China.

The Manchu conquest of China went relatively smoothly. The excessive exploitation of the extended royal family of the Ming Dynasty was widely observed by the Chinese people, most of whom welcomed a new dynasty to replace the old. In fact, the Qing Dynasty might have appeared a good candidate to replace the Ming Dynasty. It would not be fair to say that the Manchus were foreigners, as they had been ruled by the Chinese of the Ming Dynasty for two and half centuries. Rather, the Manchus could be considered a Chinese minority group.

Moreover, although "Chinese" is considered a race and a nationality today, in ancient times it identified more of a civilization. In fact, in ancient China, almost everyone could choose to be Chinese as long as he or she followed the social norms based on Confucianism. Today, the majority of Chinese in China are called "Han Chinese," which originally meant that one was Chinese during the Han Dynasty. The concept of "Chinese" in ancient times is analogous to the contemporary concept of "American."

Well-known Chinese philosopher Feng Youlan (1985, pp. 211–222) observes the following: "[W]hat the Chinese were always concerned about was the continuation and integrity of the Chinese culture and civilization . . . from the early Qin dynasty onwards, Chinese had clearly made a distinction between the 'China', or 'Huaxia', with the 'Barbarians (Yidi)' . . . such a distinction was made according to a cultural criteria rather than racial differences." Furthermore, Harrison (1969, p. 2) states that "the traditional Chinese self-image has generally been defined as 'culturalism', based on the historical heritage and acceptance of shared values, not as nationalism, based on the modern concept of the nation-state." Moreover, based on Liang Qichao's insightful writings related to celebrity over the last century (Liang, 1984), Chen (2005, pp. 36–37) offers the following summary: "From a culturalist point of view, the primary identity of the Chinese was the general acceptance of traditional Chinese culture, namely, the Confucianism that dominated the minds of the Chinese for almost 2,000 years. It is the acceptance, or not, of this culture that separated the Chinese and the Others, or the 'barbarians'. Furthermore, culturalism did not regard the boundary between the Chinese and barbarians as static or fixed. Once the 'barbarians' adopted Chinese culture, they became Chinese, and vice versa."

Before invading central China, the Manchus had largely been integrated into the Chinese culture. In other words, they were largely Chinese by definition. For example, when Qing was still in Manchuria, Huang Taiji established the format of the bureaucratic system based mainly on the model of the Ming Dynasty. Furthermore, in 1636, Huang Taiji changed his own title of Khan (the usual title of the king in a nomadic tribe) to Emperor, which as far as most people were aware was used only in China.

However, the Qing Dynasty introduced a potentially big problem: the hairstyle adopted by Manchu men differed drastically from that adopted by Chinese men. The Manchu man's hairstyle was conspicuous and unique. The hair at the front of the head was entirely shaved off above the temples, and the rest of the hair in the back was braided into a long pigtail.

From an economic efficiency perspective, it is hard to explain why Manchu men adopted such a hairstyle. The winters in Manchuria were long and cold. Thus, a man would have been likely to catch a cold if he had the Manchu hairstyle and lacked a warm hat. However, in ancient times, people were poor and many could not afford such a hat. Thus, the only plausible explanations are that such a hairstyle made a man look tougher, and that when hunting or engaging in a fierce battle, a man was not concerned that his long hair may occasionally block his eyesight and become detrimental at critical moments.

As mentioned earlier, the concept of "Chinese" in ancient times was analogous to that of "American" today. However, the different races in the United States, including whites, blacks, and Asians, are divided mainly according to their drastically different physical appearances. When the Manchus and Chinese had the same hairstyle, they exhibited only a small difference in physical appearance. However, the unique Manchu hairstyle made the two groups appear very different from each other. In other words, the Qing comprised two main groups of people who looked distinctively different when sporting different hairstyles. To resolve this potential man-made "racial problem," a policy known as the "Queue Order" was issued, demanding that all Chinese adopt the Manchu hairstyle.

However, such a policy was strongly against the Chinese Confucian culture. In particular, according to Confucius, "We are given our body, skin and hair from our parents, and we should not damage them. This idea is the quintessence of filial duty."[2] Thus, adopting the Manchu hairstyle was essentially against the Confucian Classic of Filial Piety.

According to the Queue Order, all of the Chinese were required to shave their hair into a queue within 10 days. Those who refused to do so faced the death penalty. To convey this message to the Chinese, the Queue Order was often simply stated as follows: "Keep your hair and lose your head, or cut your hair and keep your head."

Many Chinese resisted the order, and anti-Qing emotions suddenly blazed up. Most of the Chinese people shaved their heads according to the Queue Order under extreme anger and reluctance. A few simply chose to die. Lu Xun, the celebrated writer of the last century, portrays what happened pertinently: "In fact, the Chinese people in those days revolted not because the country was on the verge of ruin, but because they had to wear queues."

Qing had already conquered most of China when the Queue Order was implemented. Because an individual could not meaningfully fight against an army, violent rebellions were rare. Most of the anti-Qing movements took the form of extreme emotional resentment toward Qing. However, there were some exceptions, including a notable example that occurred in Jiading, located in present-day Shanghai. Within two months, the people in Jiading self-organized to fight against the Qing army more than 10 times. Led by General Li Cheng-Dong, the Qing troops struck back with deadly force and slaughtered the city three times. (Li Cheng-Dong was formerly a peasant rebel leader, who surrendered to the Qing army. Later on, he revolted against Qing and was killed in a battle.) In the end, more than 20,000 people in Jiading were either killed by the Qing troops or committed suicide.[3]

The Jiading revolt illustrates that the ancient Chinese held the core value of their culture dearly. However, the culture of Confucianism was not a religion, and was interpreted in different ways. Thus, it could be modified by strong outside forces, and people ultimately adjusted to the changes over time. After 10 years of strict martial enforcement, most of the Chinese began to accept queues as a part of the social custom in China.

As described earlier, China has never had a religion that governs the country. Although people have adhered strictly to Confucianism, it has never been a religion, and Confucius has never been considered a god. The preceding example of the Queue Order provides a good illustration for the reasons behind this. Consider a *hypothetical* scenario in which ancient China was a country governed by Christianity. Jesus Christ said that one's hair should not be cut. In this *hypothetical* scenario, most of the Chinese would have chosen to die rather than follow the Queue Order. However, China was not a religious country. As a result, although Confucius said that one's hair should not be cut, people could accept the Queue Order ultimately without sacrificing themselves. In fact, Confucianism was constantly subjected to modification. For example, in the Song Dynasty, the older form of Confucianism was replaced by so-called Neo-Confucianism, a new form of Confucianism based more on rationality than superstition.

As described earlier in this chapter, the five-year-old Fulin took the throne in 1643 as Emperor Shunzhi as a result of the political compromise made between his brothers Hooge and Dorgon. Between 1643 and 1650, Prince Regent Dorgon was the *de facto* ruler of China. Emperor Shunzhi's rule of China started in 1651 after Dorgon's accidental death on December 31, 1650.

The Qing conquest of China in 1644 consolidated the power of its central government, and consequently made Dorgon more powerful. Dorgon must have been conflicted over whether it was in his interest to dethrone Shunzhi so that he could have the title of emperor to himself. The power and prestige that accompanied being the emperor was extremely tempting for most people, and Dorgon was no exception. Meanwhile, Dorgon would have thought killing Shunzhi to be a sweet form of revenge for Huang Taiji (Shunzhi's father) coercing Dorgon's mother to commit suicide. However, dethronement was an extreme form of treason that might have destabilized the unity of the Manchu ruling class. It was particularly risky in such a time of turmoil, when resistances and potential insurrections persisted against the new Manchu regime.

Dorgon ultimately decided not to take the title of emperor from Shunzhi. However, it is easy to imagine that Shunzhi's early life before 1651 was full of fear and anxiety. Although Dorgon did not dethrone him, Shunzhi knew too well that Dorgon had been debating it constantly. Shunzhi knew that if he were dethroned, he would certainly be killed. Dorgon frequently bullied both him and his mother. At one point, Dorgon requested that his title be changed from "Prince Regent" to "Emperor's Uncle and Prince Regent," despite this being common knowledge.

Dorgon's reasons for this request might have been related to filial piety, the central core value in the culture of Confucianism. As discussed in the last two chapters, the Manchus were heavily influenced by the Confucian philosophy, as they had been ruled by the Ming Dynasty for about 250 years. In particular, they treasured filial piety as much as the Chinese. As filial piety emphasized that an individual should pay a great amount of respect to a senior member of an extended family, Dorgon wanted to add "Emperor's Uncle" to his official title to demonstrate his high status in relation to the emperor.

Moreover, the social norm of filial piety appeared to be more highly regarded in Manchu culture than in Chinese culture, possibly because the frequent tribal conflicts of Manchus leant this social norm more practical value. The earlier discussions of Nurhachi clarify the value of filial piety to the Manchus. Nurhachi established a kingdom with a vast territory, and did so from scratch. In fact, according to one story, when Nurhachi's father and grandfather died, they left him with 13 suits of armor. Nurhachi distributed the suits to himself, his brother, and other close relatives in his Aisin Gioro clan. They fought against their enemies in closely united forces like a single person, which greatly enhanced their military efficiency and enabled them to conquer many Jurchen tribes. Later on, Nurhachi rose to prominence by conquering all of Manchuria and a part of Mongolia. His many children and grandchildren were important reasons for his success. All of his 16 sons were brave and intelligent fighters who served as his generals, and Nurhachi trusted them completely.

However, even family members require a mechanism to unite them. It has been widely observed that family members sometimes fight fiercely when they do so out of their own self-interest. In a convenient example, Huang Taiji forced Dorgon's mother to commit suicide immediately after Nurhachi's death. There is currently a well-known story in China that parents tell their children to teach them to cooperate and help one another. According to the story, a father was going to die, and he summoned his five sons to him. He gave one chopstick to each of his sons and asked them to break it. All of his sons broke the chopsticks easily. The father then bound five chopsticks together, and asked his sons to break them. None of the five sons could do so.

For the ancient Manchus and Chinese, the mechanism for binding children together required everyone to respect the eldest male member of the family as his or her absolute authority. This social norm served to eliminate the cost of bargaining and fighting for self-interest among different family members. In a hunting tribe that often engaged in violent fighting, an individual member usually had the incentive to shirk his responsibilities to avoid injury. If every member of the family were to behave in such a way, the family would not have been a strong fighting unit in combat. The family required the authority to credibly reward or punish its members and thereby discipline them into fighting bravely and making sacrifices. This reasoning provides another explanation for why the Manchus and Chinese had an incentive to adhere to filial piety, particularly when it came to respecting their parents and grandparents.

In traditional Manchu/Chinese societies, the most senior male of the extended family was selected as the authority.[4] For example, Salaff (1976, p. 443) observes that "Chinese families have long considered themselves economic units whose head controlled the income of all members, including those adult offspring living elsewhere, and who had final say over their education, jobs, and marriages. The control of the family head lasted until the formal division of the 'economic household,' usually on the death of the patriarch himself."

The Manchus followed this tradition rigorously. For example, for the Manchus in the Qing Dynasty, it was a strictly enforced social etiquette for a servant to call his male master "grandfather." After the Manchu conquest of China, this greeting was widely used across China. For example, the waiters in a restaurant often called their important customers "grandfathers." Of course, grandfathers were not the only people to be respected according to this social custom. A father was supposed to have the authority to require his son to die if the father wished him to do so. Moreover, a senior member of a family was supposed to be well respected by the junior members, particularly among close relatives such as uncles and nephews. Therefore, against this cultural background, Dorgon had a strong motivation to add "Emperor's Uncle" to his official title of "Prince Regent."

However, it seems that Dorgon was not satisfied with being Shunzhi's uncle. When Dorgon became the almighty *de facto* ruler of Qing in 1647, he further modified his title to "Emperor's Father and Prince Regent." One can easily imagine the fury of Emperor Shunzhi over this matter. However, the 10-year-old boy had no other choice but to accept it. Even worse, such a humiliating change of title had to be conferred by Emperor Shunzhi himself.

Dorgon not only ruled China as an absolute dictator but also behaved like the emperor of the Qing Empire at almost every public occasion. In contrast, Emperor Shunzhi had to behave in a very awkward and cautious way, particularly when he and Dorgon appeared together in public. Shunzhi quickly learned about Dorgon's ruthlessness and absolute power. For example, although a large proportion of elite Qing soldiers were loyal to Shunzhi's eldest brother Hooge, Dorgon easily found an excuse to kill him and then took his concubines to add to his possessions.

After Dorgon's sudden accidental death, Shunzhi agreed to a request from Dorgon's brother and other close followers that Dorgon would be posthumously granted the title of emperor and called "Emperor Yi," and gave Dorgon an imperial funeral. Shunzhi then resolutely and quickly purged Dorgon's clique. He arrested Dorgon's brother Ajige and forced him to commit suicide. Furthermore, he consolidated his control of the Qing army. On February 1, it was officially announced that from that point forward Shunzhi would assume full and absolute imperial authority. When Shunzhi was certain that he was finally in charge, he immediately stripped Dorgon of his posthumous title of emperor, and then ordered that Dorgon's corpse be exhumed and flogged in public.[5] This act vividly illustrated Shunzhi's deep hatred for Dorgon.

The necessity to deal with Dorgon substantially sharpened Shunzhi's political and administrative skills at a very young age. Under Dorgon's reign, Shunzhi had to think hard about how to please him (or at least avoid offending him) while retaining the dignity of emperor. Indeed, even a small mistake would result in a major offense to Dorgon, which would have probably had disastrous consequences for Shunzhi and his family members. As soon as Shunzhi obtained real imperial power, he immediately became a very competent emperor.

Shunzhi was a wise emperor in that he fully understood the benefit of promoting the traditional Chinese culture while ruling the country. He spent considerable effort strengthening the indoctrination of the Confucian culture in China. In the second month after he retrieved his imperial power from Dorgon, Shunzhi sent a delegate to visit Confucius's hometown in Qufu, Shandong Province, to hold a ritual of respect for Confucius. On Confucius's birthday that same year, he led his main ministers to go to the Imperial Academy, the highest-ranking educational establishment in China, to hold another ritual of respect for the philosopher. On this occasion, despite his supreme dignity as the emperor, he knelt down at the sculpture of Confucius to personally perform the ritual of "two kneelings and six kowtows."

Moreover, Shunzhi's hatred of Dorgon might have influenced his attitude toward Chinese culture. Dorgon spent almost his entire life fighting wars. When young, he fought with swords in many battles. Later on he became a general, and in 1643 he became the chief commander of the Qing army. Dorgon's personality was influenced to a much greater extent by the nomadic culture of the primitive Jurchen tribes that took pride in violence and conquests than by the Chinese culture that highlighted peace and harmony. Therefore, possibly execrated by his repulsive reaction toward Dorgon, Shunzhi had the utmost respect for Chinese culture and adopted the Chinese style of rule as soon as he took the throne.

In the Ming Dynasty, the most senior government official rank was the "Da Xue Shi," literally meaning "grand academician" or simply "great scholar," and conferred by the emperors. The Qing Dynasty adopted this tradition. In the Qing Dynasty, although the quota for "grand academicians" was six, there were usually four "grand academicians" at any given point, including two Manchus and two Chinese. Such titles and other government structures of the former Ming Dynasty were maintained during Dorgon's reign. However, from his perspective, "grand academicians" were merely titles for his officials only.

Emperor Shunzhi showed genuine respect for "great scholars." He often discussed Confucian Classics, history, and poetry with grand academicians such as Chen Mingxia and those who exhibited outstanding performance on the Keju exams like Wang Xi. He once made the following statement both honestly and modestly: "I am extremely unfortunate. I lost my father when I was only five years old. Because I am the only son of my mother, I was very spoiled and no one was strict with me in the process of my education. Therefore, I achieved very little in terms of education. When I was 14, Prince Dorgon died and I started to assume my imperial duty. However, I often failed to understand the reports that ministers made to me. Therefore, I started to study hard. I handled the important issues of the nation from early morning to afternoon. I started reading books in the evenings. However, I still had the tendency to play, and could not memorize what I read. I started to read from late night to dawn [when he could concentrate more on his reading], and then I could memorize them. I studied hard for nine years in total. I once spit up blood [due to haematemesis]."

In contrast to Dorgon, Shunzhi relied heavily on Chinese ministers for his administration and showed complete trust in them. For example, in 1653, he appointed Hong Chengchou, a Chinese grand academician, as the governor-general of the five provinces of Huguang, Guangdong, Guangxi, Yunnan, and Guizhou, and gave him significant independent decision-making power. By putting some Chinese officials in important positions, Emperor Shunzhi not only enhanced the administrative efficiency of his government but also decreased the lopsided powers of the Manchu elites. To further consolidate his power, Shunzhi established the so-called Thirteen Offices, which handled the detailed implementations of his decisions and policies. Although Manchu nobles symbolically supervised the Thirteen Offices, the offices were manned by Chinese eunuchs who were loyal only to Emperor Shunzhi.

However, Shunzhi's actions were mainly taken to correct Dorgon's overreliance on Manchu nobles. The emperor was fully aware that Manchu nobles could play a key role in increasing the stability of his personal rule in particular and the Manchu rule of China in general. Thus, he was careful to strike a balance between the Chinese and Manchus in his government, and on occasion show at least some superficial favoritism toward the Manchus to appease the Manchu nobles who had significant powers in the Qing army. Moreover, he was resolute in imposing brutal penalties on those Chinese who broke the fundamental principles for the stability of the Manchu rule in China. For example, Chen Mingxia, the grand academician mentioned previously, proposed allowing the Chinese to return to their old hairstyle in the Ming Dynasty, and Shunzhi sentenced him to death. After that, no official dared to mention revoking the Queue Order again.

From an economics and game theory perspective, Shunzhi's decision to execute Chen was both rational and necessary for the stability of Manchu rule in China. As analyzed in the previous chapter, the stability of Manchu rule required the Chinese and Manchus to have the same hairstyle. The alternative was to create two man-made groups of people that looked drastically different. However, as the example of blacks and whites in the United States indicates, different physical appearances may result in racial tension even in a country where ancestor birthplaces are unimportant. Thus, long-term political stability required that either the Manchus adopt Chinese hairstyles or vice versa. However, not even the emperor could suggest that the Manchus adopt Chinese hairstyles, as doing so would have necessarily led to a Manchu rebellion. Therefore, the only feasible and desirable equilibrium was that the Chinese adopt Manchu hairstyles. This equilibrium could only be sustained under the "common belief" that a Chinese person who defied the Queue Order would be seriously punished. Any doubt in this belief would have led the Chinese to demand that the Queue Order be revoked. If they had done so, the Qing emperor's only choice for restoring the belief of the Chinese in the seriousness of the punishment would have been an extremely harsh and brutal response on behalf of the Qing army, such as the massacres in Jiading. Shunzhi knew that he had no other option but to order the death of Chen Mingxia. (In fact, after hearing that Chen was executed, Shunzhi cried.)

Ironically, the Queue Order might have been one of the most important reasons why the Manchus were the best rulers in feudal China. Because of the order, at least in the early period of the Qing Dynasty, the Chinese never considered the Manchus to be "completely Chinese." The Qing rulers were fully aware of this and were constantly concerned about potential insurrections from the Chinese people. According to his theory of political economy, Grossman (1991, 1999) shows that a greater likelihood of revolts influences a ruler to decrease his rent-seeking behavior. This theory indeed applied to the Manchu rulers in China. In particular, the Qing emperors imposed low tax rates and were greatly concerned about the people's welfare.

Shunzhi died at the young age of 24 after contracting smallpox, which was fatal for most Manchus at the time due to their lack of an immune capacity. Shunzhi's third son Xuanye was installed onto the throne at the age of seven. When he reached the age of 14, he began to assume imperial power and ruled the Qing Dynasty of China as Emperor Kangxi.

Kangxi continued Shunzhi's tradition of respecting Confucian culture, and considered it a powerful force in stabilizing Manchu rule in China. In particular, he promulgated the "Sacred Edicts," which were his summary of the essences of Confucian orthodoxy, to promote the education of Confucianism in the entire population of China. Kangxi also had very high achievements in Chinese literature and calligraphy and wrote very good Chinese poems. Moreover, he made a major contribution to the Chinese language by ordering the compilation of a comprehensive and authoritative Chinese dictionary, designated the Kangxi Dictionary in his honor.

The reigns of Emperor Kangxi (reign 1662–1722), his son Emperor Yong-zheng (reign 1723–1735), and his grandson Emperor Qianlong (reign 1735–1796) marked the zeniths of the prosperity of the Qing Dynasty and the history of feudal societies in China. At the end of Shunzhi's reign, the Chinese population was about 40–50 million people. At the end of Qianlong's reign, the Chinese population had increased to 313 million people. In other words, the population increased by six to seven times over the span of about 113 years. The people's welfare also improved in certain ways. For example, in 1776, the real tax per capita declined by more than 80 percent compared with most of the Ming Dynasty (Liu, 2006).

Parallel to this economic and demographic growth was an increasing integration between the Chinese culture and Manchu ruling class. Racial differences became increasingly less important in the employment of the central government. For example, most of the key civic ministers and even military generals whom Emperor Yongzheng employed and trusted were Chinese rather than Manchu. Emperor Qianlong loved Chinese literature and was an extremely prolific poet, with more than 40,000 of his poems surviving today. Qianlong was perhaps the most prolific poet in world history in terms of quantity. He also took pride in being a "preserver and restorer" of Chinese culture. He had a passion for collecting fine arts such as paintings or works of Chinese calligraphy, which contributed massively to the imperial collection of the Qing Dynasty. Qianlong's greatest achievement in Chinese literature and culture was his construction of the grandiose project known as "Siku Quanshu" ("four treasuries project of books"), which published over 36,000 volumes of books. Numerous princes and senior ministers served as chiefs of the project and 15,000 people were employed as copyists.[6]

Despite the unprecedented prosperity in the middle of the Qing Dynasty, the Manchu rulers maintained a relatively simple lifestyle and were rather constrained in exploiting Chinese peasants for their own benefit. For example, the annual expenditure on the harem of Emperor Yongzheng during the Qing Dynasty was estimated to be less than the daily expenditure on the harem of Emperor Wanli during the Ming Dynasty.[7]

According to the previous chapter, the first emperor of the Ming Dynasty, Zhu Yuanzhang, had about 0.2 million offspring. In contrast, at the end of the Qing Dynasty, only about 29,000 people had Aisin Gioro – the name of the royal family – as a last name.[8] Note that the Aisin Gioro clan started with at least Nurhachi's grandfather, who had many children. When Emperor Shunzhi began to rule China, the Aisin Gioro clan had already produced six generations. Thus, when the Qing Dynasty started in China, about 3,000 people should have had Aisin Gioro as a last name. (This is assuming that each male member of the Aisin Gioro clan had five sons, which is a low estimation given the fertility of tribal rulers. The Aisin Gioro clan would have numbered 3,125 at the end of six generations.) Thus, the members of the Aisin Gioro clan experienced a population growth of about 10 times, which was precisely the growth of the entire population of China in the Qing Dynasty. Taking the offspring of the daughters of the Aisin Gioro clan (who did not carry the family name of Aisin Gioro) during the Qing Dynasty into consideration, the population growth rate of the extended royal family was only about twice that of China as a whole.

Finally, it should be noted that assimilating the Chinese culture, levying low taxes, and adopting a simple lifestyle were only three aspects of the Manchu emperors' strategy for ruling over China. This "carrot" strategy was coupled with the deterrence of the potential "stick" strategy of a strong alliance with the Mongolian tribes. In fact, it would be an understatement to say that the Manchus formed an alliance with Mongolia. Rather, Mongolia was generally under the stable rule of the Qing Dynasty.

Throughout the Qing Dynasty, the Manchu emperors maintained the policy of marriage alliances with Mongolian tribe leaders. Such a policy had been used by previous Chinese dynasties, which referred to it as "Heqin." However, the marriage ties between the royal families of the Qing Dynasty and the nobles of numerous Mongolian tribes were much more extensive, partly due to the proximity between the original Manchu and Mongolian cultures.

Of course, marriage alliances themselves were insufficient for inducing the nomadic tribes to submit to the Manchu emperors. Thus, when the Mongolia revolts occurred, the Qing Dynasty launched a series of military campaigns to conquer various nomadic Mongolian tribes. The military attacks were massive in scale and sometimes merciless. For example, in 1759, the Qing Dynasty decimated a large proportion of the Zunghar people.

Zunghar Khanate, the country of the Zunghar people, was located in middle Asia and covered a large area from the west side of the Great Wall to eastern Kazakhstan. In particular, it included the area of China's present-day Xinjiang Province. Being a nomadic power, Zunghar Khanate had long been engaged in a rivalry with China during the Qing Dynasty. In 1755, making an opportunity out of its internal conflicts and a smallpox epidemic, the Qing army defeated the Zunghar army and caught the Zunghar Khan. The Qianlong Emperor ordered the Chinese troops to kill all of the Zunghar men and divided their wives and children among some of the soldiers. According to Qing historian Wei Yuan, 40 percent of the 600,000 Zunghar people were killed by smallpox, 20 percent fled to foreign countries such as Russia and Kazakh, and 30 percent were massacred by the Qing army.[9] The Qing government colonized Xinjiang with the migration of the Han Chinese and Uyghur people.

The Great Wall was useless during the Qing Dynasty. The Manchu rulers were not satisfied that China would not be attacked by the nomadic tribes of Mongolia. Rather, they desired firm control of Mongolia and demanded absolute loyalty from the nomadic tribes. These would serve as effective deterrents of any Han Chinese insurrections against the Qing Dynasty. Due in large part to the benevolent rules of the Qing emperors, the help of Mongolian troops in quelling the revolts of the Han Chinese was almost never required, although it was always potentially available. As an illustration, during the Second Opium War in 1860, the Qing Dynasty was aided by a cavalry of 4,000 elite Mongolian soldiers led by Mongolian general Sengge Rinchen. At the time, the world had entered into a new era in which Western countries possessed advanced firearms and artilleries. In a battle near Beijing, those 4,000 elite Mongolian cavalry soldiers were annihilated by the modern weapons of Britain and France.[10]

Notes

1 Encyclopedia Britannica: China » History » The early Qing dynasty » The rise of the Manchu.
2 Classic of Filial Piety.
3 Ebrey (1993).
4 In other words, such an authority decreases the "transaction costs" of the collaborations of household members in fighting against a common enemy. (See Pollak (1985) for a survey of the transaction cost approach to family studies.)
5 See, e.g., Oxnam (1975).
6 See, e.g., Guy (1987).
7 See, e.g., Ma (2012).
8 http://blog.ifeng.com/article/18575786.html
9 Wei Yuan, *Military History of the Qing Dynasty*, vol. 4.
10 Boulger (1893).

Part IV

An introduction to ancient Japan and the First Sino–Japanese War

13 Bushido: The soul of (ancient) Japan

The main threats to the ancient Chinese were nomadic tribes such as the Xiongnu and Mongols in their northern steppe. However, the situation drastically changed following the Qing Dynasty. During the Qing Dynasty, the whole of Mongolia had been a part of China. At the beginning of the 19th century, Japan became the Chinese people's new nightmare. The remainder of this book devotes careful attention to China's wars and conflicts with Japan, which fundamentally changed the Chinese people's "national personality." The struggle for survival led the Chinese people to adopt a national character that became increasingly similar to the Japanese personality. A thorough understanding of Japan and its history, culture, and personality should be achieved at the outset. This chapter describes the Japanese national character and its material basis.

Japan is a neighboring country to China. In ancient times, interactions between the two countries were very infrequent due to the separation caused by the sea and ocean, which were costly and dangerous to cross without modern transportation. However, Chinese culture had a significant influence on Japanese culture. The most conspicuous example is the written Japanese language, which was largely based on written Chinese.

The Japanese people's social interactions were strongly consistent with the preaching of Confucianism. For example, Alessandro Valigano, a Jesuit missionary who lived in Japan for years in the 16th century, described the Japanese culture as follows:[1]

> They are very prudent and discreet in all their dealings with others and they never weary anybody by recounting their troubles or by complaining or grumbling as people do in Europe. When they go visiting, their etiquette demands that they never say anything which might upset their host. And so they never come and talk about their troubles and grievances, because as they claim to suffer much and always show courage in adversity, they keep their troubles to themselves as best they can. When they meet or go to visit somebody, they always appear cheerful and in good spirits, and they either do not refer to their troubles at all, or, if they do, at most they just mention them with a laugh as if they did not worry about such unimportant matters. As they are so opposed to every kind of gossip, they never talk about other people's affairs or grumble about

their princes and rulers. . . For this reason (and also in order not to become heated in their dealings with others), they observe a general custom in Japan of not transacting any important or difficult business face to face with another person, but instead they do it through messages of a third person. . . As a result they live in such peace and quietness that even the children forbear to use inelegant expressions among themselves, nor do they fight or hit each other like European lads; instead, they speak politely and never fail to show each other respect. In fact they show such incredible gravity and maturity that they seem more like solemn men than children. . .

Alessandro Valigano also noted that the Japanese were very constrained in their expressions of emotion:[2] "Husbands do not beat or shout at their wives, neither do fathers (beat) their sons, nor masters their servants. On the contrary they outwardly appear very calm and deal with each other either by the messages they send or by the cultured words that they speak; in this way, even though they may be exiled, killed, or thrown out of their homes, everything is done quietly and in good order."

Alessandro Valigano's description clearly indicates the similarities between the Japanese and traditional Chinese cultures. It is plausible that Japanese culture was influenced by the Confucian culture of traditional China. Moreover, honor was particularly emphasized in the culture of ancient Japan, and was apparently more important there than in ancient China. For example, Coleridge (2011, p. 237) documents a Christian missionary's description of the ancient Japanese culture: "In the first place, the nation with which we have had to do here surpasses in goodness any of the nations lately discovered. I really think that among barbarous nations there can be none that has more natural goodness than the Japanese. They are of a kindly disposition, not at all given to cheating, wonderfully desirous of honour and rank. Honour with them is placed above everything else. There are a great many poor among them, but poverty is not a disgrace to any one. There is one thing among them of which I hardly know whether it is practised anywhere among Christians. The nobles, however poor they may be, receive the same honour from the rest as if they were rich."

However, the ancient Japanese culture differed drastically from the ancient Chinese culture in its attitude toward violence, valor, and death. Before the end of World War II, there was another crucial element to the culture: its worship of violence. This point was made well known by American anthropologist Ruth Benedict's best-selling book entitled *The Chrysanthemum and the Sword: Patterns of Japanese Culture*. Benedict (1946, p. 2) writes that the Japanese had rather conflicting personalities because they were "both aggressive and unaggressive, both militaristic and aesthetic, both insolent and polite, rigid and adaptable, submissive and resentful of being pushed around, loyal and treacherous, brave and timid, conservative and hospitable to new ways."

The seemingly conflicting personality of the ancient Japanese might have been related to the philosophy of Bushido. Bushido, which literally means "the way of warriors," also served as a behavioral code for the Japanese in general. In an influential book, Nitobe (1900) describes Bushido as "the soul of Japan."

Achieving a better understanding of Bushido requires an introduction of Japan's history and emperors. The royal family of Japan is the oldest monarchy in the world. The Imperial House of Japan was founded in 660 BC by Emperor Jimmu and continues to exist today. The emperor is called the "Tenno" in Japanese, meaning "heavenly sovereign." Consistent with the title, he has been considered the highest authority of the Shinto religion, the indigenous spirituality of Japan. Indeed, in ancient times, Japanese people considered Japanese emperors to be the direct descendants of Amaterasu, the goddess of the sun and universe in the Shinto religion.

However, despite the paramount importance of the role of emperors in Japanese culture and religion, they played only a ceremonial symbolic role and did not have real power to rule over Japan for a significant portion of its history. In particular, from 1192 to 1867, the shoguns were usually the real rulers of Japan. In Japanese, "shogun" literally means "general" or "military commander." Although shogun was a hereditary identity, they had to be nominally appointed by the emperors. A shogun's office or administration was called a "bakufu," literally meaning "tent office" in Japanese. This name originated from field commanders who summoned their officers to their tents for meetings immediately before a major battle. It also carried the innuendo that the actual administrative duties of a shogun in his "bakufu" should be temporary. However, this was not the reality. A shogun was a long-lasting job for the general, who was entitled to pass his position on to his son when he died. In other words, a shogun behaved just like an emperor in Japan: with absolute sovereignty.

Why did the shoguns not simply get rid of the Japanese emperors? Their respect for those emperors and superstitions about the royal family might have been important reasons. Also, perhaps more importantly, other warlords in Japan might not have allowed them to do so. Recall that in the Ming Dynasty, the extended royal family was not constrained in its excessive rent-seeking activities. The presence of an emperor, albeit a dummy figure, might have largely constrained the power of a shogun. Note that there was a large number of *de facto* small countries in ancient Japan, making it similar to Europe and particularly ancient Germany. Because Japan was not under the threat of nomadic tribes, it was naturally divided into many small countries. In this case, any central government represented by a shogun would have been fairly weak. Thus, the emperors had to be accepted, as they served as a credible commitment to limiting the power of the shogun central government.

A shogun ruled over Japan through a number of local territorial lords known as "daimyo." From the middle of the 15th century to the beginning of the 17th, Japan was in its Warring States or "Sengoku" period. A number of powerful daimyos ruled as *de facto* kings in their "domains" during this period. The daimyos depended on their armies to maintain their power. However, unique to ancient Japan, the main forces of those armies were groups of samurais.

A samurai was a professional soldier. It was a lifetime and hereditary occupation. The counterpart of the samurai in Europe was the knight. Both samurais and knights worshipped valor and the skills and strength used in combat.

Furthermore, "samurai" literally means "servant" in Japanese, and "knight" carries precisely the same meaning in German and old English. Because the people in Japan and Europe hardly interacted when samurais and knights coexisted, it should be a pure coincidence that these two terms for low-rank military nobility carried the same meaning in their original languages. A plausible explanation is that when a lord/king was gravely concerned about his security, he hired superb fighters to be his military followers or simply his servants.

However, samurais and knights differed significantly. For example, samurais accounted for 7–10 percent of the Japanese population, and knights accounted for less than 2 percent of the population in France. Indeed, although knights were the elite soldiers at the forefront of European battles, almost all of the soldiers in Japan were samurais. Moreover, the underlying incentive mechanisms for motivating samurais and knights were fundamentally different. First, the samurai designation was hereditary, and only a very small fraction of knighthoods were hereditary. Second, although a knight was positioned at the lowest rank of nobility in Europe, his living standard was far higher than that of a commoner. However, in Japan, samurais usually received rice as their pecuniary payment, were often poorer than peasants, and belonged to the society's low-income class. The following elaborates why the samurai system appeared to be the optimal strategy of Japanese feudal lords and why the incentive system might have worked well.

The samurai class was a product of feudalism. In economic terms, the relationship between a local lord (daimyo) and a samurai was essentially an exchange relationship, in which a daimyo provided a reward to a samurai in return for his military service and loyalty. This military service was required for external conflicts with other lords or internal peasant revolts, and a samurai was expected to fight bravely and skillfully when these conflicts arose. Meanwhile, loyalty and obedience were strictly required of samurais. Recall that the word "samurai" literally means "serve as a waiter" in Japanese, inferring that a samurai was a "military waiter/servant" to his master. Thus, samurais were part of a warrior class and were born, bred, and indoctrinated into being absolutely faithful to their lords. In ancient Japan, a local lord could usually ensure his samurai's loyalty, bravery, and self-sacrifice in a cost-effective way. In other words, a samurai mainly received payment in the forms of respect and social status rather than pecuniary rewards.

In his classic work "The Theory of Moral Sentiments" (1759), Smith makes the following statement: "The wish to become proper objects of this respect, to deserve and obtain this credit and rank among our equals, may be the strongest of all our desires." In the contemporary world, a high social status can often be achieved through extravagant consumption. In *The Theory of the Leisure Class* (1899), Veblen puts forward the theory of "conspicuous consumption." He argues that economic behavior is socially determined and driven by the human instincts of emulation and social comparison. He further argues that people often try to impress others through conspicuous consumption. In other words, a major purpose of consumption is not to satisfy an individual's biological needs, but to gain and signal social status. Further, Keynes (1936, p. 326) argues that an important aspect of conspicuous consumption can be found "in the sense that we feel them only if their satisfaction lifts us above, makes us feel superior to, our fellows." However, material consumption was not the only way to achieve a high social status in feudal Japan. For example, a high social status was given directly to samurais when daimyos had absolute power over their subjects.

Between the 12th and 19th centuries, the Japanese people were divided into a four-tier class system. At the top of the hierarchy was the samurai class, followed by the peasant class, artisan class, and merchant class at the bottom. The honor and prestige bestowed upon the samurai class was enforced on a daily basis. For example, when a samurai passed by, members of the lower classes were required to bow at him in a show of respect. A samurai was legally entitled to strike with his sword at anyone of a lower class who compromised his honor, such as a farmer or artisan who refused to bow. This right was known as "Kiri-sute gomen" in Japanese.

Wikipedia describes a classical example of "Kiri-sute gomen" as follows:[3] "In one well known incident, a commoner bumped into a samurai. The samurai pointed out the disrespect but the commoner refused to apologise. Feeling merciful, the samurai offered the commoner his wakizashi so he had a chance to defend himself. Instead, the commoner decided to run away with his wakizashi, causing further dishonour. The incident resulted in the samurai being disowned from the clan. He later regained his honour by seeking out the commoner and killing the whole family."

Because samurais obtained a high social status directly by virtue of being on top of the social hierarchy, they usually found no need to enhance it through luxurious consumption. In fact, samurais often led very simple lives. For example, Nitobe (1900, p. 50) states: ". . . a samurai . . . disdains money itself, – the art of making or hoarding it. It is to him veritably filthy lucre. The hackneyed expression to describe the decadence of an age is "that the civilians loved money and the soldiers feared death." . . . Hence children were brought up with utter disregard of economy. It was considered bad taste to speak of it, and ignorance of the value of different coins was a token of good breeding. . . . It is true that thrift was enjoined by Bushido, but not for economical reasons so much as for the exercise of abstinence. Luxury was thought the greatest menace to manhood, and severest simplicity was required of the warrior class, sumptuary laws being enforced in many of the clans."

Another important aspect of the samurai reward was that one's samurai status was passed down to future generations. This hereditary system reinforced the incentive mechanism for samurais in two ways. First, it was a great honor that further enhanced a samurai's status and sense of superiority in the society. For example, Greenfeld (2001, p. 241) writes: "The status of the samurai, sanctioned by the authority of heaven, was safeguarded from encroachment. Like the nobility in France, they were separated from the hoi polloi by the theoretically impermeable division, constituted by birth or, rather, family affiliation (for one could become a samurai by adoption), into a different, superior species of human beings."

Moreover, this hereditary system increased every samurai's concern for his reputation and honor. For example, if a soldier behaved cowardly in a battle, his fellow soldiers might have looked down on him. The soldier could have easily quit the army, and entered into a new living environment in which his cowardice was hardly known to or cared about by others. However, if a samurai behaved cowardly in a battle, his cowardice placed a permanent stigma on him for the rest of his life. A samurai usually served a single master for his whole life, and usually lived with the same neighbors and peers. Once a samurai lost his reputation for being timid or disloyal, everyone in his social circles considered him and his family members "inferior." In fact, such a stigma continued to affect his sons and grandsons even after his death. Because a samurai's position was hereditary, his sons and grandsons also became samurais. If a samurai exhibited fear in a battle, his sons and grandsons were ridiculed by their peers for having a cowardly and shameful ancestor and for being bad samurais in turn due to bad "genes." Thus, a samurai who was concerned about the dignity, honor, and welfare of his offspring had a greater incentive to be fearless on the battlefield. Consequently, samurais were willing to risk their lives in fighting for their masters to maintain their honor and prestige.

According to the Bushido culture, a samurai was expected to crave honor and pride and despise money. Most samurais indeed usually adhered to this expectation.[4] In fact, most received rice from their masters as an income, only enough to feed themselves and their family members (e.g., Greenfeld, 2001). In times of continuous peace, samurais were often members of the low-income class.

During the Meiji era at the end of the 19th century, a census was conducted in Japan and indicated the presence of 1,282,000 "high samurais" and 492,000 "low samurais" in the country. A high samurai was allowed to ride a horse and a low samurai was not. The total population in Japan at the time was about 25 million people, meaning that the samurais accounted for 7.1 percent of the Japanese population. This proportion was very high, particularly considering that few major wars had been fought in Japan since the early 17th century. This large population of samurais had a low average income, unsurprising given the long period of peace, as their services were not typically required.

During the Tokugawa shogunate period between the early 17th and mid-19th centuries, the central government forced daimyos to cut the sizes of their armies, making many samurais "unemployed." When a samurai became unemployed, he was designated a "ronin." Ronins represented a serious concern of social unrest for the Tokugawa shogunate. For example, in 1650, there were 400,000 ronins in Japan, a huge number given that the total Japanese population was only 15 million people at the time (Greenfeld, 2001). During this period, many samurais became courtiers, bureaucrats, and administrators for the governments. In general, regardless of whether a samurai was employed, he was often not rich and in fact often poorer than most peasants and artisans (Greenfeld, 2001). However, even in very harsh economic circumstances such as unemployment, samurais enjoyed a high social status that they treasured dearly.

In times of war, samurais risked their lives on the battlefield. In peacetime, they often had to endure poverty and hardship. However, they asked for little pecuniary payment in any circumstance. The territorial lords in Japan found a cheap way to pay their soldiers and officers: via honor and prestige. It cost the feudal lords little or nothing to require the peasants and artisans to pay respect to the samurais. The main concern of the peasants and artisans living at the subsistence level in ancient Japan was survival. Thus, it also cost the peasants and artisans little or nothing to pay respect to the warriors, such as by bowing to them.

However, the samurai system presented hidden costs to the daimyos. For honor and prestige to work as a payment system, the feudal lords found that they needed to make the samurai status hereditary. Although this hereditary approach cost the feudal lords nothing over the short term, it caused inefficiencies in the long term. The number of soldiers required differed drastically in different circumstances. A large number of soldiers were needed in times of war, and only a small number were needed in times of peace. Nevertheless, the hereditary system of samurais meant that the number of samurais remained stable over time, regardless of whether a war was being fought. (It should be noted that samurais were legally prohibited from working as peasants or artisans for several centuries. In fact, even if such a law had not existed, the concern for honor and social status would have made it difficult for the samurais to engage in such "inferior" occupations.)

Thus, the samurai system had its pros and cons. In ancient Japan, the feudal lords might have found the system's benefits to outweigh its costs. Because Japan was an island country, the mobility of most Japanese people was limited. Consequently, the feudal lords might have found the samurai honor system relatively easy to establish. Such a system was not developed in other parts of the world, possibly because greater population mobility rendered it much more difficult to implement. Indeed, if a samurai who lost his reputation could easily travel to a faraway place where nobody knew him, he would have cared much less about his reputation *per se*. This explains why samurais appeared in Japan but not other areas of the world.

In ancient Japan, the Bushido philosophy reflected the moral code of samurais, and emphasized loyalty, martial arts mastery, and honor unto death. The essence of Bushido can be vividly summarized by the influential and oft-recited statements of feudal lords. Some examples are provided as follows.

- Shiba Yoshimasa (1350–1410), a Japanese general and administrator during the Muromachi period: "It is a matter of regret to let the moment when one should die pass by. . . . First, a man whose profession is the use of arms should think and then act upon not only his own fame, but also that of his descendants. He should not scandalize his name forever by holding his one and only life too dear. . . . One's main purpose in throwing away his life is to do so either for the sake of the Emperor or in some great undertaking of a military general. It is that exactly that will be the great fame of one's descendants."

- Imagawa Sadayo, a famous Japanese poet and military commander: "First of all, a samurai who dislikes battle and has not put his heart in the right place even though he has been born in the house of the warrior, should not be reckoned among one's retainers. . . . It is forbidden to forget the great debt of kindness one owes to his master and ancestors and thereby make light of the virtues of loyalty and filial piety. . . . It is forbidden that one should . . . attach little importance to his duties to his master . . . There is a primary need to distinguish loyalty from disloyalty and to establish rewards and punishments."
- Takeda Nobushige, a renowned samurai of the Sengoku period: "In matters both great and small, one should not turn his back on his master's commands . . . One should not ask for gifts or enfiefments from the master . . . No matter how unreasonably the master may treat a man, he should not feel disgruntled . . . An underling does not pass judgments on a superior."
- Uesugi Kenshin (1530–1578), a Sengoku warlord: "the way of the warrior was death."

In fact, an important Bushido code stated that if a samurai failed to fulfill an important duty, then he should commit suicide. The manner of suicide, known as "seppuku," was peculiar. In performing seppuku, a samurai plunged a short blade into his abdomen and then moved the blade from left to right in a slicing motion. It was a very painful way of committing suicide. Turnbull (2003, p. 73) provides the following description: "In the world of the warrior, seppuku was a deed of bravery that was admirable in a samurai who knew he was defeated, disgraced, or mortally wounded. It meant that he could end his days with his transgressions wiped away and with his reputation not merely intact but actually enhanced. The cutting of the abdomen released the samurai's spirit in the most dramatic fashion, but it was an extremely painful and unpleasant way to die, and sometimes the samurai who was performing the act asked a loyal comrade to cut off his head at the moment of agony."

There are some cultural explanations for seppuku. For example, according to ancient Japanese culture, a samurai who cut his abdomen open released his spirit in the most dramatic fashion. However, there was also a reasonable economic rationale for the method. Because seppuku was such a painful way to die that a samurai rationally chose to die on the battlefield rather than suffer defeat and commit suicide. Thus, this extremely agonizing suicide method associated with failure further motivated samurais to fight bravely on the battlefield.

However, it should be emphasized that valor was only one aspect of Bushido. Rectitude, benevolence, politeness, truthfulness, education, and self-control were also crucial components, and as such Confucianism was its central focus.[5] Indeed, the writings of Confucius and Mencius were very important sources of the teachings of Bushido. Different from most of the ancient nomadic tribes, which usually engaged in constant battles, Japan was suitable for agricultural production, and no major wars were waged for a significant proportion of its history. Peace was made possible only when the samurais did not start battles for their own power and material interests. Therefore, Bushido served as an important tool for constraining the violent tendencies of samurais during peacetime.

This suggests that the territorial lords in ancient Japan were likely the major advocators of Bushido. The behavioral codes of Bushido were precisely what these lords desired from their samurais. For example, the worshipping of valor provided daimyos with brave fighters, the emphases of self-control and benevolence prevented samurais from becoming trouble-makers during peacetime, the emphases on thrift and the disdain for money allowed Japanese local lords to pay samurais with meager incomes, and the praising of loyalty decreased the concern that samurais would stage a coup and revolt. Of course, as such behavioral codes were also generally consistent with the interests of the general public, mainly peasants and artisans, Bushido should have been welcomed by the ancient Japanese in general. Therefore, Bushido flourished as a moral code for samurais due to the power and financial resources of daimyos and the popular support of the ancient Japanese people.

During peacetime, the samurai class was the "leisure class" in Japan. Because they were not allowed to work as peasants, artisans, or merchants, if they could not find a position in the civil government, their services were not often required. During the Tokugawa shogunate period, to prevent them from uprising or causing social unrest, the samurais were encouraged to be well educated in not only Bushido but also the more peace-loving philosophy of Confucianism, and to become the cultural elite of Japan. For example, Greenfeld (2001, pp. 241–242) writes: "Confucian philosophy equated a perfect man, a true gentleman, and a sage; so be it, decided the samurai. Confucian schools for the nobility proliferated, the first founded in 1630 by Hayashi in Edo as a private establishment, but soon transformed into the official bakufu school, Shoheiko. The daimyo followed suit, and within several decades, most samurai could polish their classical Chinese and become experts in Confucian philosophy in their own han."

There are several reasons why Bushido became the "soul of Japan." First, samurais constituted a large proportion of the population of ancient Japan (7–10 percent). Second, because the samurai status was hereditary, the fathers of samurai families were highly motivated to teach Bushido to their own children. As a result, Bushido was transmitted from one generation to the next.

Nitobe (1900, pp. 78–79) provides a good description and analysis of how Bushido became the soul of the ancient Japanese populace:

> No social class or caste can resist the diffusive power of moral influence. . .
> What Japan was she owed to the samurai. They were not only the flower of
> the nation but its root as well. All the gracious gifts of Heaven flowed through
> them. Though they kept themselves socially aloof from the populace, they set
> a moral standard for them and guided them by their example. . . The innu-
> merable avenues of popular amusement and instruction – the theatres, the
> story-teller's booths, the preacher's dais, the musical recitations, the novels –
> have taken for their chief theme the stories of the samurai. The peasants round
> the open fire in their huts never tire of repeating the achievements of Yoshitsuné

and his faithful retainer Benkei, or of the two brave Soga brothers; the dusky urchins listen with gaping mouths until the last stick burns out and the fire dies in its embers, still leaving their hearts aglow with the tale that is told. . . Debarred from commercial pursuits, the military class itself did not aid commerce; but there was no channel of human activity, no avenue of thought, which did not receive in some measure an impetus from Bushido. Intellectual and moral Japan was directly or indirectly the work of Knighthood.

Notes

1 Greenfeld (2001, p. 230).
2 Greenfeld (2001, p. 230).
3 http://en.wikipedia.org/wiki/Kiri-sute_gomen
4 Nitobe (1900).
5 Nitobe (1900).

14 Wokou: Short Japanese bandits and weak Chinese militias in the Ming Dynasty

This chapter discusses the Japanese pirates who plagued the coastal areas of China in the Ming Dynasty. It also contrasts the sharp differences in national character between the ancient Chinese and Japanese.

"Wokou" is a Chinese term meaning Japanese pirates, with "Wo" and "Kou" literally translating as "dwarf" and "bandit," respectively. In ancient China, Japan was known as "Wo Guo" ("the country of Wo") until the Tang Dynasty in the eighth century. It is not clear why such a name was used to refer to Japan. Wikipedia offers two explanations.[1] First, some historians have argued that the pronunciation of "Wo" is somewhat similar to that of "I" in Japanese. However, this explanation appears to be far-fetched, as there are many other words whose pronunciations are similar and whose underlying connotations are far more positive. Second, in ancient times, the Japanese were much shorter than the Chinese on average. For example, Wei Zhi ("Records of Wei") provided the following description of the people in a part of Japan in 297 AD: ". . . To the south, also there is the island of the dwarfs where the people are three or four feet tall."[2] (The reason why the ancient Japanese were extraordinarily short is beyond the scope of this book. A plausible explanation is that because they lived on islands and had limited regional mobility, they exhibited little genetic diversity.)

The second explanation appears to be more reasonable. However, as described earlier, the ancient Chinese were unlikely to claim superiority over others based on height. Thus, the usage of "Wo" might have simply reflected the description of a fact rather than an offensive term used against the ancient Japanese. Indeed, when "Wo" was used to refer to Japan before or during the Tang Dynasty, the interactions between Japan and China were entirely friendly. Japan often sent friendly missionaries to China, and there was no tension between the two countries. The derogatory term "dwarf Japanese" has only been used recently based on an increasing awareness of height as a Western beauty standard. In fact, the contemporary heights of the Japanese and Chinese are currently about the same on average.

Japanese pirates began to appear in Korea and some coastal areas of China in the 13th century. Because the geographical proximity between Korea and Japan was greater than that between China and Japan, Japanese pirates plagued

Korea much earlier than China. In fact, some historians have argued that Wokou first appeared in Korea to take revenge for Korea's collaboration with the Mongols in their slaughtering of the Japanese and intrusion into some Japanese islands. The invading Mongols and Koreans enslaved some Japanese, and Japan took armed action to rescue them. The Japanese expeditions in Korea were highly successful. The Japanese looted a great deal of food and other materials, which to some extent compensated for the losses they incurred when they were invaded.

However, with the exception of these few intrusions, the Japanese governments were not responsible for the activities of Japanese pirates. On the contrary, the Japanese governments spent much effort on helping to fight against the so-called Wokou. The Wokou were purely pirates and not organized by a national government. Although major military invasions from Japan into Korea took place during the Ming Dynasty, they were conducted for completely different reasons. For example, in 1227, a Korean envoy visited Japan, and the Japanese government (shogun) decapitated 90 suspected Wokou as part of a pledge to fight piracy. At the beginning of the Ming Dynasty, Prince Kaneyoshi of Japan crusaded against some Japanese pirates and rescued some Chinese captives. In 1370, he sent an envoy to China along with the rescued Chinese.

Various Japanese governments in different dynasties attempted to restrict military groups from seafaring.[3] However, Japan has a long coastline, and the Japanese governments had to allow fishermen to seafare for a living. As mentioned previously, survival was a major concern for the ancient Chinese and was also obviously critical for the ancient Japanese. When a natural disaster or war occurred, the agricultural output usually dropped considerably, causing famine and starvation. As a result, piracy was sometimes the only option for survival for many petty farmers. Some small Japanese feudal lords recognized a good opportunity for making huge profits. They recruited some farmers and fishermen who were on the verge of starvation, and provided them with some military training by hiring a few experienced fighters (former soldiers/samurais, i.e., Japanese ronin). These men were sent to loot in Korea and the coastal areas of China.

According to the Annals of the Joseon Dynasty of Korea, a group of Wokou usually had 20–400 ships, indicating that the Japanese pirate groups were usually not very large in number. The sailing distance between Japan and China was much farther than that between Korea and Japan, and seafaring in ancient times was dangerous and exhausting. A group of Japanese pirates in China typically consisted of far fewer bandits than in Korea. However, a small number of Japanese bandits who were short and not well organized often easily defeated the armies in ancient China. I visited Suzhou a few years ago. At one tourist site, I saw an inscription indicating the spot on which 300 Wokou attacked the city of Suzhou, where thousands of Chinese soldiers were stationed. Although it sounds like a joke, it actually happened.

Even if both had the same number of men of the same quality, an army should be much more effective at fighting than a gang of bandits, as army soldiers have a much better incentive mechanism that induces them to fight bravely. If a soldier was injured or killed an enemy, he was rewarded financially and/or promoted. If the soldier behaved cowardly, his officer might have executed him on the spot. However, a bandit might have had a strong incentive to put his personal interests above those of his group. A bandit would have taken his share of the plunder after the enemy troops were defeated. However, a pirate would not have taken more than his share of the loot despite killing many more enemies in comparison. Because killing an enemy entailed the risk of being injured or killed, a bandit often chose to avoid the risk. He found ways to let the other bandits fight enemies while he avoided combat and protected himself. Soldiers usually had other advantages over bandits. A soldier was usually provided with better weapons and trained by better teachers, often for longer periods.

Because a Chinese soldier was usually physically much bigger than a Wokou, the Chinese troops should have been able to defeat the Wokou easily. However, the opposite was true: the Wokou often defeated the Chinese army easily despite being outnumbered. For example, a recent best-selling book in China entitled *Those Stories in the Ming Dynasty* tells the following true story.[4] In 1555, a gang of 40 Wokou sacked a county in Zhejiang Province, and intended to run away to a port in Zhejiang Province. However, they became lost and entered into Jiangsu Province. Once there, they pillaged the areas near the two big cities of Changzhou and Suzhou. More than one month after entering China, they ran into the biggest city in southern China during the Ming Dynasty: Nanjing. The 40 bandits were ultimately annihilated outside the city walls of Nanjing, but not before inflicting about 3,000 military and civilian casualties.

Why were the Chinese troops so weak compared with a small group of foreign bandits? Somewhat surprisingly, this puzzle has not yet been well addressed. Anonymous Internet posters have suggested that the key reason for Wokou's success was the cowardice and weakness of the Chinese soldiers at the time. However, it has not been explained why the Chinese soldiers acted cowardly. This chapter attempts to provide further explanation along these lines.

Analyses in previous chapters establish the following propositions. First, it was in the best interest of the Chinese people to have a unified single country. Second, the rule of law was necessary to maintain the social order of such a large country. Third, the Chinese culture developed from Confucianism complemented the rule of law in decreasing the cost paid by the government to maintain the social order. In other words, the Chinese culture successfully turned the Chinese into docile people, which decreased the policing costs and ultimately increased the Chinese people's welfare.

The most docile people in ancient China were located in the coastal areas of China for two reasons. First, they were the farthest away from the country's northern borders. Indeed, the nomadic tribes could not access them unless they had conquered the whole of China. Second, those areas had long been the richest regions in China, and remain the richest regions in the country. When people get richer, they tend to pursue a higher social status. In ancient China, they did so by following Confucianism more rigidly and staying far away from violence and other kinds of "barbarism." A useful indicator is that the coastal provinces of China, particularly Zhejiang and Jiangsu, produced most of the top three candidates in the Keju examinations.

A strong army was obviously not necessary when the people under rule were docile and weak. Consequently, the soldiers stationed in the coastal areas of China were most likely the soldiers with the least amount of fighting spirit. In peacetime, they were lazy in terms of their military training, as they were unlikely to engage in war. When the Wokou arrived, the soldiers were completely unprepared. The weakness and cowardice of the Chinese troops in their fight against the Wokou and their defeat precisely demonstrated that Confucianism was widely integrated into the Chinese culture. The philosophy helped stabilize the social order of a single large country and prevent it from dividing into many countries. This social harmony enhanced the Chinese people's welfare throughout most of history. It also unfortunately encouraged a major weakness in the face of foreign invasions, even when the invaders were small groups of Japanese pirates. For about two centuries, the Wokou periodically and irregularly looted many of China's coastal areas.

Like most other bandits, the Wokou were brutal and bloodthirsty. The Japanese pirates committed atrocities such as killing innocents. They often raped women, and sometimes took young people (particularly women) back to Japan to force them into slavery. As China's coastal areas were far away from the northern borders and nomadic tribes, they were usually peaceful places where massive atrocities were hardly witnessed. The Wokou were synonymous with evil in those areas.

However, to the surprise of many, the Wokou problem was greatly exacerbated by the active participation of many Chinese in Wokou gangs. Historical documents have consistently indicated that an average of 70 percent of the members of each Wokou gang were Chinese (disguised in Japanese clothes and hairstyles), and that only 30 percent were actually Japanese.[5] Moreover, most Wokou organizers were rich Chinese businessmen.[6]

From an economics perspective, each Wokou group operated like a firm. Many Chinese people participated in these groups because they found that they could contribute productively. The voyage from Japan to China was long, and much money was required to build ships that could carry enough people and withstand strong torrents in the volatile ocean. As the much richer country at the time, China naturally had many more rich people with both the capacity and temptation to finance these expenditures. In fact, some of the rich Chinese in the coastal areas made a fortune from engaging in international trade with Japan.

During the Ming Dynasty, a Chinese person would have been severely penalized for any kind of involvement with the Wokou. Such a penalty included not only the individual's execution, but also the executions of his family members and potentially his close relatives. Why would a rich Chinese businessman risk his life and the lives of his family members to engage in business with the Wokou? The answer lies in a policy of the Ming Dynasty: Haijin.

When the Wokou problem appeared, the Chinese government reacted by implementing a policy that forbade Chinese civilians to trade with Japan. This policy was called Haijin. Although government trade was still allowed under Haijin, it was much less efficient than the trade driven by market forces. Consequently, the prices of Chinese goods such as silk, silk floss, fabric, iron, porcelain, cosmetics, and herbs skyrocketed in Japan. The extraordinarily high potential for profit motivated some Chinese businessmen to break the law of Haijin to export goods to Japan. It became difficult for the businessmen to hide their smuggling activities, and they became "most wanted" criminals by the government. Those businessmen who were caught were at the very least sent to jail and heavily fined. Some were even executed if their business operations were very large. Many businessmen brought their families with them to live in foreign countries, including Japan. They found that the expected profits from engaging in business with the Wokou were much higher than those from smuggling. Because they did not live in China, the Chinese police could not catch them. Thus, it made no difference to them whether they committed minor or serious crimes.

Once the Chinese businessmen became the bosses of the Wokou, they naturally considered employing some Chinese people as foot soldiers. Although the cost of recruiting a Japanese person as a pirate might have been lower than that of recruiting a Chinese person, the cost of transporting a Japanese person to China by sea was very high. Taking this into account, the total cost of recruiting a Chinese person might have been much lower than that of recruiting a Japanese person. The Japanese and Chinese both had their own advantages in a Wokou organization. The Japanese members served as the main force in battles, and the Chinese members were more familiar with China's geographical locations and the mentality of its people. Moreover, a large proportion of the Wokou jobs such as carrying the goods they robbed and escorting the captives they seized did not involve violent actions. A Chinese person was as productive as a Japanese person in performing such jobs. Thus, forming a "joint venture" of Japanese and Chinese members in a Wokou organization proved advantageous.

These joint ventures increased the Wokou activities significantly. For example, between 1369 and 1466, when most of the Wokou were Japanese, Wokou raids were carried out about once every three years. Between 1523 and 1588, the Japanese and Chinese were well integrated in Wokou gangs, and the frequency of Wokou raids increased to about once per year. However, Wokou activities sharply declined and then basically disappeared by the end of the 16th century. There are a number of reasons for this, and they are given as follows.

First, the Ming Dynasty ultimately had a strong force that fought against the Wokou effectively. The most famous general of the Chinese troops was Qi Jiguang.[7] Learning from the defeat of the Chinese troops against the Wokou, Qi Jiguang created a new army from scratch. He initially sought "high quality" soldiers. As described earlier, this was not an easy task, as the well-cultivated

Confucianism in China's coastal areas had turned the people there into docile and gentle civilians rather than tough fighters. However, Qi Jiguang had faith that he could find Chinese fighters who were tough and brave.

Lucky for Qi, an unusual riot broke out in a county in Zhejiang called Yiwu. Mines were discovered there, bringing a good deal of fortune to the previously poor county. Many people in Yiwu started working in the mines and increasing their wealth substantially.

In 1558, many people in the nearby county of Yongkang heard the news and aimed to work in the mines in Yiwu as well. However, the people of Yiwu decided to prohibit outsiders from sharing their fortunes. Many people from both counties clashed on the roads to the mines, and violence ultimately broke out. The riot lasted about four months, resulting in 2,500 casualties. The people of Yiwu ultimately drove the people of Yongkang back to their county.

Such large-scale civilian fights were very rare in the most civilized areas of China. Qi Jiguang decided to recruit most of his soldiers from the Yiwu miners. He selected 4,000 men, all of whom met his standards of being strong and tough. He then imposed strict disciplines on their military training. After only one year of rigorous training, Qi sent his new army to Taizhou Prefecture to fight a large group of invading Wokou. Qi's army took its first huge victory by killing and capturing more than 5,000 Wokou. The miraculous accomplishments of Qi's army continued after that, and some are summarized in the following table.[8]

Table 14.1 demonstrates the superiority of Qi's army over the Wokou. The underlying theories for this superiority are discussed at the beginning

Table 14.1 The casualty ratio between Wokou and Qi's army

Battle location	Number of soldiers in Qi's army during the battle	Number of Wokou in the battle	Number of soldiers in Qi's army killed during the battle	Number of Wokou killed during the battle
Baishuiyang	1,500	2,000	3	2,000 (all)
Lantau Island (Qi's army crossed the sea)			13	1,000
Nutian		10,000	0	688
Lindun			90	3,000
Fuqian			20	300
Pinghaiwei			16	2,622
Xianyou		10,000	24	1,000
Wangchangping		10,000	0	177
Caipeiling		7,000	31	1,000

of this chapter. In particular, an army is superior to a group of bandits in implementing military disciplines. Qi was extremely strict with his soldiers. During one operation, Qi's son, an officer in the army, did not obey an order carefully, allowing a large number of Wokou to escape. Qi Jiguang punished his son by executing him in public.[9]

An army had an advantage over bandits only when the soldiers were tough and fearless on the battlefields. A Japanese bandit could kill 100 Chinese weak soldiers, and conversely, a tough and fearless Chinese soldier could kill 100 Japanese bandits. This example well illustrates the importance of soldiers' bravery and a troop's discipline to the combative power of an army.

Few Wokou were taken prisoner, which should not be surprising. The Japanese Wokou, who were often former samurais, were trained to fight to the death. The "Chinese Wokou" did not want to be captured either. When a "Chinese Wokou" was caught and forced to confess when tortured, all of his family members would be executed.

The Wokou also disappeared due to a new policy put in place by the Japanese government at the end of the 16th century, when Toyotomi Hideyoshi united Japan and became its *de facto* ruler. In 1588, Toyotomi Hideyoshi implemented the policy of the sword hunt, which aimed to confiscate all of the weaponry from the hands of Japanese civilians. Toyotomi sought to mitigate the possibility of Japanese insurrections. However, this policy also helped disarm potential Japanese Wokou, who were used to fighting with unique Japanese swords and were not good at using other kinds of weapons. Toyotomi took strong and direct measures to curtail potential Wokou activities. He required the daimyos to write oaths against piracy. If a daimyo broke his oath, the Toyotomi government would confiscate his wealth and fief. Toyotomi probably implemented this policy because he was concerned that the Japanese pirates would develop into a powerful organization that would challenge his rule in Japan. The policy helped greatly in eliminating the Wokou plague from China.

The events surrounding the Wokou invasion well illustrate the national character of the ancient Chinese. The invasion was a special kind of foreign invasion in that it was organized not by the government of a foreign country, but out of the need to avoid starvation and then later the desire to accrue profits. Indeed, many Chinese were also lured by greed to join the Wokou organizations. Their decision to become Wokou indicated that racial hatred was not a major issue for a significant portion of ancient Chinese people. In this way, the Chinese culture differed significantly from other cultures that highlighted vengeance, dignity, and honor.

Notes

1 http://en.wikipedia.org/wiki/Wa_(Japan)
2 Translated by Tsunoda (1951, p. 13).
3 See, e.g., So (1975).
4 See Dang Nian Ming Yue (2006).

5 See *History of Ming (Ming Shi)* (Japan Section).
6 See, e.g., So (1975).
7 Whether Qi was the most important Chinese general/officer in the elimination of the Wokou is a different matter and debatable. For example, Hu Zhongxian was a senior officer to Qi, and spent more years focusing on Wokou issues.
8 http://baike.baidu.com/view/10438.htm
9 http://www.imdb.com/title/tt0187093/

15 The arrival of Perry, Meiji Restoration, and rise of Japan

Between 1467 and 1573, Japan was in its Warring States or "Sengoku" period, during which different daimyos engaged in constant military conflicts. The Tokugawa shogunate ended the Warring States period, leading to the unification of political powers in Japan. It also skillfully controlled hundreds of daimyos in the political arena, and established a period characterized mainly by peace and prosperity.

However, the samurai system made any central government weak. Samurai status was hereditary, and a family's samurais usually lived in the same location and were loyal to the same dynasty of daimyos. This means that the central government had a limited ability to centralize its military forces. The political structure also allowed for the continuation of the samurai system even during continuous peaceful periods. If a daimyo wanted to survive, he had to have a strong army of samurais. Otherwise, he would have been easily replaced by the shogunate, or his domain would have merged with that of another daimyo.

Due to the fragility of the central government in ancient Japan, the Tokugawa shogunate collapsed after one major shock: the arrival of Perry. Matthew Perry (1794–1858) was a commodore of the United States Navy. In July 1853, an American fleet of four ships under Perry's command arrived in Tokyo Bay. Perry's squadron was immediately surrounded by a number of Japanese ships. Perry requested the Japanese ships to disperse immediately, and told the Japanese that his fleet could vanquish them easily. To convince the Japanese that it would be in their best interest to give in, Perry demonstrated the power of his weapons by ordering his ships to shell several buildings around the harbor. This turned out to be a very cost-effective strategy, as it left the Japanese shocked by the destruction.

Perry then condescendingly presented a white flag to the Tokugawa shogunate with instructions to use it when the government decided to surrender. He also presented a letter from President Millard Fillmore to the Tokugawa shogunate demanding that it open up trade with the United States. On March 31, 1854, the Japanese ruler decided to back down, and the Kanagawa Treaty was signed between Matthew Perry and the Tokugawa shogunate. The main item of the treaty required Japan to open its two ports, Shimoda and Hakodate, for trade with the United States.

From a long-run perspective, the arrival of Perry was a blessing to Japan. It brought democracy and modernization to Japan, turning it into a strong nation. However, its immediate effect on Japan was a shocking humiliation to both the people and the government of Japan. Before this event, Japan had implemented a policy of "Sakoku" for about 200 years. "Sakoku," which literally means "close the country through a lock" in Japanese, stipulated that foreigners were not allowed to enter Japan and that the Japanese were not allowed to leave. In 1825, less than 30 years after the arrival of Perry, the Tokugawa shogunate enacted a law stating that foreigners should be expelled at all costs.

However, under the coercion of Western powers and their modern weaponry, Japan had to open up trade with foreigners. Regardless of whether the outcomes were beneficial to the Japanese economy, the Japanese people and particularly the samurai class considered the arrangement an enormous humiliation to their honor and pride. Because honor was of paramount importance to Japan, the event inflicted tremendous damage on the prestige of the Tokugawa shogunate. After the Kanagawa Treaty, other treaties were signed that further opened Japan to the rest of the world. The ensuing close interactions with Westerners in Japan intensified hatred of foreigners and brewed a bitter discontent toward the Tokugawa shogunate.

Against this background, Emperor Komei began to appear in Japan's political arena. In 1863, he issued the imperial order to expel the "barbarians," referring to Western foreigners. This action, as simple as it was, broke Japan's centuries-old imperial tradition. Indeed, Japanese emperors had played only symbolic and passive roles since 1192.

Why did Emperor Komei suddenly take such a high-profile stand? One answer is that he did it out of anger. However, although the emperor was infuriated by the bullying and condescending attitudes of the foreigners, there were many other ways for him to vent his anger. The imperial order put the Tokugawa shogunate in a very awkward position. It knew that it was not the right time to declare war against foreign powers that possessed far superior weaponry. However, the imperial order fueled the anger of the Japanese people and particularly the samurais toward Westerners. A number of Westerners were consequently attacked. The Tokugawa shogunate had to apologize and offer compensation, which further deteriorated their status and prestige among the Japanese people. However, this outcome might have been precisely what Emperor Komei wanted. He might have been wise enough to realize that it was time for the imperial house to take back the sovereign throne and allow him to assume real power in Japan.

Emperor Komei's imperial order to expel the "barbarians" received two immediate responses. First, it encouraged violent action against foreigners in Japan, which necessarily led to the Western powers taking revenge against the Tokugawa shogunate. These brutal measures of revenge, such as the bombardment of Kagoshima, resulted in further humiliation of the Tokugawa shogunate government and hence more rebellious sentiment. Second, given the increasing bullying of the Western powers and the hapless position of the Tokugawa shogunate, the Japanese people began to put their hopes of restoring their national pride and dignity on the emperor, and made their past humiliations the responsibility of the "corrupt" and "weak" Tokugawa shogunate. Indeed, the imperial order to expel the "barbarians" was spontaneously echoed by the populace slogan "revere the emperor." This slogan provided solid justification for rebellions against the Tokugawa shogunate. Indeed, it gave the emperor more legitimacy to assert his rule over Japan.

In January 1867, Emperor Komei was diagnosed with smallpox and died shortly thereafter. However, his death did not stop the rebellion. In fact, his successor, Emperor Meiji, was even more supportive of the cause of overthrowing the Tokugawa shogunate. The samurai rebels proved to be a strong force under the new emperor, and defeated the Tokugawa shogunate army after several major battles.

With Tokyo its only remaining stronghold, the shogunate knew that the outcome of the war was already decided and hence surrendered to Emperor Meiji and the rebel army. On November 9, 1867, Tokugawa Yoshinobu, the last shogun or ruler of the Tokugawa shogunate, officially handed the rule of Japan back to the emperor. Within a few months, the regime of the Tokugawa shogunate withdrew from the Japanese political arena.

The Meiji Restoration period is usually defined as the period between 1868 and 1912, the year Emperor Meiji died. It was a golden period of Japanese history, as it turned Japan from a poor feudal society into a modernized nation within a very short time. During this period, the Japanese economy took off and Japan built a strong army. Most important, the Meiji Restoration turned Japan from a country comprising numerous daimyo-controlled autonomous regions into a country with a strong central government. In fact, by the end of the Tokugawa shogunate regime, there were about 250 powerful daimyos in Japan, and each possessed a private army of loyal samurais.

In 1868, the lands that formerly belonged to the central government of the Tokugawa shogunate were seized under the control of the emperor. In 1869, the daimyos who contributed most to overthrowing the Tokugawa shogunate surrendered their fiefdoms to the emperor. Other daimyos quickly followed suit. In return, the daimyos received an income 10 percent that of their fiefs, and the Meiji government took over the payment of samurai stipends.[1]

In 1871, the so-called domains that were originally controlled by the daimyos were entirely abolished and replaced by 72 prefectures, whose governors were appointed by the Meiji government. In contrast to the daimyos, whose status was hereditary, each governor served a term of only four years with the possibility of renewal by the central government. This reform turned Japan into a fully unified country with a strong central government.

Moreover, the Japanese economy took off rapidly for four reasons. First, the Japanese cleverly took the opportunity to learn about the modern technologies of Western countries. Japan was humiliated by Western powers, leading to strong anti-foreign sentiments in the country. However, from the onset of the Meiji Restoration, the Japanese adopted an intelligent strategy of learning from their enemies. Although Japan was poor at the time, it used a significant fraction of its meager savings to employ thousands of foreign experts, which sped up the country's modernization of both its economy and army. Those foreign experts helped the Japanese learn about science, engineering, modern industrial technologies, and methods for training the country's troops and navy.

Second, although Japan had closed its doors to foreign countries for centuries under the rule of the Tokugawa shogunate, it quickly appreciated the benefits of international trade during the Meiji Restoration. Equipped with new technologies adopted from Western countries, Japan quickly began industrializing and gradually became the major exporter of manufactured goods in Asia.[2] Meanwhile, it imported a substantial amount of raw materials, which remedied its relative poverty of natural resources. Japan wisely used its comparative production advantage to reap the benefits of international trade and global markets.

Third, the Meiji government realized the value of a market economy, and encouraged free enterprise capitalism at the very beginning of the period. The market competition motivated firms to adopt better technologies and enhance production efficiencies. This consequently sped up Japan's economic growth and structural changes.

Fourth, the daimyos benefited tremendously from the economic growth, as they were the major investors in Japan's new industries. As the daimyos received substantial incomes from the Meiji government, they invested their money in the new industries, which yielded handsome returns and helped with Japan's industrial modernization. Thus, the daimyos were a major force that supported the Meiji Restoration.

The slogan of the Meiji Restoration was to "enrich the country and strengthen the military." Establishing a strong army was an important goal of the Meiji Restoration. This goal was initially a direct response to the bullying of Western powers. With the further development of Japan under the Meiji Restoration, the "strengthen the military" slogan turned into an ambition of military expansion.

One important material foundation for the rising militarism under the Meiji Restoration was Bushido, which is discussed in detail in an earlier chapter. Bushido defines the moral code of the samurai life. Samurais existed in Japan for centuries. The feudal lords in Japan, i.e., the daimyos, never really ceased to engage in power struggles before the Meiji period. They engaged in large-scale military battles during the Warring States period. The Tokugawa shogunate united Japan to a large degree, and established political stability and a peaceful society. However, theirs was essentially a period of "cold war," during which there were continuous conflicts between different daimyos and even between some daimyos and the Tokugawa shogunate. These explicit and hidden conflicts explain why samurais accounted for about 7 percent of the Japanese population even during the peaceful period under the Tokugawa shogunate. Meanwhile, the conflicts and potential conflicts kept the fighting spirit of the samurai class alive, which fostered and refined the culture of Bushido among them.

Christian missionary Saint Francis Xavier describes the ancient Japanese as follows:[3] "(The Japanese) have a high opinion of themselves because they think that no other nation can compare them in regard to weapons and valor. . . They greatly prize and value their arms, and prefer to have good weapons, decorated with gold and silver, more than anything else in the world. They carry a sword and a dagger both inside and outside the house and lay them at their pillows when they sleep. Never in my life have I met people who rely so much on their arms. . . They are very warlike and are always involved in wars, and thus the ablest man became the greatest lord."

Because most samurais were traditionally loyal to certain families of feudal lords, the samurai class was outlawed under the Meiji Restoration to strengthen the power of Japan's central government. However, the spirit of the samurais was left intact, and redefined in the form of "Japanese nationalism" in the new era. Many people of samurai origin joined the Imperial Japanese Army and were quickly promoted to the rank of officer.

Most samurais had both a strong fighting spirit and a thorough education. Because they were prohibited from working during the peaceful period of the Tokugawa shogunate, they had plenty of leisure time. To prevent potential unrest among the samurai class, the Tokugawa government encouraged samurais to spend their time focusing on education, which most samurais found agreeable. Greenfeld (2001, p. 241) observes the following: ". . . Secure in the consciousness of their social superiority, they (samurais) did not particularly care which of the symbols of their status – the swords, which they had the undisputed right to carry, or the education which they were encouraged to acquire – was to be considered central, and responded with increasing enthusiasm to the government's preference for the latter."

Therefore, the soldiers and officers of the Imperial Japanese Army had a strong fighting spirit and were well educated. They constituted the cornerstone of the Imperial Japanese Army and made it a formidable force.

The culture of Bushido permeated Japanese society as a whole. For example, Nitobe (1900) argued that although Japanese society experienced tremendous transformation under the Meiji Restoration, the traditional value of Bushido remained its core value. The Meiji government placed a great deal of emphasis on education, and many of the teachers recruited for the newly established schools were samurais. These teachers were recruited not because they were samurais, but because they were relatively better educated than most. The samurais-turned-teachers naturally taught their students about the virtues of Bushido and nationalism. For example, Greenfeld (2001, p. 275) states: ". . . the modern samurai was in some important respects superior to those of the past and could take pride in this. He was more knowledgeable and better equipped for patriotic service. The problem was that Tokugawa Japan did not give him a chance to serve."

Finally, the emerging democracy in Japan was another factor that might have contributed to the rise of militarism in the Meiji period. At first glance, one may consider it absurd to argue that an increase in democracy leads to a rise of militarism. However, it is indeed possible. Consider an extreme case in which only one member of a country, i.e., the emperor, has a dignified position while the other members work as slaves. In this case, only the emperor would claim the glory of a military victory and expansion. The other members of the country would have little interest in engaging in military conquests, as doing so would bring them only a risk of injury and death on the battlefield and present no benefits. Now consider that the country experiences an increase in democracy, leading more members of the country to feel that they are honorable members of a society. In this case, the members would call the honor and glory of their country their own, brewing feelings of nationalism.

In Japan, the rise of nationalism associated with an increase in democracy might have been fueled by emergent leaders in the new government, many of whom were the same samurais who led the rebellion against the Tokugawa shogunate. When the Japanese government sent people abroad to study in Western countries, most of the selected students were also samurais. (As in the case of teachers, they were selected not because they were samurais but because they were relatively good scholars.)[4] During their overseas journeys, those samurais were deeply impressed by the military expansions of many Western countries and the vast colonies they obtained. When they came back from abroad, they emphasized the Western successes and argued that Japan should learn from their military expansions.

A culture is usually heavily influenced by its media. As described previously, the good scholars in Japan were usually either former samurais or samurai in origin, and were much better educated than the rest of the Japanese population. The development of the Japanese media industry entailed the participation of better-educated individuals. Thus, the pioneers in the newspaper industries were mostly former samurais or samurai in origin. In other words, those who had strong spirits of Bushido and militarism controlled the Japanese media, and played an important role in propagating militarism and territory expansions.

Notes

1 See, e.g., Beasley (1972).
2 Beasley (1995).
3 Greenfeld (2001, p. 239).
4 Greenfeld (2001).

16 The First Sino–Japanese War

With the rise of Japan and decline of China, conflicts began to appear between these neighboring countries at the end of the 19th century. At that time, the "social norm" or "moral code" of the world was still that a strong country could invade or bully a weak country as long as the former had a "good excuse." A strong country could take territory from a weak country through a military victory.

Although Japan predicted that its army was strong enough to defeat the Chinese army, the Qing government thought otherwise. After its complete defeat in the two Opium Wars, China knew that it was weaker than Western powers such as the British Empire, which had superior weaponry. However, China found no reason to be afraid of Japan. China should have been well aware of Japan's experiences during the Meiji Restoration, which substantially sped up its economic development. China had already experienced the similar "Self-Strengthening Movement" between 1861 and 1895, several years before the Meiji Restoration.

During this movement, the Qing Dynasty aimed to modernize its economy and army in a number of ways, including by sending students overseas and building new schools that helped students learn about the sciences and technologies of Western countries and how to build factories, arsenals, and shipyards by importing Western technologies, equipment, and management styles.[1] Recall that the slogan of the Meiji Restoration was to "enrich the country and strengthen the military." The "Self-Strengthening Movement" in China had precisely the same goals. Both China and Japan tried to achieve their goals by learning from Western countries, and both appeared to be successful.

During the "Self-Strengthening Movement," the knowledge and technologies of Western countries were introduced to China through the importing of foreign machinery and hiring of foreign technical personnel. This period marked the beginning of China's industrialization. In particular, many industries such as the textile and cotton-weaving industries developed rapidly. The government became heavily involved in the development of many industries such as the shipping, railway, mining, and telegraphy industries. These industrial developments enriched the Chinese people and increased the government's revenues.

Moreover, a substantial increase in international trade allowed the Qing government to collect more tariffs and taxes. The increased revenues allowed the Qing Dynasty to modernize the Chinese army. An important milestone in the modernization of the Chinese military was the creation of the Beiyang Fleet. In 1894, on the eve of the First Sino–Japanese War, the Beiyang Fleet was commonly considered the most powerful fleet in Asia. The fleet had a squadron of eight armored cruisers, which had mostly been built in either Britain or Germany. The pearls of the fleet were two German-built steel turret battleships, which were equipped with the most advanced military technologies at the time.[2]

In 1894, an incident in Korea triggered a massive conflict between China and Japan, and the First Sino–Japanese War ensued. Large-scale battles between Chinese and Japanese forces took place both on land and at sea. Japan's group forces and navy achieved overwhelming victories, which can be easily illustrated by comparing the casualties: 35,000 Chinese troops were killed or wounded in the war, and the Japanese casualties totaled less than 5,000. Moreover, the Japanese navy annihilated the Beiyang Fleet and did not lose a single ship.[3]

In April 1895, after a series of fierce battles, the Qing government realized that the Chinese army was simply no match for the Japanese army, and it sued for peace. The war ended with the signing of the Treaty of Shimonoseki, which included two main items. First, China was required to cede Taiwan, the adjoining small islands of the Penghu group, and the eastern portion of the bay of Liaodong Peninsula to Japan in perpetuity. Second, China agreed to pay Japan a war indemnity of 200 million silver taels. Somewhat luckily for China, Russia, France, and Germany intervened and forced Japan to modify the treaty so that Japan returned the Liaodong Peninsula to China for an additional war indemnity of 30 million silver taels. However, the overall outcome was disastrous for China.

Why did China lose the war so completely? This question has puzzled the Chinese people since 1895. In fact, right before the war started, most Western observers perceived that China had a stronger army and would win the war. The Western media outlet Reuters interviewed William Lang, a British advisor to the Chinese army. Lang was very much impressed with various key aspects of the Qing army, such as its training, battleships, and guns. The interview took place shortly before the war started. Lang observed that "the Chinese navy was well-drilled, the ships were fit, the artillery was at least adequate, and the coastal forts were strong." Hence, he predicted that "in the end, there is no doubt that Japan must be utterly crushed."[4]

However, to the surprise of Western observers and the extreme dismay of the Chinese, the Qing army suffered a thorough defeat in the First Sino–Japanese War. Meanwhile, precisely because the difference in weaponry between Japan and China did not account for the outcome of the war, which was simply an uncontested match, the defeat was especially humiliating to the Chinese people. The main explanation for China's complete defeat among the populace was the inferiority of China's national character to that of Japan.

This inferiority complex has tortured the minds of the Chinese people for more than a century. Various hypotheses have been put forward to mitigate the bitter psychological blow and explain the reasons for China's defeat. The leading hypothesis is the corruption of the Qing government. In particular, Empress Dowager Cixi was the major scapegoat for the blame. It is a familiar story in China that Cixi took a large portion of the Chinese fleet's military fund to construct a royal summer palace. However, this explanation is too far-fetched. The Chinese population at the time was about half a billion people. The expenditure for a royal summer palace not that large in scale was unlikely to account for a major proportion of the total government revenue of such a large country.

Moreover, corruption has been commonplace throughout the world's history, and was not unique in the late Qing Dynasty. This raises three questions that may be interrelated. Was corruption a more serious problem in Qing China than in Meiji Japan? If yes, then why? Finally, what are the exact channels through which corruption adversely affects the outcome of a war?

The answers to these questions have met with a great deal of speculation. For example, Meiji had a parliament that constrained corruption. However, the substantial empirical research related to corruption in the economics and political science literature has provided no evidence that the existence of a parliament *per se* decreases corruption.

Thus, this chapter tries to advance new explanations for China's defeat in the First Sino–Japanese War, and to provide answers to the preceding three questions. Its key points are precisely the main theme of this book: soldiers' bravery and the "military professionalism" of the troops, which boil down to the national character of the late Qing China versus Meiji Japan. The following explains why the soldiers' bravery and military professionalism, which may be related to corruption, differed drastically in the two countries at the time. I then address why these factors mattered so much to the outcome of the war.

The Meiji government successfully built a modern army equipped with advanced weapons and Western-style training. Meanwhile, the ancient Bushido code dictated the culture of the Japanese military. Although the samurai class had been abolished in Japan, the combative spirit of the samurai prevailed in the Imperial Japanese Army. In such a culture, military defeat was not acceptable and surrender was unthinkable. A Japanese troop that achieved victory on a battlefield returned home with honor and glory. However, when a Japanese troop was defeated, the soldiers faced tremendous humiliation upon returning home, akin to the humiliation felt by samurais who failed to fulfill an important duty in ancient Japan. In this case, the leaders of the troop were expected to commit suicide in the form of seppuku. Therefore, a military defeat was far worse for the army officers held responsible than being killed on the battlefield. Such a feeling was also shared by most Japanese soldiers in an environment permeated by Bushido. As a result, Japanese soldiers were brave, well disciplined, and well organized in terms of their military actions.

In contrast, the morale of the Qing army was low. Its defeats at the hands of Britain and France in the Opium Wars a few decades before were shocking and humiliating in the beginning. Over time, China began to accept the defeats.

However, this acceptance was very costly in that it substantially decreased the national pride of the Chinese people, including the soldiers in the Qing army. One may argue that Japan was also humiliated by Western powers. However, the degree of humiliation in Japan was much less than that in China. The Japanese were able to place the blame on the "weak" and "corrupt" Tokugawa shogunate and take pride in the new Meiji government. As there was no such scapegoat in China at the time, the level of national pride was insufficient for the Chinese soldiers to fight bravely, and the combative spirit of the Qing army was low. For example, the central army of the Qing Dynasty was so weak that it was virtually crushed by the Taiping Rebellion. The Taiping rebels were finally annihilated only after some local troops were recruited and rigorously trained and the United States and Britain offered their help.

The Taiping Rebellion and other insurrections were large in scale by any standard. Although the Qing government ultimately managed to quell all of the rebellions, doing so proved extremely costly and exhausted its revenues. Consequently, many government officials were underpaid or paid after a long delay, which induced them to engage in corruption. The culture of corruption influenced the army over time. Army officers mainly engaged in corruption by stealing the salaries of soldiers. With the central government frequently cutting or delaying salary payments to soldiers, it became much less risky for the officers to engage in corrupt behavior because the soldiers did not know whom to blame.

Such corruptive activities in the Qing army were devastating to the fighting spirit of the soldiers. Indeed, the pursuit of personal gains that permeated the army culture transferred over when a war broke out, influencing the soldiers to behave cowardly and avoid risking their lives. When victorious, the officers of a troop were praised and awarded by the government far more often than ordinary soldiers. Although the soldiers knew that their officers were stealing their salaries, they had no hard evidence to accuse them. (In fact, even if evidence had been available, it would have been hard for the soldiers to accuse their generals given the rampant army and government corruption.) What soldier would be willing to sacrifice his life to fight for an officer who stole his salary? When soldiers behave like cowards, their army becomes easy to defeat. This point is addressed more rigorously with the application of game theory later on.

How to account for the disastrous fate of the Beiyang Fleet? A marine who operates a large battleship is often responsible for a small portion of the overall military operations, and he does not run any risk of doing his job *per se*. Bravery is not often an issue, or at least not an important factor, in a navy's military success or failure. The key point here is the "military professionalism" that distinguished the Japanese marines from the Chinese and hence the Japanese navy from the Beiyang Fleet. This point can be well elaborated based on the O-ring theory developed by Michael Kremer, a professor of economics at Harvard University.

The O-ring theory emphasizes that in the industrial specialization process, the qualities of different intermediate goods are highly complementary in producing the quality of the final consumption good. For example, a computer will not work even if only one of its thousands of components fails. Kremer (1993) uses the example of the space shuttle *Challenger*, which exploded because one of its millions of components, the O-ring, malfunctioned under very high temperatures.

The essential insight of the O-ring theory can be well applied to a battleship. Even a small navy battleship is a weapon far more complicated than a foot soldier's gun. Engaging a battleship in combat requires close collaboration and complete trust between the different soldiers and marines on the ship. The training of every marine in his individual task is very important and often hard for an officer to monitor. Thus, "military professionalism" is extremely important to a battleship's combative power. For example, suppose a battleship has 100 marines. If just one marine does not operate well, the artillery fired by the battleship may miss the target. The Japanese marines exhibited a much greater degree of military professionalism and performed much better in training and combat. Thus, a Japanese battleship might have had much greater fighting power than a Chinese battleship, even if the two ships were produced by the same British producer and shared the same quality.

In a major ship battle, a fleet consists of a large number of battleships, and coordination between the different battleships is crucial. Successful coordination depends on not only the skills of the marines involved, but also the willingness of the captain to sacrifice himself. One battleship will inevitably take more risks than others in combat. The degree of risk is often decided at the discretion of the individual battleship captain. O-ring theory can again be applied in this situation. A Japanese captain might have put the victory of the whole fleet above his personal safety. Even if the captain himself avoided injury, he would have had to commit suicide if his fleet was defeated. In contrast, a Chinese captain might always try to blame others for a military defeat, and consequently receive little punishment from the corrupt Qing government when brought to trial.

O-ring theory can also be applied to ground forces. Coordination between different armed soldiers is important. In this case, even if an individual Japanese soldier were only slightly better than an individual Chinese soldier in terms of bravery and military professionalism, the combative power of the Japanese troop was much greater as a whole. Consider two machines (A and B), each of which has 100 components. If every component of Machine A is a little bit better than its counterpart in Machine B, then Machine A is likely to function much better than Machine B. This explains the huge difference in casualties between the Chinese and Japanese troops in the First Sino–Japanese War.

The central point in the preceding argument is that a typical Japanese soldier fought much more bravely than a typical Chinese soldier. The game theory concepts developed by John Nash can be used to clarify this logic. John Nash received the 1994 Nobel Prize in Economics, and rose to even greater fame after the release of the 2001 Oscar-winning biographical drama film *A Beautiful Mind*, which is based on Nash's life.

Nash was a first-rate mathematician worldwide. He was a strong contender for the Fields Medal, the most prestigious award in mathematics, and only narrowly missed receiving it. However, possibly to his own surprise, Nash made an even greater contribution to economics than he made to mathematics. His main contribution was non-cooperative game theory, which is described as follows.

Although *A Beautiful Mind* describes non-cooperative game theory in brief, it misses the main point and can be misleading. A crucial concept of game theory is the Nash equilibrium, which has two key components: strategy and belief. A Nash equilibrium exists if no player has the incentive to deviate from his or her strategy given the belief that the other players will not deviate (Nash, 1950). As this definition is fairly abstract, some examples are necessary to clarify the concept.

The "prisoner's dilemma" is a famous example of the Nash equilibrium concept. The police apprehend two criminal suspects (A and B). The police know that the suspects committed a serious crime, but have little evidence to prove it in court. The two suspects could be sentenced to 10 years in prison if sufficient evidence exists to prove that they committed the crime. A confession would be sufficient evidence. However, given the little evidence obtained, the court can only send each criminal to prison for one year. The police concoct the following strategy to induce the two suspects to confess. They separate the suspects into two different rooms and visit each of them, offering the following deal: if one testifies in court for the prosecution of the other and the other does not, the one who testifies will go free and the other will be sentenced to prison for 10 years. If both choose to testify, then each will receive an eight-year sentence. The prisoner's dilemma is summarized in the following table.

What should the two suspects do? The conceptual framework of the Nash equilibrium provides a useful way of answering this question. In this example, the only Nash equilibrium is that both of the suspects betray their partners, consequently sentencing themselves to prison for eight years each. In particular, note that (Loyal, Loyal) is not a Nash equilibrium. If one prisoner believes that the other is "loyal," then it is in his interest to confess to ensure his own freedom.

Despite its simplicity, the preceding example illustrates the concept of the Nash equilibrium and its two crucial components: strategy and belief. The following example illustrates the usefulness of the Nash equilibrium in a more complicated scenario. It shows that the importance of soldiers' bravery and military professionalism can be explained from the perspective of confidence. Consider a team of two warriors (X and Y). The warriors are fighting a common enemy, and their strategies and payoffs are summarized in the following table.

Table 16.1 Prisoner's dilemma

A/B	Loyal	Betray
Loyal	(−1, −1)	(−10, 0)
Betray	(0, −10)	(−8, −8)

Table 16.2 Two warriors' game (A)

A/B	Fight bravely	Be a coward
Fight bravely	10, 10	0, 5
Be a coward	5, 0	2, 2

In this example, if both warriors fight bravely, they will achieve a victory and consequently obtain the greatest level of happiness (10, 10). If Warrior A fights bravely and Warrior B behaves cowardly, both warriors will be beaten by the enemy and Warrior A will be killed in action. In this case, the "payoffs" of A and B are 0 and 5, respectively. If Warrior B fights bravely and Warrior A behaves cowardly, both warriors will be beaten by the enemy and Warrior B will be killed in action. If both warriors behave cowardly, they will lose the battle and possibly have the chance to escape. In this case, each warrior would obtain a low payoff of 2.

Note that in this example, there are two potential Nash equilibriums. The good equilibrium is obviously the case in which both warriors fight bravely. In this equilibrium, each warrior expects that the other warrior will fight bravely, and such an expectation can be self-fulfilling. However, there is also a bad equilibrium in which both warriors behave cowardly. In this equilibrium, each warrior expects the other warrior to behave cowardly, and such an expectation can also be self-fulfilling. For example, if A believes that B will be a coward, then his fighting bravely alone will generate a payoff of 0, which would be less than the payoff of behaving cowardly as well (i.e., 2). Thus, A will choose to be a coward if he believes that B will also be a coward.

There is an old Chinese saying that describes the bad equilibrium vividly: the defeat of an army is like a falling mountain. When a soldier expects that no one else will fight and hence that his army will be defeated, he will try to run and escape. If every soldier expects the same outcome, they will compete to run away, and the escaping army will look like a falling mountain in defeat.

Because most Chinese people had weak personalities and lacked a sense of nationalism at the time, the Chinese soldiers fought cowardly and exhibited little military professionalism in the face of a malfunctioning disciplinary system. In relation to the preceding numerical example, the Chinese soldiers were caught in the bad equilibrium.

Indeed, Paine (2003, p. 362) summarizes her observations of the war as follows: the Chinese "common soldiers had little incentive to fight." Furthermore, one Japanese government's record of the war[5] describes some of the Chinese generals as tall and strong, and claims that they superficially looked like they were commanding their armed forces effectively. However, as soon as the generals heard gunshots, they became "weak worms," and some even put on women's clothing as disguises to help them escape.

Bushido carried a good strategy to rule out this bad equilibrium: a defeated samurai had to commit suicide. According to this strategy, a Japanese soldier rationally expected all of his fellow Japanese soldiers to fight bravely. For example, it is well known that many Japanese soldiers committed suicide after Japan lost World War II. Although one may consider this a waste of human life, the hidden rationale is that it ruled out the bad equilibrium.

The Japanese soldiers might have faced a different scenario, according to which the preceding numerical example can be modified as follows (see Table 16.3).

In this case, even if one believed that his partner would behave cowardly, it would still be in his best interest to fight bravely. The payoff of fighting bravely is 3, which is greater than the payoff of being a coward (i.e., 2). Of course, if one believed that his partner would fight bravely, he would obviously choose to fight bravely as well, generating the highest payoff of 10. Thus, the only equilibrium in this example is reached when both soldiers choose to fight bravely.

Indeed, Liang Qichao once compared the Chinese and Japanese in terms of how they sent their children and close relatives off to war. The Chinese often cried when they saw their loved ones off. In contrast, the Japanese often appeared to be overjoyed to see their loved ones off, much like one reacted to seeing a loved one succeed in the Keju examinations in ancient China. Moreover, the "greeting" the Japanese gave to their loved ones was often akin to "don't come back alive" or a prayer that they would die in battle.[6]

In the First Sino–Japanese War, the Chinese troops were obviously caught in the bad equilibrium in which every soldier expected his fellow soldiers to behave cowardly, particularly in the later stages of the war. In contrast, the Japanese culture enabled its troops to choose the good equilibrium in which everyone fought bravely. Consequently, the Japanese troops easily defeated the Chinese troops, and the Qing government had to plea for peace talks at an extremely heavy cost.

The analysis presented in this chapter is consistent with that of Nitobe (1900), who offers the following observation (p. 90):

> It has been said that Japan won her late war with China by means of Murata guns and Krupp cannon; it has been said the victory was the work of a modern school system; but these are less than half-truths. Does ever a piano, be it of the choicest workmanship of Ehrbar or Steinway, burst forth into the Rhapsodies of Liszt or the Sonatas of Beethoven, without a master's hand? Or, if guns win battles, why did not Louis Napoleon beat the Prussians with his Mitrailleuse,

Table 16.3 Two warriors' game (B)

A/B	Fight bravely	Be a coward
Fight bravely	10, 10	3, 0
Be a coward	0, 3	2, 2

or the Spaniards with their Mausers the Filipinos, whose arms were no better than the old-fashioned Remingtons? Needless to repeat what has grown a trite saying that it is the spirit that quickeneth, without which the best of implements profiteth but little. The most improved guns and cannon do not shoot of their own accord; the most modern educational system does not make a coward a hero. No! What won the battles on the Yalu, in Corea and Manchuria, was the ghosts of our fathers, guiding our hands and beating in our hearts. They are not dead, those ghosts, the spirits of our warlike ancestors. To those who have eyes to see, they are clearly visible. Scratch a Japanese of the most advanced ideas, and he will show a samurai. The great inheritance of honor, of valor and of all martial virtues is, as Professor Cramb very fitly expresses it, "but ours on trust, the fief inalienable of the dead and of the generation to come," and the summons of the present is to guard this heritage, nor to bate one jot of the ancient spirit; the summons of the future will be so to widen its scope as to apply it in all walks and relations of life.

Notes

1 See, e.g., Feuerwerker (1958).
2 See, e.g., Wright (2001).
3 Paine (2003).
4 Fairbank, Liu, and Twitchett (1980, p. 269).
5 The record of Japan-Qing War (日清战争实记).
6 http://news.xinhuanet.com/mil/2014–04/14/c_126386397_3.htm

Part V

National humiliations in the late Qing Dynasty and the New Culture Movement

17 National humiliations at the end of the Qing Dynasty

China reached the peak of its economic prosperity, population growth, and hegemony in world politics in the middle of the Qing Dynasty. However, the good fortune of the dynasty came to an end by around 1840, after which China suffered repeated national humiliations and defeats by foreign powers for about a century.

The Industrial Revolution began in Britain in 1760. The underlying reasons why it did not spread to China are complicated and beyond the scope of this book.[1] Some historians and economists have attributed its absence in China to the nations' differing political structures. Political fragmentation led European countries to compete with one another, which yielded more economic and political freedom, a greater emphasis on commerce, and hence the formation and rise in importance of a merchant class. Most important, it fostered scientific development and innovation along with their applications in industrial production.

Moreover, the Keju system might have induced the most talented young men to work on the classics of Confucianism rather than new technological innovations. As Baumol (1990) emphasizes, entrepreneurial choices are sensitive to the material returns and social statuses of different occupations. By this logic, the Keju system, which had benefited China and helped it maintain its status as a large country, ultimately had a negative effect on its economic growth.

Some historians have put forward similar views. For example, Balazs (1964, p. 18) states that "the state's tendency to clamp down immediately on any form of private enterprise (and this in the long run kills not only initiative but even the slightest attempts at innovation), or, if it did not succeed in putting a stop to it in time, to take over and nationalize it. Did it not frequently happen during the course of Chinese history that the scholar-officials, although hostile to all inventions, nevertheless gathered in the fruits of other people's ingenuity? I need mention only three examples of inventions that met this fate: paper, invented by a eunuch; printing, used by the Buddhists as a medium for religious propaganda; and the bill of exchange, an expedient of private business."

The Industrial Revolution was made possible by major technological innovations, such as the invention of new machines and methods for using basic materials and energy sources. This technological progress transformed the British manufacturing industry from hand and home production into machine and factory production, drastically increasing productivity. In 1840, the productivity of the British manufacturing industry far exceeded that of China. The theory of international trade posits that this tremendous difference in productivity offered significant comparative advantages for both China and Britain in different sectors of production, and therefore an enormous potential for international trade profit for both countries.[2]

However, national pride hindered China's incentive to trade with Britain. The Qing rulers considered even the idea of importing from foreign countries to undermine the image of China's superiority over all other countries. Thus, the Qing government virtually banned imports into China. Given the illegality of imports, the merchants of Britain and other Western countries focused on the product that was most profitable to sell to China: opium. The Qing government responded by taking harsh measures against those who smuggled opium into China. This led to the Opium War between the two nations, and China was thoroughly defeated in 1840 owing to Britain's far superior weaponry. China's excessive national pride therefore led only to a major national humiliation. China lost Hong Kong Island and the Kowloon Peninsula, which contained only small fishing villages at the time, to Britain in the first two Opium Wars (1856–1860). Although this loss was materially insignificant to the large Qing Empire, the wars symbolized the beginning of numerous national humiliations for China that would continue for a century.

The ancient Chinese people did not have a strong sense of nationalism for two main reasons. First, the Chinese territory was so large that it usually covered all of the lands that were suitable for people to live comfortably and reachable by transportation technologies at the time. Second, foreigners rarely posed serious threats to China due to its large size. Even when foreigners conquered China, they were foreign only at the time of invasion and often became Chinese quickly once they came to rule the country. Liang Qichao (1989, p. 66), a well-known Chinese scholar, describes this Chinese mentality as follows: "we Chinese are not by nature an unpatriotic people. The reason Chinese do not know patriotism is because they do not know that China is a state."

However, this scenario changed completely after the First Opium War in 1840. China was repeatedly defeated by foreign powers, including Britain, France, and Japan. Moreover, China lost Outer Manchuria, a large area of land comprising 350,000 square miles (910,000 square kilometers) of Chinese territory, to Russia without daring to fight. In fact, an Internet search reveals that many Chinese people today feel bitterly resentful over the loss of Outer Manchuria to Russia. Somewhat surprisingly, 100 years ago, the loss was relatively minor compared with the national humiliations suffered by the Qing Dynasty for two main reasons. First, Outer Manchuria had long cold winters, which most Chinese at the time felt unsuitable for living. Consequently, very few Chinese lived in Outer Manchuria despite its large size. In contrast, many Russians found it a far better place to live than Siberia, and hence stepped in to settle there. Second, the Chinese people did not have a strong sense of national territory *per se* at the time.

Among the numerous national humiliations suffered by China during the late Qing, the two events that affected the emotions of the Chinese people most also influenced the evolution of the Chinese "national character." The first was the First Sino–Japanese War in 1895. The second was the 1900 Boxer Rebellion and the ensuing invasion of eight foreign countries, which is discussed in the remainder of this chapter.

Although foreigners invaded China sporadically, the ancient Chinese were rarely discriminated against and ill treated for long periods. Indeed, with the exception of some periods during the Yuan Dynasty, race was largely not an issue in ancient China. Nevertheless, this changed drastically after the First Opium War in 1840, when the Chinese began to feel bullied by foreigners.

Some foreigners entered into China and interacted with the Chinese people, exacerbating the Chinese people's awareness of their humiliation. Some Westerners led lifestyles that were completely different to that of the Chinese and often went against the Confucian culture. Because the armed forces of their countries easily defeated the Qing armies, some foreigners in China were often domineering. They looked down upon the Chinese and effectively treated them as slaves, which over time resulted in strong anti-foreign sentiments in China.

The Boxer Rebellion broke out in many areas of China at the end of the 19th century. This massive movement was a response of national pride and a direct consequence of the clash of civilizations between the traditional Chinese culture and the Western culture of Christianity. As described previously, many Chinese people resented the swaggering attitude of some foreigners in China. Although it is difficult to be a loser, it is much harder when the loser must maintain close social interactions with the victor.

Although Christian missionaries from Western countries did many nice things in China, their preaching directly conflicted with the traditional Chinese culture. Most Christian missionaries in China were zealous and intended to "save the souls" of the Chinese people. They played an important role in China's initial modernization, as they built hospitals and schools and brought modern medicines and scientific knowledge into the country. In a recent empirical study, Bai and Kung (2015) show that the activities of the Protestant missionaries in early 20th-century China significantly increased the degree of urbanization and the establishment of modern industrial enterprises in China.

However, with little knowledge of Christianity, most of the Chinese at the time could not appreciate the good intentions of the missionaries. Even if they could have, they were strongly against the preaching of Christianity, as it posed a serious challenge to the traditional Chinese culture of Confucianism. When Qing officials tried to interfere with their preaching activities, the missionaries invoked their privilege of "extraterritoriality." Although doing so conveniently circumvented the harassments of local officials, it unintentionally reinforced the sense of inferiority of many Chinese and hence their hatred of the foreigners.

Against this background, the Boxer Rebellion occurred between 1899 and 1901, spurred on by the intention to drive all foreigners out of China. Because rebels around the world had been severely penalized throughout history, rebellions occurred only if the potential returns were extremely high. These returns could usually be achieved only by overthrowing incumbent rulers. The Boxer Rebellion was a rare exception. In 1899 or so, the Boxer rebels numbered about 300,000 men.[3]

However, the rebels had no intention of overthrowing the Qing government. If they intended to do, they had a good chance of defeating its troops, who were not only weak and corrupt but had also lost the honor and prestige bestowed upon them by the public due to their numerous humiliating defeats at the hands of foreign countries. On the contrary, the rebels were determined to support the Qing government by helping it fight against foreigners. Thus, the Chinese personality, which had been extremely weak and submissive, started to become tougher at the end of the 19th century. Driven by their burning hatred of this patriotic movement, the Boxer rebels killed hundreds of foreign Christian missionaries and tens of thousands of Chinese Christian converts.

The Qing government was too weak to quell the large-scale rebellion, and hence strategically and temporarily chose to side with the rebels. The foreign troops of eight nations invaded and occupied Beijing, Tianjin, and some areas of northern China for one year. The troops had absolute power over the Chinese civilians and committed horrendous atrocities against them, placing a permanent scar of humiliation on the Chinese people and further changing the Chinese personality from weak and submissive to tough and defiant. Recall Lord Acton's statement that "[p]ower tends to corrupt and absolute power corrupts absolutely." This statement applied well to the foreign troops in China during the Boxer Rebellion.

The foreign troops committed three main atrocities: looting, killing, and rape. Looting was the most prevalent and conspicuous atrocity. Some of the Western media claimed that the foreign soldiers engaged in "an orgy of looting." The British Legation held auctions on looted goods every afternoon, and sarcastically and shamelessly declared that "looting on the part of British troops was carried out in the most orderly manner."[4] In fact, many Christian missionaries also engaged in looting, and the Catholic Beitang or North Cathedral became a virtual storage room for looted property.

Killing was also common for both the Boxer rebels and civilians. Even after the war ended, foreign troops undertook punitive expeditions to the countryside to look for Boxer rebels, but could not usually distinguish them from ordinary peasants. Consequently, many innocent civilians were summarily executed. According to General Chaffee, "It is safe to say that where one real Boxer has been killed . . . 55 harmless coolies or laborers on the farms, including not a few women and children, have been slain."[5] At least 30,000 Chinese people were killed. For example, Klein (2008, p. 5) observes the following: "A particularly atrocious incident that combined all of these features was the capture of Liangxiang by a German contingent and a small British detachment on September 11, 1900, in which around one quarter of the small town's population was killed."

In fact, some foreign troops considered killing Chinese a national honor. On July 27, 1900, during the departure ceremonies for the German troops, German emperor Kaiser Wilhelm II made the following statement: "Should you encounter the enemy, he will be defeated! No quarter will be given! Prisoners will not be taken! Whoever falls into your hands is forfeited. Just as a thousand years ago the Xiongnu under their King Attila made a name for themselves, one that even today makes them seem mighty in history and legend, may the name German be affirmed by you in such a way in China that no Chinese will ever again dare to look cross-eyed at a German."

Soldiers from the Western countries raped thousands of Chinese women. In the area of Tongzhou, 573 women committed suicide either after being raped or to avoid being raped.[6] E. J. Dillon, a journalist from *The Daily Telegraph*, witnessed the mutilated corpses of Chinese women who had been raped and then killed by foreign troops. The foreign soldiers obviously exhibited little discipline. The French commander described the rapes as the "gallantry of the French soldier." Based on these kinds of observations, George Lynch, a foreign journalist, stated that "there are things that I must not write, and that may not be printed in England, which would seem to show that this Western civilization of ours is merely a veneer over savagery."[7]

The Japanese soldiers represented an exception. Prostitutes were reportedly brought from Japan for the purpose of preventing the Japanese soldiers from raping Chinese women.[8] The Japanese soldiers might have been more disciplined, and were reportedly astonished at the rapes committed by soldiers from other foreign countries. The soldiers found it difficult to restrain themselves in such an environment. When recollecting his experiences of the Second Sino–Japanese war in the 1940s, one former Japanese soldier admitted that witnessing rape drove him to behave like a "mad dog" and stimulated his sex drive in the manner of pornography.

The Boxer Rebellion did not result in a particularly large amount of human casualties considering that China was a country of nearly half a billion people at the time. However, the atrocities committed by foreign troops against Chinese civilians in China's capital city brought an unforgettable national shame to the country. Although the Boxer Rebellion was the first mass movement made in direct response to national humiliation, it ended up increasing that humiliation. However, an often-unnoted outcome of the rebellion is that it began to change China's national character. A central argument of this book is that China's national personality evolved from weak and submissive to tough and defiant, and the turning point might have been the Boxer Rebellion in 1900.

Notes

1 See, e.g., Diamond (1997), Hall (1985), Hicks (1969), Mokyr (2007), Montesquieu (1989), Pirenne (1925), Pomeranz (2000), and Rosenberg and Birdzell (1986).
2 See, e.g., Krugman, Obstfeld, and Melitz (2012).

3 See, e.g., Preston (2000).
4 http://en.wikipedia.org/wiki/Boxer_Rebellion
5 Thompson (2009, p. 204).
6 http://zh.wikipedia.org/wiki/%E4%B9%89%E5%92%8C%E5%9B%A2%E8%BF%9
   0%E5%8A%A8
7 Preston (2000, p. 284).
8 See, e.g., Ebrey, Walthall, and Palais (2008, p. 301).

18 New Culture Movement

The national shame the Chinese experienced during the late Qing period was too much for them to bear, and ultimately brought down the Qing Dynasty. In 1912, the Republic of China was established. The Chinese people had high expectations for this new republic, but it turned out to be a total disappointment. As a result of the numerous wars waged between local warlords, the development of the Chinese economy did not accelerate, and on the contrary slowed down in the new republic era. Given the weakness of the central government, China could not prevent Mongolia from becoming independent. Moreover, the Chinese felt continually oppressed and bullied by foreigners. At the national level, the Chinese government continued to sign "unequal treaties" with foreign powers. In people's daily lives, foreigners were overbearing toward the Chinese. For example, the media widely reported on signs hanging in locations reserved exclusively for Westerners that read, "Chinese and dogs are not allowed."[1]

Many Chinese wondered how to save themselves from further national humiliation. Immediately after the Opium Wars, China was convinced that its inferior technology was the reason for its defeat. After the First Sino–Japanese War, most Chinese people found flaws in the political institution of the Qing government, and some even suspected the Manchus of being genetically inferior rulers of China. However, to the dismay of the Chinese, China continued to have a weak economy and military in the republic era.

Out of their desperate search for China's "way out," some Chinese intellectuals began to suspect that the problem was the Chinese people themselves. However, they quickly ruled out the possibility that the Chinese were genetically inferior to Westerners. The intellectuals observed that although the Japanese and Chinese were genetically similar, the Japanese economy had developed spectacularly, and Japan thoroughly defeated Russia in a major war in 1905. They reasoned that the inferiority of the Chinese culture was the only explanation, and lamented the weakness and selfishness in China's national character. Consequently, the New Culture Movement broke out in the middle of 1910s.

The most influential channel transmitting the ideas of the New Culture Movement was *New Youth*, a magazine edited by Chen Duxiu and other young intellectuals at Peking University. Chen Duxiu was the Dean of the Faculty of Arts at Peking University, and later became the co-founder of the Chinese Communist Party. Numerous articles in the magazine laid the blame for China's weakness on Confucian culture. In particular, Chen Duxiu called for "Mr. Confucius" to be replaced by "Mr. Science" and "Mr. Democracy."

One may consider Chen's argument absurd. The Confucian culture does not prevent one from learning science. For example, many Chinese scientists who follow Confucianism strictly have made outstanding achievements in their areas of scientific research. Furthermore, the Confucian culture does not contradict democracy. A convenient example is Taiwan, which has a fully developed democratic system. No event in Taiwan has indicated that the Confucian culture hampers democratic development.

What did Chen Duxiu mean by his comments? The answer may be provided in an important article he wrote entitled "Our Final Awakening." In particular, the article states the following:[2] "We, having been living in one corner of the world for several decades, must ask ourselves what is the level of our national strength and our civilization. This is the final awakening of which I speak. To put it another way, if we open our eyes and take a hard look at the situation within our country and abroad, what place does our country and our people occupy, and what actions should we take? . . . Our task today can be said to be the intense combat between the old and the modern currents of thought. . . A constitutional republic which does not derive from the conscious realization and voluntary action of the majority of the people is a bogus republic and bogus constitutionalism. It is political window-dressing, in no way like the republican constitutionalism of the countries of Europe and America, because there has been no change in the thought or the character of the majority of the people, and the majority of the people have no personal feeling of direct material interest."

Chen Duxiu's argument makes some sense. For example, if everyone were extremely selfish, nobody would ever vote. Voting usually involves some cost, such as the time required to go to the voting station. Furthermore, the single vote of one individual never affects the outcome of a major election. In some elections the results between two competing parties are extraordinarily close. For example, in the United States presidential election of 2000, the outcome of the contest between Republican candidate George W. Bush and Democratic candidate Al Gore ultimately depended on close election results in the state of Florida. Bush and Gore received popular votes of 2,912,790 and 2,912,253, respectively, a difference of only 537 or less than 0.01 percent of the total vote. However, even in this extreme case, one person's vote would not have changed the outcome.

What Chen Duxiu really meant is that the Chinese people should change their national character. The same logic applies to China's potential military conflicts with foreign countries. If a war were to break out and Chinese soldiers did not exhibit bravery on the battlefield, China would lose the war. In other words, democracy does not automatically generate brave soldiers and military victories. Thus, many believed that the way out of China's problems was to adopt the Western cultural ideals of nationalism and the worship of valor and self-sacrifice.

Arthur Henderson Smith was an American missionary who spent 54 years in China. He wrote a book in 1894 that carefully describes the characteristics of the Chinese personality at the time. In particular, Smith (1894, pp. 109–112) offers the following observations: "The attitude of the government is handsomely matched by that of the people, who each and all are in the position of one who has no care or responsibility for what is done with the public property so long as he personally is not the loser. . . Of what we mean by 'right of way' no Chinese has the smallest conception . . . whatever the dynasty might happen to be, the feeling of the mass of the nation would be the same as it is now a feeling of profound indifference." Smith (1894, p. 112) provides the following explanation for this observation: "The key-note to this view of public affairs was sounded by Confucius himself, in a pregnant sentence found in the 'Analects': 'The Master said: He who is not in an office has no concern with plans for the administration of its duties.' To our thought these significant words are partly the result, and to a very great degree the cause, of the constitutional unwillingness of the Chinese to interest themselves in matters for which they are in no way responsible."

Indeed, in ancient times, when nomadic tribes were the major threat to China, the Chinese people craved the stability of a large country. The best way to maintain that stability was to keep ordinary people out of public affairs, as doing so would have substantially decreased the likelihood of public outcry and social unrest. However, in the new environment of the Republic of China, such a personality was not conducive to the functioning of democracy.

Some Chinese intellectuals became strong adherents of social Darwinism, which theorized that a weak race would be dominated and enslaved by a strong race. Against this background, the New Culture Movement broke out in full swing. After China's defeat in the Sino–Japanese War, some Chinese intellectuals began inferring that China's weakness stemmed from its weakness as an "institution." Although these intellectuals did not know the exact problem with the "institution," they speculated that it was rooted in traditional Chinese culture. Indeed, once China had the institution of a republic and a formal constitution, it followed that if the republic did not function well, the problem must have been rooted in the Chinese culture. Despite not having a better alternative option, many Chinese intellectuals believed that China should abandon the Confucian culture.

This was vividly reflected in a short story written by Lu Xun (1881–1936) entitled "The True Story of Ah Q," which is well known to almost every Chinese person today and an important reason why Lu Xun was the most influential Chinese writer of the 20th century.

In the story, Ah Q is a poor man with little education. He receives pleasure from bullying those who are physically weaker, and at one juncture teases and sexually harasses a nun. Many people are annoyed by his rudeness and bad manners. As a result, he is often bullied and beaten by those above him in rank, strength, or power. Ah Q deals with being bullied by acknowledging his spiritual superiority to his oppressors, even as he faces total defeat and severe humiliation. Lu Xun used this story to communicate that Chinese people were essentially similar to Ah Q when they were bullied and humiliated by foreign powers. He lamented that, like Ah Q, the Chinese people behaved timidly and did not fight back bravely.

The Confucian culture was most suitable to ancient China and facilitated the unification of the Chinese people into one country. As a result, it was used to credibly deter the potential threat of the war-like nomadic tribes to the north. The traditional Chinese culture of Confucianism was useful in controlling violence. If most civilians had considered "honor" and "dignity" to be more important than their lives, there would have been a great deal more violence between different individuals and groups, which might have ultimately divided China into many countries. In other words, without the traditional Chinese culture, China might have been divided into hundreds of small countries, which the nomadic cavalry would have ravaged one by one.

During the 20th century, firearms were developed sufficiently enough to completely rob the horsemen of their combative advantages. The traditional Confucian culture therefore lost much of the material foundation for its existence. Moreover, it encouraged people to be benign to others and discourage the use of violence, which was not conducive to producing brave soldiers.

The popularity of "The True Story of Ah Q" by Lu Xun illustrates that the Chinese were already well aware that they were being bullied by foreigners and lived in shame. The ancient Chinese adopted a weak national character, and could have lived peacefully without sacrificing their dignity. However, the world suddenly changed so drastically that many Chinese people realized they could no longer live with honor and dignity if they did not adopt a different culture.

Many Chinese envied Japan's Bushido culture. The previous chapter cites Liang Qichao's comparison of the Chinese and Japanese reactions to sending children and close relatives off to war. Liang notes that the Japanese often appeared to be overjoyed to see their loved ones leave for the battlefields, offering "greetings" to their loved ones akin to "don't come back alive" and praying that they would die in battle. Western culture showed a similar attitude. For example, in the famous Russian novel *War and Peace* by Leo Tolstoy, the following conversation takes place between Nikolay Bolkonsky and his son Andrey on the eve before the latter must leave to fight in a major battle (pp. 116–117):

> "Remember one thing, Prince Andrey, if you are killed, it will be a grief to me in my old age. . ." He paused abruptly, and all at once in a shrill voice went on: "But if I learn that you have not behaved like the son of Nikolay Bolkonsky, I shall be . . . ashamed," he shrilled.
> "You needn't have said that to me, father," said his son, smiling.

This passage indicates that the Japanese and Western cultures valued valor more than one's life or the lives of one's children. From an evolutionary perspective, one may argue that such a culture goes against human nature. However, when a potential enemy belonged to such a culture, a country needed to cultivate the same kind of social norm to have a chance at defeating the enemy on the battlefield.

Despite the country's chaotic politics and stagnating economy, the sense of national shame and Chinese dignity surged in the new era of the Republic of China. The New Cultural Movement was possibly the most important reason for this. However, there was another reason: the establishment of the republic brought more democracy into China, however symbolically, which greatly enhanced the awareness of the Chinese that everyone in China should be equal and not treated as subhuman by foreigners in their own motherland. As a result, the Chinese became more sensitive to the overbearing and bullying attitudes of foreigners,[3] which changed the Chinese culture and toughened the country's national character over time.

The May Fourth Movement in 1919 is often considered a milestone of the New Cultural Movement. It was a public demonstration of Chinese students and intellectuals that directly aimed to obtain more benefits for China via international negotiation. Although street demonstrations have become commonplace, in the 1910s, such a form of fighting for China's interest was something new, at least for the Chinese. In ancient times, a demonstration against a nomadic tribe's incursion would have been considered ridiculous. The international environment underlying this street demonstration and important historical event should be clarified.

The beginning of the 20th century saw a rise of "moralism" or a sense of justice in the international environment, which was reflected in at least two ways. First, in 1917, the Bolsheviks led by Vladimir Lenin overthrew the imperial autocracy of Russia and established a communist region that later became the Soviet Union. In terms of its ideology, communism strongly promotes the social and economic equality of every individual in the world. The Soviet Union ostensibly forfeited all of its privileges in China that Russia obtained through "unequal treaties." Second, the United States was growing into a major world power. Because it consisted of migrants from around the world, the spiritual foundation for its establishment as a nation was the commonality of race. Its core value was the essence of Christianity and the equality of different races, at least relative to other Western powers. Against such a background, in January 1918, United States President Woodrow Wilson put forward the principle of "Fourteen Points," which included the following points in particular:[4]

- A general association of nations must be formed under specific covenants for the purpose of affording mutual guarantees of political independence and territorial integrity to great and small states alike.
- A free, open-minded, and absolutely impartial adjustment of all colonial claims, based upon a strict observance of the principle that in determining all such questions of sovereignty the interests of the populations concerned must have equal weight with the equitable claims of the government whose title is to be determined.

Indeed, the United States was charitable to China. For example, it used two thirds of the war indemnity it received from China during the Boxer Rebellion to construct a major university in China (Tsinghua University) and offer scholarship to Chinese students to study in the United States. Several other Western countries including Britain, France, and Belgium quickly followed suit in sponsoring Chinese students to study in their countries.

In parallel to this rise of moralism, the form of international warfare changed fundamentally during World War I, a war fought between two large groups of nations rather than two individual countries. At least to some extent, the alliances were formed based on ideologies, and it was reasonable to expect that the United States would be on the side of the countries that were bullied by stronger nations. Many Chinese intellectuals made this observation, and felt that the Chinese government could have taken a tougher stance against the oppression of foreign powers.

The May Fourth Movement broke out on May 4, 1919, representing an important milestone of China's rising nationalism and the progress of the New Culture Movement. This cultural and political movement was triggered by an event that occurred immediately after World War I. In simple terms, World War I was a major war between two alliances: the Allied (Entente) and Central Powers. The former included Britain, France, the United States, and Japan, and the latter included Germany and the former Austria–Hungary Empire. During the later stages of the war, China joined the Allied Powers by declaring war on Germany in 1917. China initially offered to send 40,000 soldiers to France. France and Great Britain rejected the offer, but found that China could contribute in another way: by sending laborers to Europe. Thus, China sent about 100,000 laborers to France and other European countries, which helped the soldiers of other Allied Power countries fight. In November 1918, the war ended in a total victory for the Allied Powers.

Before World War I, Germany enjoyed many economic privileges in China's Shandong Province, especially the Kiautschou Bay concession. After the war, China expected to take these privileges back. However, the peace treaty proposed after the war, i.e., the Versailles Treaty of April 1919, awarded Germany's rights in Shandong Province to Japan. This proposal might have stemmed from two factors. First, Japan launched its military campaign against Germany in Shandong. Although the scale of the military operation was relatively small, it led to some Japanese troop casualties, which might have influenced the Allied Powers to think that Japan made much more of a contribution to the war than China. Second, Japanese forces occupied the areas of Shandong where Germany troops were stationed. Thus, the Allied Powers might have thought it would be difficult to request the Japanese troops to retreat.

Many Chinese were furious over this outcome, which triggered the historical event of the May Fourth Movement. On the afternoon of May 4, 1919, 3,000 university students marched from their campuses in Tiananmen Square, shouting patriotic slogans. They denounced the Chinese government's weakness, and called for Chinese delegates in Paris not to sign the Versailles Treaty. They also burned the residence of a major Chinese official whom they believed was collaborating with the Japanese. The Chinese government quelled this demonstration and arrested a number of student protesters.

Although the May Fourth Movement did not appear to be a major event given the size of China, it had a profound spiritual effect. It was an outcome of rising Chinese nationalism and an increasing deviation from Confucianism, and it reinforced these two trends in the country. Further, it gave birth to the Chinese Communist Party (CCP).

The CCP was established in China in 1921 with the secret help of the Soviet Union. One of its co-founders was Chen Duxiu. As described earlier in this chapter, Chen Duxiu was a prominent leader of the New Culture Movement, and realized that a new culture had to be introduced in China to turn its people into brave fighters and unselfish government officials. Chen found this culture in communism. For example, the "International Anthem of International Communist Movement" featured the following opening lyrics:

Stand up, damned of the Earth
Stand up, prisoners of starvation
Reason thunders in its volcano
This is the eruption of the end.
Of the past let us make a clean slate
Enslaved masses, stand up, stand up.
The world is about to change its foundation
We are nothing, let us be all.
This is the final struggle
Let us group together, and tomorrow
The Internationale
Will be the human race.

Although the "International Anthem" mainly captured the poor's struggle against the rich, it championed a strong combative spirit against any bully, including oppressive foreign powers.

Receiving financial support and guidance from the Soviet-controlled Comintern, the CCP was founded in Shanghai in 1921. Comintern is an international communist organization that was established in Moscow in 1919 with the following aim: "by all available means, including armed force, for the overthrow of the international bourgeoisie and for the creation of an international Soviet republic as a transition stage to the complete abolition of the State."[5] Its establishment was perfectly consistent with the principles of Marxism. For example, according to "The Communist Manifesto," "the working class has no country. Proletarians of all countries, unite!" Indeed, China was a weak country that desperately needed help from foreign powers. Thus, many Chinese intellectuals considered the Soviet Union, a country founded on the ideology of communism, a natural source of potential help.

Notes

1 See, e.g., Bickers and Wasserstrom (1995). A "No dogs and Chinese allowed" sign appeared in Bruce Lee's film Fist of Fury.
2 https://www.milestonedocuments.com/documents/view/chen-duxiu-our-final-awakening/text
3 For example, the signs reading "No Chinese or dogs allowed" in locations reserved exclusively for Westerners became extremely offensive to the Chinese.
4 See, e.g., https://www.mtholyoke.edu/acad/intrel/doc31.htm.
5 http://en.wikipedia.org/wiki/Comintern

Part VI

Japanese atrocities and the transformation of the Chinese personality

19 Japan's invasion of Manchuria

Japanese troops invaded Manchuria in 1931. Why did it engage in such a large-scale invasion? Where did the Japanese soldiers suddenly come from? Answering these questions requires consideration of the Russo–Japanese War.

The Russo–Japanese War took place between February 1904 and September 1905, in large part due to the Russian invasion of Manchuria during the Boxer Rebellion. In 1900, 100,000 Russian troops invaded Manchuria. The Qing government sent its elite troops, the Manchu bannermen, to fight against the Russian invasion. Although the Qing troops fought bravely, the Russian troops possessed much better weapons and killed most of the Manchu bannermen in battle. Moreover, the Russian soldiers looted many villages, committed atrocities against Chinese civilians, and burned down their houses. The Russian troops then occupied Manchuria without further effective resistance from the Chinese.

However, Russia's major rival at the time was not China but Japan. Russia and Japan were both interested in the areas of Manchuria and Korea. In 1903, Japan tried to make a deal with Russia to co-occupy (i.e., "dominate") Korea and Manchuria, respectively. However, Russia rejected the offer.

Failing to reach an agreement, Japan went to war with Russia, which might have underestimated the strength of the Japanese army. The main battlefields comprised the area around the Liaodong Peninsula and the city of Shenyang in southern Manchuria. The fighting was fierce and large in scale, and both sides suffered huge losses. An estimated 34,000–52,623 Russia military members died, and 74,369 Russian soldiers were taken captive. In contrast, Japan saw military deaths totaling 59,000.[1] However, very few Japanese soldiers were captured, as most adhered to the samurai code.

Japan secured a complete victory overall. The Russo–Japanese War ended with the Treaty of Portsmouth, signed by Japan and Russia on September 5, 1905. The treaty included the following main clauses: Russia ceded the southern half of Sakhalin Island to Japan, turned over its leases of Port Arthur and the Liaodong Peninsula to Japan, and withdrew its troops from Manchuria. Thus, in a sense, China was a beneficiary of the Russo–Japanese War. However, despite the material gains it created for the country, the war is considered a national disgrace in China. Most Chinese feel humiliated that a war between two foreign countries was fought on Chinese soil and resulted in Chinese civilian casualties.

The Russo–Japanese War had a number of significant long-term consequences. First, Russia lost much of its international esteem. Before the war, Russia was considered one of the most formidable countries. Its army was the largest in the world and was equipped with advanced weapons. After the war, Russia was looked down upon by many Western powers, particularly Germany and the Austria–Hungary Empire. These European countries came to believe that the Russian army was weak. As a result, a small conflict led the Austria–Hungary Empire to launch a military attack against Russian ally Serbia, triggering World War I. Second, the Russian people were humiliated by the defeat, and consequently the Russian emperor lost much of his domestic prestige. Many Russian people could not get over the humiliation and discontent for a long time, and this became an important reason for the success of the Communist Revolution in Russia in 1917.

Finally, although Russia ceded the southern half of Sakhalin Island to Japan, the benefits that Japan received from the treaty did not meet the expectations of most Japanese. Indeed, Japan gained much more from its victory over China in the First Sino–Japanese War. The Japanese public had expected that Japan would receive at least all of Sakhalin Island and be paid a large war indemnity. However, the Japanese populace might not have been aware of the essential difference between the two wars. In the First Sino–Japanese War, the Chinese troops were no match for the Japanese troops, and the Qing government knew that prolonging the war would only lead to many more Chinese casualties and more humiliating defeats. However, in the Russo–Japanese War, the Russian and Japanese troops were much more evenly matched. Moreover, Russia was a large country and had many more troops available to send from Europe to Manchuria to continue the war and ultimately defeat Japan. In fact, Russian Emperor Tsar Nicholas II decided to negotiate peace mainly to focus on dealing with domestic matters such as social unrest.

Japan's victory in the Russo–Japanese War instilled a much greater sense of nationalism in the Japanese. At this new zenith of Japanese national pride, the preceding reasoning would have been very unpopular among the Japanese public in spite of its accuracy. Consequently, many Japanese were frustrated and felt bitter about the Treaty of Portsmouth, which was negotiated under the mediation of American President Theodore Roosevelt at the Portsmouth Naval Shipyard in Kittery, Maine, in the United States. Some Japanese were angrily suspicious of the United States' show of favoritism for Russia. Their dissatisfaction and frustration were important reasons behind Japan's decision to officially annex Korea in 1910. Out of possible concern over the anger and bitterness of the Japanese public and possibly to remedy Japan's dissatisfaction with the Treaty of Portsmouth, the Western powers protested little against the brutal annexation.

Japan's victory in the Russo–Japanese War and annexation of Korea boosted its sense of nationalism and the confidence of the Imperial Japanese Army. Japan's next goal was the conquest of northeast China, namely Manchuria. Manchuria was a convenient goal for Japan because a large Japanese troop, the Kwantung army, had already been stationed there for a long time.

One legacy of the Russo–Japanese War was that Japan received the Kwantung Leased Territory and areas adjacent to the South Manchurian Railway from Russia. The Kwantung Leased Territory was an area in the southern part of the Liaodong Peninsula in Manchuria. The South Manchurian Railway ran through the largest city of Manchuria Shenyang (referred to as Mukden in Japan at the time) to the major city of Changchun, and the land on the two sides of the railway tracks was also leased as territory to Japan. The Kwantung army was established for the proclaimed purpose of defending these territories. However, the Kwantung army grew increasingly tempted to take over the entire territory of Manchuria.

Zhang Zuolin had been the warlord of Manchuria since 1916. He realized that the Kwantung army was his most important neighbor, and he had a good relationship with Japan. With the support and military assistance of the Kwantung army, Zhang's army became increasingly stronger and defeated the armies of other warlords in several large-scale civil wars. Zhang's power became increasingly consolidated and he became the supreme ruler and *de facto* King of Manchuria. Moreover, in June 1926, Zhang's army captured Beijing, and soon afterward several other warlords supported him to become the Grand Marshal of the Republic of China, assuming the power of the president.

However, the Kwantung army grew discontented with Zhang Zuolin. The Japanese felt that Zhang was becoming arrogant toward them, and ultimately lost hope of controlling Manchuria through him. Therefore, the Kwantung army decided to take over Manchuria via straightforward invasion. To minimize the cost of the invasion, the Japanese chose to kill Zhang Zuolin. Indeed, as Zhang Zuolin had been the only absolute dictator of the Manchurian army for many years, he was by far the most effective military leader of the Chinese troops in northeast China. Without his leadership, the Chinese officers and soldiers would have been much less well organized in the potential Japanese invasion and might not have had the determination to fight against the formidable Kwantung army in the first place.

On June 3, 1928, Zhang Zuolin took a train from Beijing to Shenyang. When his train arrived at the outskirts of Shenyang, a bomb exploded on the rail track underneath the train and killed Zhang. About two decades later, it was revealed that Colonel Komoto Daisaku of the Kwantung army planted the bomb.

Zhang's death was a devastating blow to the Manchurian army and was kept secret for two weeks. (In fact, Zhang Zuolin's official date of death was June 21, 1928, 18 days after his actual death.) This was done to decrease the likelihood of instability and insurrection within the Manchurian army. The transition of power was peaceful. Zhang Zuolin's eldest son and designated successor, Zhang Xueliang, succeeded the position of the supreme ruler of Manchuria.

Despite the lack of hard evidence, everyone believed that Zhang Zuolin was killed as the result of a plot concocted by the Kwantung army. It was not hard for Zhang Xueliang to figure out the motive for the plot. Out of both his hatred of the Japanese for murdering his father and the fear of a potential invasion of the Kwantung army into Manchuria, Zhang Xueliang made a decision that shocked China: he surrendered to the Kuomintang government in Nanjing.

Shortly before Zhang Zuolin's death, the National Revolutionary Army under the command of Chiang Kai-shek approached Beijing, forcing China's official central government to surrender and dissolve. The next goal of the National Revolutionary Army was the expedition toward Manchuria. Japan had long supported Manchuria's *de facto* independence from China, and hence was the most likely resource to offer help upon request. The National Revolutionary Army might not have been able to defeat the Manchurian army if the latter had strong support from the Kwantung army.

In retrospect, if Zhang Zuolin had not been killed, the Manchurian and Kwantung armies would have probably formed a strong alliance. Such an alliance would have increased Zhang Zuolin's dependence on Japan and put Manchuria at greater risk of being taken over by Japan. However, his concern for wealth and status might have outweighed his patriotism. In fact, Zhang Zuolin accumulated a large amount of wealth and built a chateau-style home. He had at least five formal wives and many children, all of whom led luxurious lives. A defeat at the hands of the National Revolutionary Army would have probably robbed him and his family members of their extravagant lifestyles.

However, forming such an alliance was not an option for Zhang Xueliang. First, he felt an overwhelming hatred for the Japanese for killing his father. Second, an alliance with Japan would have given many officers of the Manchurian army a good justification to revolt against him. The officers would have rightfully accused Zhang Xueliang of not being filial toward his father, to whom the officers claimed a strong loyalty. Thus, Zhang Xueliang's only choice was to seek the help and support of the Kuomintang and National Revolutionary Army.

Although Manchuria under Zhang Zuolin's rule was close to an independent state, it was nominally a part of the Republic of China and had flown its banner for years. Kuomintang established a new government and replaced the old national banner with a new flag of the Kuomintang, which it has used since 1917.

On July 1, 1928, only one week after Zhang Zuolin's official date of death, Zhang Xueliang announced that he had agreed to the reunification between Manchuria and the rest of China. A representative from the Kwantung army informed Zhang Zuolin that Japan was not happy with his announcement and asked him to reconsider his decision. Zhang rejected the demand. On December 29, 1928, Zhang Xueliang announced an important gesture of the unification: the old official national flag would be replaced with the flag of the Kuomintang, indicating his acceptance of Manchuria as an official jurisdiction of the Nationalist Government of China.

This move did not deter Japan from invading Manchuria. The Kwantung army believed for good reason that it could defeat the Manchurian army easily regardless of whether it had the help and support of the Kuomintang government. The Kwantung army only needed an excuse for the planned invasion. On September 18, 1931, an explosion occurred close to a railroad owned by

Japan's South Manchuria Railway near Shenyang. This explosion, of course, was a plot of the Kwantung army. The Japanese army immediately accused Chinese dissidents of the railway sabotage, and a large-scale invasion of the Kwantung army into Manchuria ensued.

The Chinese troops almost permitted the Japanese invasion based mainly on the order of the Kuomintang government. Chiang Kai-shek explained that if the Chinese forces fought back, a war would be waged between China and Japan that China would surely lose, and China would have to cede territory to Japan. However, if China did not offer any resistance, the international community would have deemed the Japanese occupation of Manchuria "inappropriate," and Japan would have had to withdraw its troops from Manchuria under international pressure. Although Chiang's explanation has always angered many Chinese, it makes a lot of sense in retrospect. Despite the accusation that Chiang was a traitor to China, the policy of not resisting the Japanese army was indeed a very clever strategy. In retrospect, if China had refrained from entering into military conflicts with Japan in 1894 and the First Sino–Japanese War never happened, the Qing Dynasty would not have lost the territory of Taiwan to the Japanese empire.

Note

1 Dumas and Vedel-Petersen (1923).

20 Japanese rule of Manchuria
Why was it a success?

Soon after Japan's occupation of Manchuria, it established the puppet state of Manchukuo (meaning the Manchu State) on February 18, 1932. To make it appear more legitimate, Japan installed the last emperor of the Qing Dynasty, Pu-Yi, as the Head of State and Emperor of Manchukuo. Manchukuo was governed as a constitutional monarchy, meaning it was administered by the prime minister and the ministers of the state cabinet. However, the Chinese ministers and Pu-Yi were dummy figures. In a documentary film, one senior Japanese official likens the relationship between Manchukuo and Japan to the relationship between the moon and earth, respectively. If the moon (Manchukuo) intended to deviate from its trajectory, it would be destroyed by its own choice.

The Japanese military officials of the Kwantung army were the *de facto* rulers of Manchukuo. Moreover, a peculiar system was designed and implemented in the state's government structure: many vice-ministers of the state cabinet were Japanese and held real government power. Similar to the Japanese annexation of Korea in 1910, this structure helped pave the way for the Japanese annexation of Manchuria when the time was right.

Most of Zhang Xueliang's army followed Chiang Kai-shek's order to retreat out of Manchuria. However, a small fraction led by General Ma Zhanshan decided to disobey the order. Ma commanded 20,000 Chinese troops and engaged in fierce battles with the Kwantung army. However, the Japanese troops, who were armed with artillery and tanks and received close air support, had strong advantages over Ma's troops. One Japanese soldier died for every ten of Ma's soldiers. After a few battles, Ma realized that further resistance was futile and agreed to defect to Manchukuo to save the lives of the surviving soldiers in his army. However, only four months after the defection, Ma rejoined the rebel forces.[1]

One must admit that the Japanese rule of Manchuria, or Manchukuo, was a remarkable success. There are a number of indicators to this effect.[2] First, the population size of Manchuria was 30 million people in 1931, and increased to about 50 million people in 1941. In other words, 10 years after the Japanese occupation, the population in Manchukuo had increased by about 67 percent, indicating that Manchuria attracted considerable migration from other parts of China during the period. Second, the economic growth of Manchukuo was nothing less than a miracle. In 1931, immediately before the Japanese occupation, Manchuria's only industry was the Shenyang Arsenal, which was unsurprisingly owned by the warlord Zhang Xueliang. After the Kwantung army occupied Manchuria, Japanese investment flooded into the area, which in turn encouraged local investments that led to spectacular growth in the area. In 1941, the total industrial output in Manchuria already exceeded that of Japan, whose population size was 40 percent larger. Third, through the channel of the Manchukuo government, the Japanese government invested heavily in Manchuria's public infrastructure. For example, in 1945, Manchuria contained 11,479 kilometers of railway. In contrast, the total length of railway in China totaled only 22,000 kilometers in 1949. Fourth, a large number of the cities in Manchuria were modernized during the Japanese occupation. In 1931, the urban population accounted for 11.5 percent of the total population. In 1942, this figure jumped to 23.8 percent. Fifth, the Manchukuo government expanded the public education system substantially. Moreover, Confucianism was made an important aspect of the curriculum.

All of these achievements provide hard evidence that the material welfare of the Chinese people in Manchuria improved considerably in the state of Manchukuo established by Japan. They would not have occurred if there had not been a relatively peaceful environment in Manchuria. Indeed, various groups of anti-Japanese forces known as the "Anti-Japanese United Army" (AJUA) was crushed quickly by the joint forces of the Kwantung army and the Chinese army of Manchukuo. In 1932, the number of AJUA troops was estimated at between 120,000 and 300,000. However, this number declined steadily to 50,000 in 1934, 40,000 in 1935, 30,000 in 1936, 20,000 in 1937, and 10,000 in 1938. From 1935, the AJUA was almost entirely under the leadership of the CCP. However, it was annulated entirely, with about 1,000 remaining members fortunate enough to escape to the Soviet Union.[3]

The anti-Japanese guerilla forces under the CCP were extremely successful in China after Japan's full-scale invasion in 1937. Why were their fates drastically different in Manchuria and in other parts of China? The answer is simple: the Japanese army committed atrocities and particularly mass-scale rape on Chinese civilians in other parts of China, but did not do so in Manchuria. The underlying reasons for this are explained in a later chapter. The policy difference led to drastically different outcomes for the Japanese invaders.

According to accurate statistics provided by the Yasukuni Shrine of Japan, the Japanese military deaths from 1937 to 1945 totaled 2,325,165. About 2.12 million of these deaths were Japanese soldiers. The remaining soldiers were recruits from Korea and Taiwan, which were part of Japan at the time. In a later chapter, a scientific calculation reveals that most of the Japanese casualties in World War II were inflicted by Chinese troops and guerilla forces operating under the CCP. The Imperial Japanese Army launched numerous massive attacks on the Chinese communist troops, and even implemented the notorious "kill all" policy in the regions where the Chinese communist army actively operated.

However, the number of Chinese communist troops continued to increase as a result.

In sharp contrast, the Japanese army in Manchuria was far more successful at quelling insurrections. This is surprising for several reasons. First, the AJUA was fairly strong at the beginning, at least compared with the CCP guerilla forces in other parts of China after Japan's invasion in 1937. The main AJUA force initially comprised former troops of Zhang Xueliang. They refused to follow the order to retreat out of Manchuria, mainly due to the grief and humiliation they had suffered over the loss of their homeland. They were quickly joined by patriotic students and peasants. Many bandits also joined the AJUA because the Japanese army was trying to annihilate them as well. Against this background, the CCP found a good opportunity to organize and command the AJUA, which was in need of such leadership. The CCP was indeed very successful at taking over the AJUA, and most of its high- and middle-ranking officers, including former bandits, soon agreed to join the party. Beginning in 1935, the AJUA was almost entirely under the leadership of the CCP, which included a number of brave and talented heroic figures such as Yang Jingyu and Zhao Shangzhi. Moreover, the group had a major advantage. Due to its geographical proximity to the Soviet Union, the AJUA received substantial aid that supported it not only for ideological reasons but also because a strong anti-Japanese force in Manchuria served as a "buffer" against a major potential enemy of the Soviets.

The AJUA made good use of the CCP's leadership, well-armed and well-trained former troops of Zhang Xueliang, Soviet weapons, and skills of former bandits in the mountains to secure a number of military victories. However, thanks to the assistance of the newly recruited army of the puppet state of Manchukuo, the Kwantung army prevailed within a few years.

The Japanese army did not commit atrocities against innocent civilians in Manchuria. Although the AJUA forces sometimes imposed heavy casualties on the Kwantung army, the Japanese did not vent their anger on Chinese civilians or allow their soldiers to rape Chinese women in compensation for the risks they took on the battlefields. As a result, the Manchurian civilians came to accept the Japanese as their rulers over a mere several years, partly because the "national character" of most Chinese people remained weak. In fact, the Japanese army ultimately caught Yang Jingyu due to the betrayal of several Chinese farmers.

In contrast to the policy of the Japanese army in other parts of China, the Kwantung army treated its Chinese captives well. Ma Zhanshan was such an example. The resistance forces organized by Ma resulted in heavy casualties for the Kwantung army. However, when Ma decided to surrender out of desperation, the Japanese army not only accepted his surrender but also treated Ma with dignity and materially rewarded him. Ma was immediately appointed as the Governor of Heilongjiang Province and a senior minister of Manchukuo. Ma rebelled again only four months after the defection, which was a major disappointment and humiliation for the Kwantung army. However, by that time the Kwantung army had established a reputation of treating defectors well, which was enormously beneficial for Japan and the puppet state of Manchukuo over the long run. Kim Il-Sung, who later became the leader and absolute dictator of North Korea, was an officer of the AJUA. In his autobiography, he recalls that Japanese military intelligence was very successful in alluring some members of the AJUA to defect to the Japanese side, which was detrimental to the AJUA. The reputation of the Japanese army for treating surrenders and captives well ultimately provided ample positive returns.

Finally, one important factor that made the rule of Manchukuo popular among the Chinese is that the occupation of the Kwantung army in Manchuria resulted in the near elimination or at least a drastic reduction of the bandits that had plagued the people there for decades. Prior to the Japanese invasion, there were an estimated 1,000 groups of bandits in Manchuria, a region of only about 30 million people. This means that every 3,000 persons (including children and the elderly) had to feed one bandit group regularly on average. There were no clear divisions among the different bandit groups in terms of the areas in which they conducted their criminal and violent activities, meaning that a household often faced a potential threat from several groups.

Relatively rich families were constantly fearful of bandit raids and robberies, and were afraid of being kidnapped and ransomed. Bandits often plundered whole villages or towns at once and raped women in the process. Every household was a potential victim, and innocent people were often killed. In Olson's (1993, 2000) terms, these "roving bandits" inflicted a tremendous amount of pain on the people of Manchuria.

The following example is meant to give readers an intuitive idea of the seriousness of the bandit problem in Manchuria. The warlord of Manchuria, Zhang Zuolin, joined a bandit gang at the age of 21. His initiation was quite dramatic: he was hunting in a mountain when he saw a seriously wounded bandit on horseback. He killed the bandit and took his horse, which provided him with a valuable possession that allowed him to join a bandit gang. The Chinese national hero Ma Zhanshan had also been a bandit before joining the army. Zhang Jinghui, who served as the Prime Minister of Manchukuo from May 1935 to August 1945, had also been a bandit in his early years.

When the Kwantung army occupied Manchuria, it launched massive attacks on the bandits, inducing most of them to join the AJUA. After the defeat of the AJUA, the Japanese army annihilated most of the bandits. From the perspective of many ordinary Chinese in Manchuria, their material living standards improved enormously after the establishment of Manchukuo. They were encouraged to work harder and invest more because they were no longer concerned that their hard-earned money would be stolen. They also worried much less about their personal safety because the murder, kidnap, and rape rates were lowered.

Although Manchukuo was a puppet state of Japan, most people there felt that they were ruled by the Chinese. Indeed, during the turmoil of the few decades after the collapse of the Qing Dynasty, many Chinese very much missed the benevolent rule of the Manchu emperors. Confucianism was highlighted in the education system, which brought dignity to the Chinese. Therefore, Manchukuo turned out to be very successful. In fact, the National Anthem of Manchukuo, the lyrics of which translate into English as follows,[4] aimed to persuade the Chinese in Manchuria to accept this new state from a Confucian perspective. (Note that of the following lyrics, "virtue and li" (etiquette), "family in order" and "state well-ruled" are all key components emphasized in Confucianism.)

> There is the new Manchuria on Earth,
> Manchuria is our new land.
> Let us make our country to be upright and free of sadness,
> with only love and no hate.
> Thirty million people, thirty million people,
> at ten times more we should still be free.
> With virtue and li, rectified am I;
> with family in order and with the state well-ruled, there are nothing more
>   I want.
> For now, may we assimilate with the world;
> for the future, may we follow the ways of the Heaven and Earth.

Notes

1 For this and other descriptions of Ma Zhanshan, see, e.g., Gunther (1942).
2 For more information, see Yamamuro (2006) and http://www.sznews.com/culture/content/2009–07/01/content_3879949.htm.
3 See, e.g., Hsu and Chang (1972).
4 http://en.wikipedia.org/wiki/National_Anthem_of_Manchukuo

21 The Second Sino–Japanese War

Japan had ambitions to expand its territory beyond Manchuria. Indeed, China's choice to not resist Japan's invasion into Manchuria could be interpreted as a clear signal that China believed its own army to be no match for the Japanese army. The war-like Japanese generals obviously received this signal as well. Consequently, Japan found it too tempting not to expand its territory to incorporate the entirety of China. At the very least, Japan was willing to engage in warfare to force China to accept the independence of Manchukuo.

The condemnation of the international community presented a minor concern for Japan's aim to conquer China. Thus, Japan began creating a series of "incidents" in China in 1931. During this period, China was frequently provoked by Japanese troops and engaged in small-scale military conflicts after which it always made compromises and lost its territories piece by piece, often annexing them to Manchukuo.

However, an incident that occurred on December 12, 1936, left Chiang Kai-shek no further room to tolerate Japan's continuous provocations. This was the "Xian Incident,"[1] in which two Chinese generals arrested Chiang Kai-shek in Xian for his weak response to the Japanese invasion. One of the generals was Zhang Xueliang, who is described in the previous chapter. The other was Yang Hucheng, who was the commander of Kuomintang's northwest army. Yang's headquarters were in Xian, which was close to the stronghold of the CCP's Red Army. Yang was positioned at the frontline, crusading against the communists as the general of the Kuomintang army.

Zhang did not fight against the Japanese invasion in Manchuria, and ultimately led a large army out of the region. In 1933, his army engaged in combat with Japanese troops in the First Battle of Hopei. The scale of the battle was small and the military loss of the Manchurian army was not significant. Chiang Kai-shek made good use of the Manchurian army by sending it to join forces with Yang to fight against the Chinese communist army.

Several years before, the Chinese communist army suffered a devastating defeat in southern China, leading to a massive military retreat known as the "Long March." It was an extremely difficult journey, as the Chinese communist troops were in constant pursuit of the Kuomintang army. To avoid the strong force of the enemy, the Red Army escaped in a circling retreat to the west and north. However, the route included the most difficult terrain of western China, and many soldiers died of hunger. About 90 percent of the soldiers had died when the Red Army finally reached its destination of Yan'an in Shanxi Province more than a year later.

In 1937, there were only about 30,000 Red Army soldiers in Yan'an. Although the joint forces of Yang and Zhang's armies outnumbered the Red Army at least 10 to 1, the Chinese communist troops easily defeated their offense. These defeats did not discourage Yang and Zhang. On the contrary, the two Kuomintang generals were so impressed with the Red Army's fighting capabilities that they believed China could defeat Japan if its forces joined the Kuomintang.

However, they knew that Chiang Kai-shek and most members of the Kuomintang would not share their belief. Indeed, the troops of the Kuomintang outnumbered the Chinese Red Army by about 100 to 1 and had much better weapons. Therefore, most of the Kuomintang generals and officials believed that there was no need to collaborate with the CCP.

The Xian Incident occurred against this background. Yang and Zhang arrested Chiang Kai-shek when he visited Xian in December 1936. They forced him to agree to the proposal for a united front between the Kuomintang and CCP against the Japanese invasion of China. Chiang agreed to their demands under coercion.

The Xian Incident benefited the Chinese communists greatly, as their assaults at the hands of the Kuomintang forces ceased afterward. Moreover, the event portrayed Chiang as a weak leader and even a traitor to the Chinese people. Indeed, in his diary, Chiang described his experience in the incident as the greatest humiliation of his life. Thus, there was little room for him to tolerate further provocation from Japan.

The Marco Polo Bridge Incident occurred in July 1937.[2] The Marco Polo Bridge (or Lugou Bridge) was located in the Fengtai District of Beijing. In 1937, the bridge served as a border between the Chinese and Japanese troops. Beginning in June 1937, Japanese troops carried out intensive exercises close to the bridge. This made the local Chinese government nervous, and it asked the Japanese to give advance notice for each exercise. The Japanese agreed.

On the night of July 7, 1937, Chinese troops noticed Japanese military actions taking place near the bridge. Because they had not received any notice from the Japanese that day, they did not know whether it was an assault or an exercise. Perhaps as a way of judging the possibilities, some Chinese soldiers fired a few ineffectual gunshots. The Japanese troops responded immediately and there was a brief exchange of fire between the two sides.

The next morning, the Chinese army received a call from the Japanese army, stating that a Japanese soldier was missing in action from the night before. The Japanese asked permission to send troops to search for the soldier in Wanping, an area on the Chinese side. The Chinese troops denied the request, but offered the services of Chinese troops stationed in Wanping to help the Japanese search for the missing soldier. They also mentioned that the search could be accompanied by a Japanese officer. The Japanese accepted the offer.

However, as the two sides discussed the search, a group of Japanese soldiers suddenly approached Wanping and tried to break the defenses on the Chinese side. The soldiers failed to break the defenses. However, the Japanese army issued an ultimatum two hours later.

In the late afternoon of July 8, 1937, two Japanese officers requested access to Wanping to conduct an investigation, and the Chinese side agreed. However, only 10 minutes after the officers entered Wanping, the Japanese troops opened fire at the Chinese side with machine guns and a group of Japanese soldiers attacked the Marco Polo Bridge. A small-scale battle ensued on the bridge, and the Chinese troops managed to withhold the offense of the Japanese army.

There was a temporary ceasefire between the two sides on July 9, 1937. However, the truce was quickly violated, and the military conflicts between the Chinese and Japanese troops escalated. Chiang Kai-shek then announced that the heightened tensions of the Marco Polo Bridge Incident were the "last straw" for the Kuomintang government. This outcome might have been exactly what the Japanese army was hoping for. A full-scale war broke out between China and Japan.

The first major battle was the Battle of Shanghai, which took place in Shanghai and its surrounding regions between August 13, 1937 and November 26, 1937.[3] About 300,000 Japanese troops and at least 600,000 Chinese troops participated in the battle. Although the Japanese army was outnumbered, the Japanese soldiers were much better trained and organized. Moreover, they were equipped with 3,000 airplanes and 300 tanks and supported by 130 naval ships. In contrast, the Chinese troops had only 250 airplanes and 16 tanks, and did not have any naval ships. The combined arms of the Japanese troops were much stronger.

The Battle of Shanghai lasted for more than three months and resulted in huge casualties for both sides. The exact numbers of casualties are not well counted and vary by source. The English version of Wikipedia provides the following information: the Chinese causalities numbered 333,500 with at least 200,000 deaths, and the Japanese causalities numbered 92,640 with 70,000 deaths. Thus, the casualty ratio between the Japanese and Chinese troops was about 1:3.6.

This ratio was a shock to the Japanese army. Indeed, during the First Sino–Japanese War in 1894, the casualty ratio between the Japanese and Chinese troops was about 1:10. In 1894, the Chinese and Japanese troops were equipped with similar arms. In 1937, Japan's military strength far exceeded that of China. The Qing court had much firmer control over the Chinese army in 1894 than Chiang had over the Chinese warlords in 1937. Moreover, Japan had a strong navy, and China had no armed forces on the sea.

Given these reasons, the only plausible explanation for the considerable improvement in the fighting capacity of the Chinese army is that the personality of the typical Chinese soldier became tougher during the Second Sino–Japanese War. Between 1894 and 1937, the Chinese people's sense of nationalism strengthened increasingly as foreign powers continued to humiliate and bully the country.

Although the fighting spirit of the Kuomintang troops was probably still significantly weaker than that of Japanese troops in 1937, the "cultural gap between
China and Japan" or more specifically the "the gap of the toughness of personality between the Chinese and Japanese" narrowed substantially between
1894 and 1937.

Nevertheless, the Kuomintang government knew that its army could not
match the Japanese army. Thus, Chiang Kai-shek's strategy was to seek sympathy
and help from the international community to force the Japanese troops out of
China. Chiang reasoned that international intervention would be more effective
if the Chinese troops could inflict greater casualties on the Japanese army. It
was a very clever strategy that ultimately worked in the early 1940s and helped
China win the Second Sino–Japanese War in 1945.

Nevertheless, this strategy was not effective in 1937. The foreign powers
merely paid China lip service, encouraging the country and issuing verbal con-
demnations of Japan. For example, in November 1937, Kliment Voroshilov, a
marshal of the Soviet Union, told Chinese delegates in Moscow that the Soviet
Union would definitely send troops to help China at the most critical moment
of the Sino–Japanese War. On November 30, 1937, Chiang Kai-shek sent a
telegram to Kliment Voroshilov and Stalin, expressing his gratitude and making
the following statement: "The most critical moment has already arrived, and
China did its best. The Chinese troops retreated to Nanjing, China's capital
city. China can now depend only on the strength of the Soviet Union. I am
eagerly expecting your wise decision to send Soviet troops to China." To the
dismay of Chiang and many Chinese, the Soviet Union did not want to engage
in a major war with Japan at the time, and never arrived to help China.

As the Japanese troops approached Nanjing, Chiang Kai-shek faced a difficult
decision. At the time, China was essentially controlled by a group of warlords,
with Chiang the strongest among them. However, Chiang lost 60 percent of
his elite troops at the Battle of Shanghai. In particular, out of the 25,000 junior
officers trained by the Whampoa Military Academy between 1929 and 1937,
about 10,000 were killed at the Battle of Shanghai.

Chiang Kai-shek knew that it would be futile to defend Nanjing. He was
convinced by the suggestion of his German advisers that China's best chance
at winning the war was to draw the Japanese army deep into China. This would
have forced the Japanese army to divide itself into smaller units to defend itself
in the many areas within China's vast territory. At that point, the Chinese troops
could have annihilated the groups of Japanese invaders one by one. Mao Zedong
shared this strategy in his well-known article entitled "On Protracted War."

According to the national interest and Chiang's personal interest, it made
sense not to defend Nanjing. If Chiang had used the remainder of his elite
troops to defend Nanjing, they would have probably been annihilated in the
capital city, resulting in a devastating loss to the Chinese army. Moreover, Chiang
would not have been able to obtain sufficient military support to remain supreme
leader of China if he had lost the elite troops that would have controlled the
other warlords. This would have led to a loss of the central government and

hence chaos in China. Thus, Chiang decided to abandon Nanjing as China's capital, and many people evacuated the city in addition to some important facilities.

However, Chiang could not consider the option of not defending Nanjing at all. If he had chosen to do so, he would have been portrayed as a coward and even as a traitor by the media and particularly CCP propaganda. Thus, he required some troops to defend Nanjing so that he could claim the city had been defended before being abandoned. He ultimately decided to assign a relatively small number of troops to defend Nanjing. The approaching Japanese troops numbered 240,000 men. By some estimates, only about 60,000 Chinese troops were left to defend Nanjing. These soldiers knew before the battle began that their defense was simply for show.

The battle of Nanjing began on October 9, 1937. After only a few days, the confidence of the Chinese troops began to crumble. Some troops began fleeing conspicuously from the most heated battlefields and simply refused to obey the orders from senior officers to stay in their combat positions. In their panic, some soldiers robbed civilians of their clothes so that they could escape in disguise.

On December 13, 1937, Nanjing fell to the Imperial Japanese Army. The conquest of the capital city was immediately followed by the Nanjing Massacre,[4] which shocked the world. Japanese troops ruthlessly killed an estimated 200,000–300,000 civilians and unarmed soldiers and raped 20,000 women. As the next chapter explains, these atrocities were a main reason why Japan lost the war, as they encouraged the participation of the United States. (As Japan was convinced that the United States would join the war in any case, its attack on Pearl Harbor was simply a preemptive attempt at disabling the country's efforts.)

Japan's motivations for engaging in the Nanjing Massacre are not entirely clear, and are discussed at greater length in the next chapter. One possibility is that the Japanese generals were inspired by the Yangzhou Massacre at the beginning of the Qing Dynasty, which defeated the determination of many Chinese to fight against the Manchus. However, the personality of the Chinese people had changed substantially since the First Opium War, and the humiliations from foreign countries had greatly aroused their nationalism.

Thus, from the perspective of the Japanese army, the Nanjing Massacre had mixed effects. Some Chinese soldiers were fearful of the cruelty of the Japanese troops, which was what the Japanese army had hoped for. This effect was significant in the short run. However, the massive killings and rapes committed in the Chinese capital humiliated the Chinese people and fueled their hatred of the Japanese invaders, making many Chinese troops more determined to fight. Indeed, from a long-run perspective, the Chinese personality reached a significantly higher level of toughness after the Nanjing Massacre. The two effects were demonstrated in the battles that immediately followed.

Between March 24 and April 7, 1938, the Battle of Taierzhuang broke out in the border areas of Shandong and Jiangsu Provinces.[5] This battle is usually considered to mark the largest victory of the Kuomintang army in the Second

Sino–Japanese War. According to the Kuomintang's claim, the military deaths of Chinese and Japanese troops totaled about 20,000 and 24,000, respectively. Moreover, it claimed that the Chinese troops destroyed 30 Japanese tanks. (It was a Chinese victory even according to the Japanese.) The Nanjing Massacre did not appear to deter some Chinese troops from fighting against the Japanese invasion. On the contrary, it might have significantly boosted the fighting spirit of some Chinese troops. China received much more international sympathy after the Nanjing Massacre. In particular, the Soviet Union sent its air force to help China in the form of a "Soviet Volunteer Group." This air force played an important role in fighting against the armored Japanese troops and boosted the confidence of the Chinese troops. By 1941, the Soviet Union had sent 885 aircrafts to China along with many excellent Soviet pilots. By the time of their withdrawal in 1941, 227 of these "volunteer" pilots had sacrificed their lives in China.

However, many generals of the Kuomintang army were indeed afraid of the combative capacity and ruthlessness of the Japanese troops, and this resulted in a man-made natural disaster in China. Despite a small-scale victory at the Battle of Taierzhuang, the Kuomintang army could not stop the rapid advance of the Imperial Japanese Army toward the Chinese hinterland. To prevent the Japanese troops from moving into western and southern China, Chiang Kai-shek issued a radical order to open up the dikes on the Yellow River near Zhengzhou, the capital city of present-day Henan Province. Consequently, waters flooded large areas of Henan, Anhui, and Jiangsu Provinces.

This event is often described as the "largest act of environmental warfare in history." It slowed down the Japanese troops' advances and might have even inflicted some military casualties. However, it also brought tremendous disaster to tens of millions of Chinese civilians. Even by the Kuomintang's own official estimation, 800,000 people immediately drowned in the floodwaters. Tens of millions of Chinese farmers lost their land, leading to widespread famines in those areas in the years to come. It is estimated that at least 3 million people starved due to the event.

Between June 11 and October 27, 1938, another large-scale battle waged during the Sino–Japanese War, the Battle of Wuhan, took place in the metropolitan city of Wuhan and its adjacent areas.[6] It was a very fierce battle that resulted in enormous casualties on both sides. As in many other battles, the exact number of casualties is debatable. The English version of Wikipedia reports that the Japanese and Chinese casualties numbered 107,000 and 225,000, respectively.[7] Hence, it concludes that the battle was a pyrrhic victory for Japan, and that the Chinese troop casualty ratio improved significantly over the Battle of Shanghai in 1937. The Battle of Changsha also took place in the capital city of Hunan Province between September 13 and October 8, 1939, where the Kuomintang army was victorious.[8] According to the Kuomintang's estimation, the Chinese and Japanese causalities numbered 40,000 and 30,000, respectively. In other words, the Chinese troop casualty ratio improved even further over the Battle of Wuhan.

After the Battles of Wuhan and Changsha, the Sino–Japanese War reached a stalemate. This outcome was precisely what China had hoped for. Because China's population size was many times larger than that of Japan, many more potential Chinese troops would have been able to gradually annihilate Japanese troops by dragging out the war in China's vast territory over a long period. This strategy was commended by American General Joseph Stilwell, who summarized it as "winning by outlasting."

In parallel with the brutal battles between the Kuomintang and Japanese imperial armies, the CCP organized tenacious resistance in areas that were already occupied by Japanese troops. In those occupied areas, the Japanese army could only effectively control cities, major towns, and to a lesser extent the railroads due to a lack of manpower. This left convenient room for the CCP to organize anti-Japanese forces in the country's vast rural areas. The horrendous atrocities committed by Japanese troops fueled many Chinese people's hatred of the Japanese, generating a large number of potential soldiers who would be fearless on the battlefields. Consequently, the amount of Chinese communist troops, who were usually guerrillas, mushroomed rapidly. They engaged in frequent harassment and sabotage operations in the occupied areas, and attacked the Japanese troops in guerrilla welfare. The communist guerrillas often fought the Japanese on the move. When the Japanese troops spread their forces out in search of the guerrillas, the guerrillas often ambushed or encircled small groups of Japanese troops and decimated them one by one. The historical documents related to Chinese guerrilla warfare against Japan are scarce, particularly those written in English. However, this form of warfare appeared to be very effective. For example, the Japanese troops in the occupied areas often implemented the notorious "Three Alls Policy" ("kill all, loot all, and burn all"), probably because they were suffering substantial losses as a result of the Chinese guerrilla warfare.

On December 8, 1941, to the great joy of China, the United States Congress declared war against Japan. The underlying reasons for the United States' participation in the war against Japan are not entirely clear, and are discussed in greater detail in the next chapter. However, the direct reason is well known: Japan attacked the United States navy in Pearl Harbor. The United Kingdom also declared war against Japan shortly afterward. Beginning in 1942, China and the United States formed a strong alliance against Japan that radically changed the course of the war.

In early June 1942, only six months after its country's declaration, the United States navy scored a decisive victory against the Japanese navy in the Battle of Midway. This battle inflicted tremendous damage on the Japanese fleet, and resulted in the sinking of four Japanese aircraft carriers. From that point forward, the United States navy dominated the Japanese navy.

Beginning in 1942, the United States considerably increased its military aid to the Kuomintang army, which increased its fighting capacity. Moreover, it substantially enhanced the confidence and morale of the Kuomintang troops. For example, in the Burma Campaign of 1944–1945, Chinese troops fought alongside United States and United Kingdom troops. Doing so allowed the Chinese to fight against Japanese troops on equal terms and sometimes even dominate them.

On August 9, 1945, the Soviet Union troops invaded Manchuria and soundly defeated Japan's Kwantung army. The battle lasted only about 10 days. The Soviet troops killed 83,737 Japanese soldiers. On August 6 and 9, 1945, the United States dropped two atomic bombs on the Japanese cities of Hiroshima and Nagasaki, respectively. These new weapons instantly killed about 240,000 Japanese, most of whom were civilians. Due at least in part to these two shocking events, Japan surrendered to the allied countries, including China, on August 15, 1945.

The number of Chinese civilian deaths in the Second Sino–Japanese War has been estimated to be at least 20 million. However, China recovered all of the territories it lost to Japan in the Treaty of Shimonoseki, including Taiwan and the Penghu group. Furthermore, Manchuria was restored to China.

Japan was on the losing side throughout the Pacific War, in which the Sino–Japanese War played a major role. In addition to losing Taiwan, the Penghu group, and Manchuria, Japan lost the south Sakhalin, Kuril Islands, and Korea. Moreover, almost all of the large Japanese cities were devastated as a result of the American army's air strikes.

Notes

1 See, e.g., Taylor (2009).
2 See, e.g., Dorn (1974).
3 See, e.g., Hsiung (1992).
4 See, e.g., Lu (2004).
5 See, e.g., Hsu and Chang (1972).
6 See, e.g., MacKinnon (2008).
7 http://en.wikipedia.org/wiki/Battle_of_Wuhan. It is based on a documentary entitled *The Battle of Wuhan*: http://www.youtube.com/watch?v=PGM-QARKzIg.
8 See, e.g., Van De Ven (2012).

22 Japanese atrocities and American participation in the Sino–Japanese War

Japan suffered a complete defeat in World War II, in large part due to the involvement of the United States. In fact, it has been argued that the United States played the leading role in the Pacific War. However, the following question has rarely been carefully addressed: why did the United States go to war with Japan?

The answer to this question appears to be straightforward. In December 1941, Japan attacked Pearl Harbor in the American state of Hawaii. However, this answer is overly simplistic. The more fundamental question is: why did the Japanese attack Pearl Harbor?

Indeed, if Japan were certain that the United States would take no military action otherwise, then it would have made no sense to attack Pearl Harbor. The only other explanation is that Japan intended to invade the United States while engaging in a full-scale war in China. Such an explanation is clearly absurd.

The Japanese rulers must have been convinced that the United States would go to war against Japan, and that their attack on Pearl Harbor was simply a preemptive strike. No matter how the Japanese government evaluated the potential military capacity of the United States, it should have been fully aware that America's retaliation would be very costly to Japan. Therefore, it should have received reliable information that the United States was likely to attack Japan, possibly through its complicated system of spies in America and around the world.

In fact, many people might have shared the Japanese military government's opinion of America's intentions. For example, well-known American journalist and author Edgar Snow (1905–1972) expressed this opinion at a conspicuous public occasion. In his biography of Snow, Hamilton (2003, p. 133) observes the following: "At a June 1941 book-signing party for The Battle for Asia in the Gimbel's Philadelphia store, Snow, puffing reflectively on his pipe, predicted the United States would be at war with Japan in four months, almost certainly within a year." This means that Snow predicted that the United States would go to war with Japan six months before the attack on Pearl Harbor.

Although there is no accounting for why Snow made such a prediction, he had good connections with the governments of many countries, which suggests that his prophecy was probably well founded. In fact, he became well known to the Western world because in the 1930s he was virtually the only American with good access to Chinese communist leaders. Snow also made other accurate predictions. For example, based on several sources,[1] the website *Your Dictionary* observes the following:[2] "The publication in 1937 of his book Red Star Over China quickly earned Snow the reputation of the Western world's expert on Communists in China. An international bestseller, Snow's prophetic account of the guerrilla movement and its leaders predicted that they would ultimately win the civil war. He reported with exuberance on the discipline and idealism of the insurgents; he recounted Mao's version of his pre-1936 career and of the Communist program for China; he suggested that Mao's policies enjoyed widespread support in the countryside; and he depicted the Communists as a formidable nationalist and anti-Japanese force, not the bandits claimed by Chiang Kai-shek. Another prophetic work, The Battle for Asia, published in 1941, predicted many of Japan's military victories and foresaw the challenge to the whole colonial system that would result from World War II."

It is reasonable to argue that Japan perceived that the United States would soon go to war against Japan. Some evidence supports this argument, and Wikipedia summarizes it as follows: "In an effort to discourage Japanese militarism, Western powers including Australia, the United States, Britain, and the Dutch government in exile, which controlled the petroleum-rich Dutch East Indies, stopped selling iron ore, steel and oil to Japan, denying it the raw materials needed to continue its activities in China and French Indochina. In Japan, the government and nationalists viewed these embargos as acts of aggression; imported oil made up about 80% of domestic consumption, without which Japan's economy, let alone its military, would grind to a halt. . . . Faced with a choice between economic collapse and withdrawal from its recent conquests (with its attendant loss of face), the Japanese Imperial General Headquarters began planning for a war with the western powers in April or May 1941."[3]

On April 13, 1941, the Soviet Union and Japan signed a peace treaty known as the Soviet–Japanese Neutrality Pact.[4] In particular, Article Two of the treaty states the following: "Should one of the Contracting Parties become the object of hostilities on the part of one or several third powers, the other Contracting Party will observe neutrality throughout the duration of the conflict." The Soviet Union was pleased with the pact because it expected that war with Nazi Germany was imminent, and it was trying to avoid a two-front war with Japan. Japan signed the pact because it noticed that its relationship with the United States was rapidly deteriorating and hence expected that a war between the two countries was probable (Paul, 1994). Thus, Japan was also eager to maintain a peaceful relationship with the Soviet Union, and this eagerness was reflected in Japanese Foreign Minister Yosuke Matsuoka's trip to Moscow to sign the treaty.

In April 1941, the same month when the peace treaty between the Soviet Union and Japan was signed and eight months before Japan attacked Pearl Harbor, the United States government ordered the withdrawal of its citizens from China. Due to a stalemate between the Japanese army and Kuomintang troops, it was not the most dangerous period of the Second Sino–Japanese War for Americans to be living in Chinese cities. Therefore, it was reasonable to infer from the American withdrawal that the United States government perceived a coming war with Japan.

If such was the case, why did the United States and other Western countries act in a way that would encourage such a war? This question becomes especially difficult to answer when the following three factors are considered.

First, although the United States was already an economic powerhouse and possibly the largest economy in the world at the time, its military strength remained relatively weak. This was partly due to its fortunate geographical location. The United States was separated from the military powers of Germany, Japan, and the Soviet Union by vast oceans, and its neighbors Canada and Mexico posed no serious military threat. In contrast, Japan was armed to the teeth, and its naval strength definitely surpassed that of the United States in terms of both the quantity and power of its warships and other weaponry. In addition, the Japanese soldiers were brainwashed by the spirit of Bushido, and the entire country was highly militaristic. Therefore, when the United States decided to go to war with Japan, the USA should have fully been aware that many of its young people would sacrifice their lives on the battlefields, and that defeat was not a foregone conclusion.

Second, Britain was fighting fiercely with Germany at the time. A large fraction of the elite class in the United States comprised white Anglo-Saxon Protestants (WASPs). Because the ancestors of the WASPs were located in Britain, the United States would have battled Germany outright if it decided to enter the war. Jewish people were influential in American politics, and were obviously concerned about the Jews who were being tortured in the concentration camps of Nazi Germany. Thus, they would have sided with the WASPs in lobbying the United States government to focus its attention on Europe rather than Asia based on America's decision to enter the war.

Third, although the Japanese soldiers in China were considered evil, Japan had not done anything to harm the interests of the United States. The United States did have one colony in Asia at the time: the Philippines. However, Japan did not attack the Philippines before the Pacific War broke out, and the colony was not crucial to the American national interest. Indeed, immediately after the end of World War II, the United States granted the Philippines independence in 1946.

Why was the United States so determined to fight against Japan? This chapter suggests that the heinous atrocities committed by the Japanese troops in China crossed a moral line for most of the American people, who were deeply influenced by the Christian culture. In other words, many Americans felt strongly that the Japanese soldiers' atrocious behavior in China was no longer tolerable.

During World War II, Japanese troops committed horrendous atrocities against Chinese civilians. It is difficult to arrive at an accurate number of the civilians who were killed or raped. However, it is safe to say that the murders and rapes committed by Japanese troops were beyond comparison with those committed during any other war of the last century. In this chapter, I argue that these war crimes were likely the most important reasons why the United States joined the fight against Japan.

The Nanjing Massacre, also known as the Rape of Nanjing, is the best-known example of Japanese atrocity in China. The stories of the massacre are still often told. The website *Gendercide.org* provides the following summation:

> On 5 December, even before Nanjing's fall, Prince Yasuhiko Asaka – uncle of Emperor Hirohito – issued a secret order to "Kill all captives." When Nanjing was taken, "All military-age men among the refugees were taken prisoner," whether or not they had actually been soldiers . . . At wharves along the Yangtze River, tens of thousands of these prisoners – up to 150,000 in all – were massacred in cold blood . . . Atrocious tortures were also inflicted on the captive men. "The Japanese not only disemboweled, decapitated, and dismembered victims but performed more excruciating varieties of torture. Throughout the city they nailed prisoners to wooden boards and ran over them with tanks, crucified them to trees and electrical posts, carved long strips of flesh from them, and used them for bayonet practice. At least one hundred men reportedly had their eyes gouged out and their noses and ears hacked off before being set on fire. Another group of two hundred Chinese soldiers and civilians were stripped naked, tied to columns and doors of a school, and then stabbed by zhuizi – special needles with handles on them – in hundreds of points along their bodies, including their mouths, throats, and eyes. . . ." [5]

The most notorious part of the Nanjing Massacre was perhaps the mass-scale rapes of Chinese women. Wikipedia provides the following description:[6]

> The International Military Tribunal for the Far East estimated that 20,000 women were raped, including infants and the elderly. A large portion of these rapes were systematized in a process where soldiers would search door-to-door for young girls, with many women taken captive and gang raped. The women were often killed immediately after being raped, often through explicit mutilation or by stabbing a bayonet, long stick of bamboo, or other objects into the vagina. Young children were not exempt from these atrocities, and were cut open to allow Japanese soldiers to rape them.
>
> On 19 December 1937, Reverend James M. McCallum wrote in his diary: "I know not where to end. Never I have heard or read such brutality. Rape! Rape! Rape! We estimate at least 1,000 cases a night, and many by day. In case of resistance or anything that seems like disapproval, there is a bayonet stab or a bullet . . . People are hysterical . . . Women are being carried off every morning, afternoon and evening. The whole Japanese army seems to be free to go and come as it pleases, and to do whatever it pleases."
>
> On March 7, 1938, Robert O. Wilson, a surgeon at the American-administered University Hospital in the Safety Zone, wrote in a letter to his family, "a conservative estimate of people slaughtered in cold blood is somewhere about 100,000,

including of course thousands of soldiers that had thrown down their arms". Here are two excerpts from his letters of 15 and 18 December 1937 to his family: "The slaughter of civilians is appalling. I could go on for pages telling of cases of rape and brutality almost beyond belief. Two bayoneted corpses are the only survivors of seven street cleaners who were sitting in their headquarters when Japanese soldiers came in without warning or reason and killed five of their number and wounded the two that found their way to the hospital."

"Let me recount some instances occurring in the last two days. Last night the house of one of the Chinese staff members of the university was broken into and two of the women, his relatives, were raped. Two girls, about 16, were raped to death in one of the refugee camps. In the University Middle School where there are 8,000 people the Japs came in ten times last night, over the wall, stole food, clothing, and raped until they were satisfied. They bayoneted one little boy of eight who have [sic] five bayonet wounds including one that penetrated his stomach, a portion of omentum was outside the abdomen. I think he will live."

In his diary kept during the aggression against the city and its occupation by the Imperial Japanese Army, the leader of the Safety Zone, John Rabe, wrote many comments about Japanese atrocities. For 17 December: "Two Japanese soldiers have climbed over the garden wall and are about to break into our house. When I appear they give the excuse that they saw two Chinese soldiers climb over the wall. When I show them my party badge, they return the same way. In one of the houses in the narrow street behind my garden wall, a woman was raped, and then wounded in the neck with a bayonet. I managed to get an ambulance so we can take her to Kulou Hospital . . . Last night up to 1,000 women and girls are said to have been raped, about 100 girls at Ginling College Girls alone. You hear nothing but rape. If husbands or brothers intervene, they're shot. What you hear and see on all sides is the brutality and bestiality of the Japanese soldiers."

There are also accounts of Japanese troops forcing families to commit acts of incest. Sons were forced to rape their mothers, fathers were forced to rape daughters. One pregnant woman who was gang-raped by Japanese soldiers gave birth only a few hours later; although the baby appeared to be physically unharmed (Robert B. Edgerton, *Warriors of the Rising Sun*). Monks who had declared a life of celibacy were also forced to rape women.

Of course, the war atrocities committed by the Japanese troops were not limited to Nanjing. For example, one can easily imagine that Japanese soldiers committed massive killings, rapes, and lootings in their implementation of the "Three Alls Policy." There have been numerous writings about those events, mostly in Chinese.

The atrocities committed by Japanese troops were so horrendous that they crossed the line of moral standards for many Americans, especially United States President Franklin D. Roosevelt. Because Nanjing was the capital city of China, people of all nationalities observed the massive killings and rapes. There were many Christian missionaries located in the rural areas of China, and the atrocities committed by Japanese soldiers in those areas did not escape their eyesight. One Internet article states the following:[7]

> The Japanese invasion of China (1937) was accompanied with horrendous atrocities against Chinese civilians. Reports from missionaries in China had a profound impact on American public opinion. Thus when President Roosevelt began a series of diplomatic efforts including embargoes to force Japan out of China, he received considerable support in still largely isolationist America.

Recall that during the Boxer Rebellion at the end of the 19th century, many Chinese people had a deep hatred for Christian missionaries in China. However, the same type of Christian missionaries ironically played a key role in persuading Americans to join the war against Japan only 40 years later, saving China to a large extent.

Why were Americans particularly angry and disgusted with the Japanese soldiers' atrocities? Americans had a moral standard that surpassed that of most other countries. The core value of American culture then and now has been Christianity, which has little tolerance for the murder of innocent civilians and mass-scale rape. One may be quick to point out that most European countries had also adopted Christianity. However, churches had often been a part of the political arena in Europe for hundreds of years, which might have marred the purity and essence of the Christianity they practiced to an extent. In contrast, the United States was a relatively new country, and its churches had rarely been used for political purposes and personal gain.

Moreover, that Americans had formed a large country with a federalist system might have reinforced their sense of justice and sympathy for the weak. From an economics perspective, a main benefit of forming a large country in the contemporary world is that a larger country enables people to better insure themselves against all kinds of disasters such as floods, droughts, and hurricanes.[8] However, when a disaster does inflict damage on a region, what guarantee is there that the people in other regions will be willing to help? Christianity provides a moral foundation for such a guarantee, along with a strong sense of justice and fairness.

The American people's strong sense of justice went beyond their national borders, which ultimately induced them to sacrifice the lives of many of their young men in the fight against Japan. For example, one article entitled "China's Emergence as a Great Power Began with FDR" states the following:[9] "It was the US refusal to recognize the Japanese conquest of Manchuria, as well as the former's desire to dominate China (along with US insistence that Japan pull its troops off the Asian mainland), that eventually placed the two countries on a collision course. This led to the dramatic events of December 1941 – and turned the Second World War into a truly global conflict."

President Franklin D. Roosevelt won a battle against the isolationists in the United States Congress on November 4, 1939, to revise the Neutrality Act, which allowed China to purchase weapons from the United States. In May

1940, the United States government launched a secret program that provided China with a modern air force. In particular, Roosevelt signed an "executive order" that encouraged some United States military pilots to resign and then participate in a covert operation of fighting against Japanese troops in China. This group of American "volunteers" later formed the well-known "Flying Tigers" led by Claire L. Chennault, and inflicted heavy casualties on the Imperial Japanese Army in China. Moreover, Japan witnessed the Americans' Pacific fleet move to Pearl Harbor, which it might have considered a signal that the United States was entering into the war.

The final trigger of the Pacific War was the so-called Hull note, which was a proposal that the Secretary of State of the USA, Cordell Hull, delivered to the Empire of Japan on November 26, 1941. It requested the complete withdrawal of Japanese troops from China, and in exchange for that the United States would end the oil embargo against Japan. However, for some mysterious reasons that are still not fully understood, this proposal was regarded as an ultimatum, and hence the Hull note was sometimes referred as Hull Ultimatum. For example, Steil (2013, p. 55) states: "the Japanese government made the decision to move forward with the Pearl Harbor strike after receiving the ultimatum."

The actions of the United States just described and many others not well documented by the history literature should have led Japan to infer (correctly or incorrectly) that the United States would sooner or later join forces with China in fighting against Japan. Based on this reasoning, Japan decided to launch a surprise attack on the United States with the hope of neutralizing its navy. Indeed, if the United States was going to enter into the war, it would have been unwise for Japan to wait for the Americans to attack first.

Japan's attack on Pearl Harbor occurred on the morning of December 7, 1941. Since then, a conspiracy theory has surfaced that President Roosevelt and high Unites States government officials had advance knowledge of the attack, and allowed it to happen on purpose to force the isolationists and those in the Congress who proposed a war with Germany to support the war against Japan. This theory may carry some validity, and has been supported by some evidence.[10] It has also been suggested that the Roosevelt administration took the precaution of removing its aircraft carriers, which were the most important pieces of the navy, from Pearl Harbor before the attack occurred, a rare coincidence if unintentional.

Regardless of whether these theories are true, they suggest that many people had been well aware that President Roosevelt and high United States government officials had a strong preference to engage in a major war with Japan. However, without the Pearl Harbor attack, many Americans would have been against such a war, which resulted in the deaths of hundreds of thousands of young American men. Most countries recognized that the Japanese navy possessed the most powerful fleet in the world at the time. The United States navy scored a decisive victory against the Japanese Imperial Navy at the Battle of Midway. However, luck had a great deal to do with the victory. The United States Central Intelligence Agency broke the Japanese code of telegraphs, allowing the Unites States navy to set up an ambush against the Japanese fleet.

However, the luck and effort involved in naval cryptology could not have been anticipated before the war. Furthermore, the higher priority of the United States was to help the United Kingdom and France fight against Nazi Germany. Many Americans believed that it would be unwise and risky for the United States to fight two major wars at the same time.

United Kingdom Prime Minister Winston Churchill flew to Washington, D.C., immediately after the Pearl Harbor attack. After passing along his condolences for the Americans who were killed and injured in the attack, Churchill immediately sought assurance from Roosevelt that the United States would continue to make the war with Nazi Germany its priority. Churchill made this request because he knew that most Americans, or at least their elites, would support it despite the attack from Japan.

However, a large proportion of Americans were furious at the Japanese troops' horrendous atrocities against Chinese civilians, and ultimately joined the Chinese and others to fight against the Japanese army. Their anger and disgust might have been important reasons why the United States used nuclear weapons against Japan. In one TV interview with an American pilot who bombed Japanese cities during the Pacific War, the pilot said that he had heard about an island in the Pacific Ocean where Japanese soldiers not only raped the native women but also mutilated them afterward. He said that he had felt no guilt at all when he dropped the bombs, which killed many Japanese civilians. Those hideous rapes and murders might have been the key factors that allowed the United States government to overcome its moral obstacles and drop two atomic bombs on two Japanese cities in 1945.

In summary, an unintended consequence of the Japanese atrocities in China was that they became the fundamental reason why the United States entered into the war against Japan. As such, they accounted for Japan's defeat, which was ensured by America's participation.

Notes

1 Farnsworth (1996), Hamilton (2003), and Thomas (1996).
2 http://biography.yourdictionary.com/edgar-snow
3 https://en.wikipedia.org/wiki/Pacific_War
4 http://www.ibiblio.org/pha/policy/1941/410413a.html
5 http://www.gendercide.org/case_nanking.html
6 http://en.wikipedia.org/wiki/Nanking_Massacre
7 http://histclo.com/country/other/china/chron/cc-miss.html
8 For example, see Asdrubali, Sorensen, and Yosha (1996).
9 http://www.rooseveltinstitute.org/new-roosevelt/china-s-emergence-great-power-began-fdr
10 See, e.g., Greaves (2010) and Sweeny (1946). More references can be found at http://en.wikipedia.org/wiki/Pearl_Harbor_advance-knowledge_conspiracy_theory.

23 Japanese atrocities and the growth of Chinese communist troops

Yukio Omata, a reporter for the Imperial Japanese Army, wrote a book entitled *Memoirs of a Japanese Army Reporter: The Nanjing Massacre*. One of the chapters of the book is titled "Hand Over the Girl!" It begins as follows: "A (Japanese) troop moved into a small town called Sanchanghe. The representatives of the town came to greet the troop, holding Japanese flags that had just been made. All of the Chinese soldiers fled, and the Japanese troop entered the town without firing a single shot. . . The captain of the Japanese troop hastily demanded that they 'needed girls.' A town representative replied, 'This town does not have prostitutes. But if you are fine with girls from ordinary families, we can find some in the nearby villages.' A few days later, about a dozen young girls were gathered to provide sexual services for the Japanese soldiers."[1]

The preceding passage was written by a Japanese reporter and mainly for Japanese readers. It describes the behavior of the Imperial Japanese Army in China as being quite civilized. Because the Chinese army did not resist the Japanese soldiers, the soldiers did not have to go door to door, raping all of the Chinese women in the town.

If the Chinese had shown resistance against the Japanese army, particularly if it resulted in severe Japanese troop casualties, the outcome would have been very different. The following is a passage from another article that describes the mass-scale rapes in Nanjing:[2]

Of all the hideous crimes committed by the Japanese, none were worse than those situations in which women, victims of the same killings as the men, were first forced to endure sexual assault and rape by the Japanese! Frequently, after being raped, the women suffered a cruel death at the hands of Japanese soldiers. "Sometimes the soldiers would use bayonets to slice off the women's breasts, revealing the pale white ribs inside their chests. Sometimes they would pierce their bayonets into the women's genitals and leave them crying bitterly on the roadside. Sometimes the Japanese took up wooden bats, hard reed rods, and even turnips, forced the implements into the women's vaginae, and violently beat them to death. Other soldiers stood by applauding the scene and laughing heartily." (Military Commission of the Kuomintang, Political Department: "A True Record of the Atrocities Committed by the Invading Japanese Army," compiled July 1938) . . .

It is impossible to list all the reams of documents regarding atrocities involving rape committed by the Japanese in Nanjing. But the most shocking materials are in the form of pictures taken by the Japanese themselves. Captured Japanese soldiers were caught red-handed with photographs of their female victims. . .

After raping the women of Nanjing, Japanese soldiers would often force them to lift up their dresses to reveal their genitals and to have photographs taken. Some particularly bestial soldiers shamelessly squatted beside the women who had undergone the most severe and humiliating abuse and forced their victims to pose for "group photographs." In one of the worst cases, a picture was found of an abused woman who was forced to use her own hands to reveal her genitals for the Japanese to photograph. . .

In fact, many of those photos can be easily found on the Internet, and continue to humiliate the Chinese even today. Nanjing was the capital of China, and the representatives of foreign countries often observed the Japanese soldiers' behavior. The atrocities were even worse in the remote countryside. For example, Chen (2004) conducted a comprehensive survey of the atrocities committed by the Japanese troops in Hunan Province, where the Japanese army suffered substantial casualties in several major battles. Chen's survey was based mainly on newspaper articles published in Hunan during the war. For example, he writes (2004, p. 72): "The only 'work' of the Japanese devils was searching for women. They went after women either in groups or alone, day and night, at any locations. . . They raped women of all types, irrespective of beauty and ugliness. Underage girls, old ladies in their eighties, the disabled . . . no one would be spared. Even pregnant women were targets of their sexual violence. When they caught a man, he would be ordered to help them look for women. Thus, even some of the women who fled to the mountains were found by Japanese soldiers."

Chen (2004) lists some examples as follows.

- A 20-year-old girl was raped by five Japanese soldiers. She could not move for several days afterwards.
- Six women in the Peng family were raped. Some were menstruating at the time, but were not spared. All of the men of the family were forced to drink the blood of the women's menstruation. When one of them refused, a Japanese soldier stabbed him and killed him immediately. The knife completely penetrated his chest, and the Japanese soldier had to place a foot on his chest to draw the bayonet from his body.
- The Yang family had three sons whose wives were gang-raped by nine Japanese soldiers. The father and eldest son asked the solders to stop and were immediately killed. The second eldest son became furious witnessing his wife being raped, and used a bench to knock the Japanese soldier who was raping his wife into unconsciousness. The soldiers then killed him and his younger brother, and burned the house to ashes.
- A young women of the Luo family had been married for about a year and had an infant boy. She was raped by Japanese soldiers. After the rape, the soldiers stabbed her vagina with a bayonet, killing her and covering the room with blood.

Chen's (2004) list goes on and on, as do other lists in numerous other books on the atrocities committed by the Japanese troops. In addition, Chen (2004) observes that when the Japanese soldiers raped Chinese women, they coerced their husbands into kneeling by their wives' sides to watch. These horrendous atrocities revolutionized the Chinese people's national character, especially for those Chinese who had directly experienced them. Faced with such unbearable shame and humiliation, the "personality" of the Chinese people changed fundamentally. The Chinese were no longer fearful of trouble, injury, or even death. Given the enormous loss of human dignity they had experienced, they did not much prefer being alive to being killed.

Indeed, Chen (2004) gives the following two examples of how a man chose to die after witnessing his loved ones being raped by Japanese soldiers.

- Gao Niansheng's parents were killed by the Japanese, and his wife was raped. His 16-year-old daughter was gang-raped, and a Japanese soldier penetrated her genitals with a bayonet and killed her. Gao was so ashamed and resentful that he committed suicide by drowning himself in a river.
- Li Baochang's mother, wife, and daughter were all caught by the Japanese soldiers, who raped them immediately. During the rape, Li took a gun from one soldier and killed six men before he was killed by additional soldiers.

Against this background, the CCP took the opportunity to expand its forces by leading and organizing Chinese people to fight against the Japanese invaders. Before the Second Sino–Japanese War broke out, the Red Army in northern Shaanxi had about 30,000 men. After the war broke out, a small part of the Red Army was left behind in northern Shaanxi, and the rest was split up and sent to the areas occupied by the Japanese. The Chinese who were bullied, humiliated, and tortured by Japanese troops were in desperate need of the leadership of the CCP, and the CCP was happy to organize them effectively in their fight against the Japanese. Such a mutual relationship is vividly illustrated by the following story about "trackers." I heard this story from Steven Cheung, who is arguably the best-known Chinese economist and has made significant contributions to the field of institutional economics.

The so-called trackers were those who helped people pull their boats upstream with a towrope for a living. Before the advent of steamships, a boat was often difficult to move upstream, especially when fully loaded. If the boat owner wanted to continue his voyage, he had to rely on the help of trackers. Trackers were well paid, but their job was very difficult. Pulling a boat forward usually required all of their strength. Anyone who observed them working knew exactly how hard the job was: trackers bent their bodies, carried thick ropes, and trudged forward with each step, occasionally vomiting blood due to fatigue and exhaustion.

Because pulling a boat against the current of a river was incredibly difficult, each boat often required more than one tracker. However, the trackers' selfishness often problematized their coordination. One tracker might have tried to take it easy, hoping that the efforts of the others would be sufficient to pull the boat forward. However, if every tracker had done the same, the boats would not have been towed. This is a typical "free rider" problem in economics: if an individual can enjoy a benefit accrued from a collective effort, he often has little incentive to exert an effort himself.

To resolve this "free rider" problem, the trackers adopted the following strategy: they hired a supervisor, who was delegated the right to beat those trackers whom he perceived as lazy or not working hard enough. The irony of this scenario is that the supervisor was essentially an employee hired to beat his bosses. The trackers used this strategy because they knew it was the only way to ensure that they would work efficiently, and therefore made all of the trackers better off. In reality, the presence of such a supervisor ensured that every tracker spent all of his strength and energy towing a boat. Consequently, although he was given the right to do so, the supervisor rarely needed to beat any tracker.

The pivotal role of the CCP in the organization of the anti-Japanese movement follows the same logic. Consider the simple example of five Chinese men, all of whom witnessed their wives being raped by Japanese soldiers. Deeply furious and humiliated, they sought revenge on the Japanese troops. However, successful revenge requires more than anger and hatred. If the men had attempted to fight against the Japanese army individually, they would have effectively been committing suicide. If they formed a coalition, they might have become a formidable force. How could the five men have coordinated themselves most efficiently in the battle against the Japanese? Although most of the Chinese deeply hated the Japanese soldiers, they also wanted to continue to live, implying that they might have preferred others to fight more bravely on the battlefield. In such circumstances, they needed a fair boss to discipline them into fighting bravely against the Japanese troops, just as the trackers demanded a fair supervisor. Moreover, they often demanded the best leaders.

In economic terms, the analysis here is similar to the analysis of the nature of a firm. The early chapters of this book introduce the Coase theorem and its extension, the political Coase theorem, which serves as the book's major theoretical foundation. In fact, Ronald Coase made another important contribution to economics: his analysis of "the nature of the firm." Coase (1937) argued that firms exist because using the market involves significant transaction costs. If the transaction costs were zero, individuals would not form partnerships, companies, or other business entities. Instead, they would trade bilaterally through contracts, and production would be carried on without any firm or organization involved. However, in reality, the transaction costs are almost never zero and are often substantial. They justify the existence of firms, which considerably save on transaction costs.

There are different types of transaction costs in business activities, such as search and information costs, bargaining costs, the costs of keeping trade secrets, and policing and enforcement costs. In military operations, many individuals have to perform tasks together and engage in complicated interactions. In such cases, the "transaction costs" among them are usually much higher. Thus, from an abstract and theoretical perspective, a military unit can be likened to a firm or an organization.

Coase (1937) emphasized the essential role of entrepreneurs in the organization of firms. He posited that holding other things constant, a firm tends to be larger if an entrepreneur can further decrease its organization and transaction costs. Moreover, this idea relates to social Darwinism in the sense that only the "fittest" entrepreneurs can survive in market competitions. The fiercer the market competition, the more important the competence of an entrepreneur.

Who were the best "military entrepreneurs" in the battles and struggle against the Imperial Japanese Army in China? The answer is clearly the CCP or Chinese Red Army, particularly in terms of guerilla warfare. There are a number of reasons why CCP members made for brave soldiers and good leaders of the masses, who deeply hated the Japanese invaders. First, these men joined the CCP in support of the ideology of fighting against oppression and "liberating the entire human race" rather than pursuing personal gains. Indeed, prior to 1937, the CCP was on the verge of annihilation. Hence, the remaining members of its troops usually shared a strong communist ideology. Second, the CCP had been a branch of Comintern, which effectively severed as a credible commitment to largely preventing any Chinese leader in CCP from pursuing personal gains. Third, most of the soldiers in the Chinese Red Army experienced many tough battles and survived the extremely arduous journey of the Long March. They were possibly the toughest soldiers in the world at the time, an important factor in leading new recruits in guerilla warfare. Indeed, if the leader of a guerilla troop is extremely brave and skilled at fighting, he may motivate his soldiers by example, which may be the best way to lead others. For example, in explaining the tenacity and effectiveness of German troops in World War II, Shils and Janowitz (1948, p. 286) emphasize the existence of "hard core" soldiers, who "placed a very high value on 'toughness'. . ."

Because the Chinese people faced very fierce and brutal enemies, they had no choice but to seek the most competent "military entrepreneurs." Regardless of whether they liked or hated communism, the CCP and Red Army become their only choices. Only the strong leadership of the CCP presented a chance of defeating the almighty Japanese army.

Moreover, just as an entrepreneur of one firm must develop good connections with those of others, the "military entrepreneurs" in different regions were interdependent. This gave the CCP a major advantage. As an organization, the CCP was highly efficient, and its members were highly disciplined. Discipline was highly emphasized in communist parties at the time, and the CCP was certainly no exception. For example, in a short and important speech entitled "An Essential Condition of the Bolsheviks' Success," Vladimir Lenin repeatedly emphasizes the role of "truly iron discipline in our Party . . . the iron discipline needed for the victory of the proletariat."[3] Such an emphasis was even reinforced by Joseph Stalin. In a short article entitled "The Foundations of Leninism," Stalin uses the term "iron discipline" 12 times.[4] In fact, Stalin's family name was Jughashvili. He changed it into Stalin, which translates to "man of steel" in Russian.[5] The discipline of the Soviet army was indeed as unforgiving as iron. For example, during the Battle of Moscow in World War II, about 8,000 Soviet soldiers were executed for perceived cowardice.[6]

Finally, from an international perspective, the CCP gave the Chinese people an intrinsic connection to the Soviet Union. At the time of the Japanese invasion, China was a weak country and many Chinese seriously doubted whether it could defeat Japan alone, particularly before the breakout of the Pacific War and the involvement of the United States. Against this background, the CCP, being a branch of Comintern, became an attractive feature to many Chinese. Indeed, when Japan invaded Manchuria in 1931, the CCP immediately declared war against Japan in the name of "the Soviet Republic of China." (Of course, such a gesture was not taken seriously by Japan, as the Chinese Red Army was in the middle of being surrounded and annihilated by the Kuomintang army.) The capital of the CCP was Yan'an (or Yenan) in Shaanxi Province, which attracted many patriotic young Chinese intellectuals. One of them described his feeling upon approaching the city as follows: "At last we saw the heights of Yenan city. We were so excited we wept. We cheered from our truck. . . . We started to sing the 'Internationale', and Russia's Motherland March."[7]

The combative power of the Chinese communist army is well illustrated by the Battle of Pingxingguan, which took place at Pingxingguan in Shanxi Province on September 25, 1937. In this battle, 6,000 Chinese communist troops led by Lin Biao annihilated about 1,000 Japanese troops. Moreover, the Chinese troops suffered smaller numbers of casualties despite the Japanese troops being equipped with much more advanced weaponry.

It seems that the Japanese army knew very well that the Chinese communist troops, which were renamed the "Eighth Route Army" and "New Fourth Army" in the Anti-Japanese War, were much tougher fighters than the Kuomintang army. In the 1990s, a Chinese man who studied in Japan, Fang Jun, interviewed a number of Japanese who had served as soldiers in the Sino–Japanese War. Based on the interviewers, Fang (1997) wrote a book entitled *The Devil Soldiers I Know Of.* The author asked one interviewee, a former Japanese soldier in China, about the enemies that Japanese troops feared the most. The former soldier identified the *Ming-Tuan*, a group of local peasants turned soldiers. He added that those people had a deep hatred for the Japanese because the Japanese soldiers might have killed their fathers and raped their wives, and that this hatred made them extremely brave. The former Japanese soldier also said that the Eighth Route Army of Chinese communist troops had much more combative power than the Kuomintang army. He said that the Japanese troops could easily distinguish the Eighth Route Army from the Kuomintang army at the beginning of a battle simply by listening to the gunfire. The Kuomintang army usually fired many shots to show off their good weapons. In contrast, the Eighth Route Army would not open fire until the Japanese troops approached within 150 meters.

The former soldier added that a Japanese troop of 2,000 soldiers would not have hesitated to attack a Kuomintang troop of 3,000 soldiers, and that there were plenty of examples of a small Japanese troop defeating a large Chinese troop. However, he observed that when a Japanese troop of 1,000 soldiers met an Eighth Route Army of 800 soldiers, the Japanese soldiers were often defeated and demoralized.

It should be emphasized that the Chinese communist troops mainly engaged in guerilla warfare against the Japanese army. Their main strategies were to annihilate the Japanese troops by striking them in an off-guard position and attacking their isolated garrisons. The details of the guerilla warfare were little documented, mainly because the guerilla soldiers usually tried to run away quickly after an ambush. Although only a few Japanese soldiers were usually killed or wounded per battle, their casualties were significant given their large numbers. (This is explained further in the next chapter.) The success of the Chinese communist troops was reflected by their enormous growth. In July 1937, when the Sino–Japanese War broke out, the Chinese communist army had only 30,000 soldiers. In 1945, by the time the Japanese surrendered, the communist army had 1.2 million soldiers and the CCP had a membership of 2.7 million people. (It should be noted that once a person joined the CCP, he or she was unable able to leave. Thus, joining the CCP was a large and risky commitment.)

The CCP was successful during the eight-year Anti-Japanese War for three main reasons. First, the heinous atrocities committed by the Japanese army generated immense hatred for the Japanese soldiers among the Chinese people, which in turn provided an infinite pool of potential soldiers for the Chinese communist army. One documentary film portrays a CCP soldier who was instructed to form a guerrilla troop in an area occupied by the Japanese army. He was initially shocked by the order because he was instructed to go alone. However, as soon as he arrived in the area, he realized that it would not be a problem. Despite being the only man with a single gun, he quickly recruited 80 young men within a few days. The young men demanded no financial compensation for the grave risks they were going to take. Their hatred of the Japanese soldiers was so tremendous that they were willing to risk their lives for a slim chance of exacting their wrath. The soldier summoned some local landlords and rich peasants and asked them to donate weapons. He again experienced no difficulty, and immediately received 40 guns as donations. The rich landlords had also been enormously humiliated by the Japanese soldiers who raped their wives and daughters. Because they were still relatively rich, they were not willing to become guerilla fighters, but were more than happy to devote weapons and their wealth to the cause of killing Japanese soldiers. Of course, the local people were happy to provide the new guerrilla troop with food and clothing.

In fact, many historians have wondered how the Chinese communists paid their guerilla fighters to risk their lives fighting against the Japanese under extremely harsh circumstances. Some even suspected that the communists at their headquarters in Yan'an engaged in considerable opium trafficking, and that their customers included Japanese merchants in China. For example, Hastings (2007, p. 413) states: "Mao and the Communists engaged in the opium trade. How else could they pay their troops? Nothing else that would grow in Yan'an was marketable. In such a situation, you do what you must."

This analysis is reasonable. Money was an important factor for motivating the Kuomintang troops even during the Battle of Taierzhuang, a source of pride for the Chinese. A recent television series about the Second Sino–Japanese War includes a scene between Li Zhongren (the commander-in-chief of the battle) and Major General Sun Lianzhong. Li asks Sun to form a squad to risk their lives in attacking the Japanese troops. Sun replies that he cannot. Li tells him that he will help, and immediately gives him 100,000 taels of silver.[8]

However, as the atrocities committed by the Japanese troops became increasingly horrendous, many Chinese fought for revenge rather than money. In fact, in most of the anti-Japanese endeavors, Chinese communists found that the soldiers did not require money as payment. Many soldiers' close relatives were killed and raped by Japanese troops. Their hatred and humiliation motivated them to join the Chinese communist guerilla forces without demanding any pecuniary payment. They hoped only for a chance, however slim, of taking revenge on the Japanese soldiers.

Second, communism was usually an attractive "religion" to the poor, oppressed, and bullied. The CCP has enormous capacities for political organization and propaganda. In particular, a system was designed in the basic army unit of the Chinese communist troops to enhance the soldiers' solidarity. Shils and Janowitz (1948) develop a theory of military effectiveness. They argue that an army is a social group, and that the soldiers' relationships within the company, i.e., their primary group, are of paramount importance in determining the degree of the soldiers' bravery and hence their combative power.

A "political commissar" system was designed to enhance the solidarity of primary groups of communist troops in both the Soviet Union and China. A political commissar (or political officer) is the political leader of a basic army unit of about 100 soldiers, and is responsible for the political education of communist ideologies, ensuring the loyalty of the troops to the CCP and their solidarity. A political commissar held a rank equal to that of the unit commander to whom he was attached.[9] For example, one Japanese study conducted in 1941 investigates the Sino–Japanese War and highlighted that "The most distinctive feature of the Communist Army . . . is the existence in each unit of propaganda agitators and organizers."[10]

Moreover, this propaganda was greatly facilitated by the atrocities committed by the Japanese troops. For example, one communist organization leaflet distributed in the county of Shansi in 1938 read as follows: "Comrades! Japan had invaded our Shansi, killed large numbers of our people, burned thousands of our houses, raped our women in countless numbers, robbed us of our food and wealth, tramped on the graves of our ancestors, forced our wives and children to flee . . . and made the joy of peace impossible. . . Everybody! Rise up and join a guerrilla self-defense unit! . . . Defend our anti-Japanese patriotic people's government!"[11]

Due to the superb organisation of the CCP, its guerilla soldiers were very brave and disciplined on the battlefield despite their lack of guns and ammunition. Over time, the anti-Japanese CCP guerrillas became a powerful force and kept growing. Many CCP guerrillas were killed in battle, but there were always more young Chinese men eager to join the guerrillas. In fact, it became a social norm at the time for every CCP guerrilla soldier to consider his gun as "his first life," meaning that he could never lose his gun as long as he was alive. The soldier considered his personal life as "his second life," meaning that it was less important than his gun. It was much easier to recruit a new guerrilla and replace him than to obtain a new gun.

Third, the CCP benefited tremendously from the alliance between the Kuomintang government and the private armies in different regions of China. Due to the Japanese army's slaughter and defeat of Kuomintang's troops, most of the Kuomintang army and government retreated to the corner of southwestern China. The private armies of local governments proved to be no match to the formidable Imperial Japanese Army. As a result, they had to cooperate with the CCP and sometimes provide Chinese communist troops with arms.

For example, Johnson (1962, p. 59) states: "In spite of the shrinkage of the guerilla areas and the severe losses suffered in them, the Communist reaped certain advantages from the fact that there was now hardly a village left in Hopei or Shansi that was not half-burned or worse. The revolution spread and became irreversible in the years 1941–42. Instead of breaking the tie between the Eight Route Army and the peasantry, the Japanese policy drove the two together into closer alliance. . . The Army's strength and the size of the guerilla areas very soon surpassed those of 1940."

In economics, inefficient firms are under pressure to be "taken over" by more efficient firms with the increase of market competition. Otherwise, they would suffer a loss and be forced out of the market. In fact, the Kuomintang army also tried to engage in guerilla warfare, but was mostly annihilated by the Japanese army. The essence of this logic applies to the alliance between the Chinese communist troops and the troops of local rich landlords. The rich landlords were fully aware of the substantial conflicts they had with communists. However, compared with their tremendous shame and hatred of the Japanese soldiers for raping their wives and killing their children, money suddenly became a trivial issue. The landlords put some of their "investments" into the much more efficient "military enterprise" of the Chinese communist troops so that more Japanese soldiers would be wounded and killed.

Notes

1 Omata (1988, p. 25).
2 http://www.cnd.org/njmassacre/njm-tran/njm-ch10.htm
3 http://www.marxists.org/archive/lenin/works/1920/lwc/ch02.htm
4 https://www.marxists.org/reference/archive/stalin/works/1924/foundations-leninism/ch08.htm
5 http://wiki.answers.com/Q/What_does_Stalin_mean?#slide=2

6 http://www.bbc.co.uk/history/worldwars/wwtwo/hitler_russia_invasion_01.
   shtml
7 Chang and Halliday (2005).
8 http://news.ifeng.com/history/phtv/wdzgx/detail_2011_01/11/4222136_3.
   shtml
9 http://en.wikipedia.org/wiki/Political_commissar
10 Tada Corps (1941), translated by Johnson (1962, p. 79).
11 Johnson (1962, p. 4).

24 Who killed 2.12 million Japanese troops in World War II?

Yasukuni Shrine is a Japanese imperial shrine dedicated to those who died in service of the Japanese empire. In 1874, Emperor Meiji composed a poem that read as follows: "I assure those of you who fought and died for your country that your names will live forever at this shrine in Musashino."[1] This poem was written in the spirit of Bushido, which highlights honor rather than material rewards for samurais.

The shrine provides a reliable figure of the number of Japanese casualties in World War II. It indicates that the Japanese military deaths from 1937 to 1945 numbered 2,325,165. About 2.12 million of these casualties were Japanese soldiers.[2] The remaining 210,000 soldiers were mainly recruits from Korea and Taiwan, which were part of the Japanese empire at the time. Who killed these 2.12 million troops? How many Japanese were killed by the Chinese communist army? The answers to these questions indicate how the atrocities committed by Japanese troops affected the number of Japanese troops killed.

Quite surprisingly, the literature provides no satisfactory answer to these highly politicized questions. First, the Chinese communists and Kuomintang have debated their relative contributions to their victory in World War II since 1945, and continue to do so. Both sides have claimed to be the main fighting force against the Japanese troops. Second, most of the Japanese felt superior to the Chinese, and hence suffering major casualties to Chinese troops was simply unacceptable to their self-esteem. In contrast, most Japanese do not feel ashamed at losing the war to the United States army, which possessed more advanced weaponry and even nuclear weapons. Thus, most Japanese have strongly preferred attributing their casualties to the United States army.

Due to these kinds of political and emotional factors, different sources have provided various answers to the aforementioned questions. Therefore, this chapter attempts to provide a new estimation and more convincing answers. It obtains its estimation based on reliable figures. First, Yasukuni Shrine indicates that the Japanese military deaths from 1937 to 1945 numbered 2,325,165, and that about 2.12 million of those comprised the deaths of Japanese soldiers. These numbers should be reliable, as the name of a Japanese man who did not die in a military conflict would not be displayed in such a highly regarded sacred place.

Second, the number of United States military deaths suffered during the Pacific War totaled 111,606. This figure has been publicly stated without any debate.[3] Thus, it should be fairly accurate.

Third, the military deaths of the Japanese and American armies in four major battles during the Pacific War have been documented fairly accurately. Table 24.1 lists the causalities suffered in some of the major battles.[4]

The casualty ratio of the armies between Japan and the United States can therefore be calculated as follows:

$$204,811/108,168 = 1.893427$$

As previously mentioned, 111,606 United States soldiers died in the war with Japan, and 253,142 soldiers were injured. Therefore, the total number of United States military casualties suffered in the Pacific War can be calculated as follows:

$$111,606 + 253,142 = 364,748$$

This means that the number of United States military casualties suffered in the four battles listed in Table 24.1 over the total number of casualties is:

$$108,168 \div 364,748 = 30 \text{ percent}$$

This figure of 30 percent should be representative. Thus, it can be assumed that the ratio of Japanese to United States military casualties for the entire Pacific War was 1.89:1. In addition, it can be assumed that the ratio of military deaths between the United States and Japanese armies equaled the ratio of Japanese to United States military casualties. Based on these results and assumptions, the number of Japanese military deaths in battles with the United States can be calculated as follows:

$$1.893427 \times 111,606 = 211,321$$

After World War II, most Japanese people admitted that they lost the war to the United States, which possessed and used more advanced and nuclear

Table 24.1 The casualty ratio between Japanese and American soldiers

	Japanese casualties	U.S. casualties
Saipan (Jun–Jul 1944):	23,811	16,612
Leyte (Oct 1944)	49,000	15,584
Iwo Jima (Feb–Mar 1945)	22,000	26,821
Okinawa (Apr–Jun 1945)	110,000	49,151
Total	204,811	108,168

weapons. However, most Japanese considered it an insult to state that Japan had lost the war to China. Indeed, since the First Sino–Japanese War in 1895, "Chinese" had been a word synonymous with "weak" and "coward" in Japanese, and even "clown" in children's games. This mentality might have accounted for Japanese articles claiming that United States forces killed 1.5 million Japanese troops in the Pacific War. The preceding calculations show that such claims are not true, as the 100,000 American casualties would have placed the ratio at an absurd level of 15:1.

Of course, the United States' contribution to winning the Pacific War went far beyond annihilating 211,000 Japanese troops. The US navy annihilated the Japanese navy, and its air force attacked many strategic positions in Japanese cities. Both of these actions were crucially important for winning the war. A critical factor in the surrender of the Japanese was the United States dropping two nuclear bombs on Japan. However, these attacks did not result in many military deaths. Although a fleet was expensive to build, there were few soldiers on a battleship. Most of the victims of the American air strikes and nuclear bombs were Japanese civilians.

Another important ally to China in the Anti-Japanese War was the Soviet Union, which engaged in two major battles with Japan. The first comprised the Battles of Khalkhin Gol, which were waged between Japan and the Soviet Union near the Khalkhin Gol River at the Sino–Mongolian border. Although the Soviet Union was victorious by consensus, the number of Japanese casualties was unclear. For example, Japan claimed that its military deaths totaled 8,440.[5] However, the Soviet Union sometimes claimed that it killed and wounded 60,000 Japanese soldiers in the battle, implying that it killed about 20,000 Japanese soldiers given the typical killed-to-wounded ratio of 1:2.[6] To avoid overestimating the number of Japanese casualties caused by Chinese troops, it can be assumed that the Japanese suffered 20,000 military deaths at the Battles of Khalkhin Gol.

In August 1945, the Soviet Union declared war against Japan and sent its troops into Manchuria. This was a massive campaign that annihilated 83,737 Japanese troops despite lasting only 12 days. Thus, the number of Japanese military deaths caused by the Soviet Union can be calculated as follows:

$$20,000 + 83,737 = 103,737$$

The Soviets took about 560,000–760,000 Japanese POWs and sent them to work in labor camps. An estimated 50,000–60,000 Japanese POWs died in the camps.[7] It is unclear whether the Yasukuni Shrine accounts for those deaths. (Indeed, most of those deaths occurred in Russia after the Japanese surrender in 1945.) I decide to consider it to avoid any possibility of overestimating the number of Japanese casualties caused by Chinese troops. Moreover, I assume that the number of Japanese POW deaths totaled 60,000.

Finally, Australia, India, and the United Kingdom also fought against Japan in World War II, and suffered military deaths totaling 9,470, 6,860, and 5,670, respectively.[8] These three countries exhibited poor combative power against the

Imperial Japanese Army. For example, at the Battle of Singapore in 1942, 80,000 British and Australian joint forces surrendered to the Imperial Japanese Army of merely 30,000 soldiers after only one week's battle.[9] This indicates that the three countries did not have strong fighting forces, and that the casualty ratio between these countries and Japan was 1:1 at most. As such, the military deaths of Japanese troops caused by these countries could not have exceeded the following sum:

$$9,470 + 6,860 + 5,670 = 22,000$$

Based on the preceding analysis and calculations, Table 24.2 summarizes the total military deaths suffered by Japan at the hands of countries other than China by category.

Recall that the number of military deaths suffered by Japan during World War II totaled 2,120,000. Thus, the total Japanese military deaths caused by Chinese troops can be calculated as follows:

$$2.12 \text{ million} - 397,058 = 1,722,942$$

Moreover, if the soldiers of foreign origins (mainly Korean) are taken into account, the military deaths suffered by the Imperial Japanese Army from 1937 to 1945 totaled 2,325,165. Using this figure, the total Japanese military deaths caused by Chinese troops can be calculated as follows:

$$2,325,165 - 397,058 = 1,928,107$$

Therefore, the Chinese army killed a total of 1.72–1.93 million Japanese soldiers during the Sino–Japanese War.

The preceding calculations are based on a new method that has not yet been applied in the Chinese and Japanese historical literature. However, its results are consistent with the research of some historians. For example, Hsu and Chang (1972) also report that the deaths of Japanese soldiers in China during World War II totaled over 1.7 million.

According to Wikipedia, "Both Nationalist and Communist Chinese sources report that their respective forces were responsible for the deaths of over 1.7 million

Table 24.2 Japanese military deaths caused by the other countries

Military deaths caused by the United States	211,321
Military deaths caused by the Soviet Union	103,737
Military deaths caused by Australia, India, and the United Kingdom	22,000
POW deaths	60,000
Total	397,058

Japanese soldiers."[10] However, this debate seems surprising. It has been officially claimed that the Kuomintang army suffered 1.32 million casualties in World War II, a figure that has been widely accepted with little controversy.[11] Although the casualty ratio between the Japanese and Kuomintang armies is debatable, it is commonly agreed that the Kuomintang suffered many more casualties than the Japanese in most battles. At the Battle of Shanghai, where the casualties were well counted, the casualty ratio between the Japanese and Kuomintang armies was 1:3.6. However, the Kuomintang army might have performed better after the Nanjing Massacre. Thus, a reasonable estimate of the casualty ratio between the Japanese and Kuomintang armies would be 1:3. Because the number of Kuomintang military deaths during World War II totaled 1.32 million, the number of Japanese military deaths suffered in battles with the Kuomintang army can be estimated as follows:

1.32 million/3 = 440,000

This provides enough information to calculate the number of Japanese troops killed by Chinese communist troops such as the Red Army and CCP guerrillas. If only the Japanese soldiers are counted, then the result is as follows:

1,722,942 – 440,000 = 1,282,942

If the soldiers of Korean and Taiwanese nationals are counted, then the result is as follows:

1,928,107 – 440,000 = 1,488,107

Therefore, during the Sino–Japanese War, Chinese communist troops killed a total of 1.28–1.49 million Japanese soldiers.

One question remains: How could the Chinese communist troops have possibly accomplished this? Recall that in July 1937, after the Long March, the number of Red Army soldiers totaled about 30,000. At least one third of these soldiers were assigned to defend the headquarters of the Chinese communists in Yan'an. How could 20,000 Chinese communist troops have killed 1.28 million Japanese soldiers?

A troop of 20,000 men clearly could not have inflicted casualties totaling more than 10,000 in one battle, particularly if the enemy possessed much better weapons, as they did when the Chinese communists faced Japanese troops. However, the Chinese communist troops grew quickly in number.

In 1945, by the time the Japanese surrendered, the communist army and guerillas had a total of 1.2 million soldiers. The Sino–Japanese War lasted eight years, during which numerous battles were fought. For example, according the "Complete History of People's Liberation Army," the Chinese communist and Japanese troops fought each other in 125,165 battles.[12] By this estimation, if 10 Japanese soldiers were killed in each battle on average, then the Japanese would have suffered 1.25 million military deaths at the hands of the Chinese communist army and guerillas.

The most famous offense launched by the Chinese communist army and guerillas against the Japanese was the Hundred Regiments Offensive, which lasted from August 20 to December 5, 1940. The Chinese guerillas damaged the railways and other supply lines by blowing up bridges and tunnels and ripping up track, annihilating the Japanese troops by catching them off guard and attacking isolated Japanese garrisons. This offense killed 20,645 Japanese troops and 5,155 puppet troops. Other Chinese guerilla attacks were far less pretentious than the Hundred Regiments Offensive, which Mao Zedong criticized for its pretentiousness. However, the vast number of guerilla attacks inflicted heavy casualties on the Japanese army.

The number of CCP troop casualties suffered during World War II can only be crudely estimated. Some estimates place the total number of Chinese military deaths in World War II to be 3.5 million.[13] As the Kuomintang army suffered 1.32 million deaths, the number of CCP troop deaths can be estimated as follows:

3.5 million – 1.32 million = 2.18 million

However, the heavy CCP troop casualties did not prevent the army from growing. The atrocities committed by the Japanese troops generated an extreme hatred in the Chinese, producing a virtually infinite number of potential soldiers for the Chinese communist army. As long as it could provide weapons, the Chinese communist army could recruit any number of soldiers who would fight bravely on the battlefields and whose enormous shame and extreme hatred would make them willing to die for the chance to take revenge on Japanese soldiers.

Where did the weapons of the Chinese communist troops come from? The answer to this question is beyond the focus of this book and deserves careful future research. Some possible answers are provided as follows. One answer is that the Chinese troops captured weapons from the Japanese troops after each victory. Another possible channel involved capturing weapons from the so-called Collaborationist Chinese Army (or simply "puppet army"), which consisted of Chinese soldiers employed by the Japanese army. As the Japanese troops occupied more areas of China, they needed more manpower to administer those areas. They recruited some Chinese to form an army that would deter revolts and safeguard the railways and other supply lines to the Japanese troops at the frontlines. However, many soldiers in the puppet army only wanted to "earn a living" and exhibited low morale in combat. In fact, it is reasonable to believe that many of the soldiers hated the Japanese troops, as some of them had witnessed their wives and daughters being raped by Japanese soldiers. These soldiers often became a relatively easy target of Chinese communist guerillas. According to the "Complete History of People's Liberation Army," the Chinese communist guerillas captured 512,933 puppet army soldiers, indicating an additional supply of 512,933 guns for the Chinese communist army.

Furthermore, CCP guerillas often used whatever weapons they could obtain. For example, Johnson (1962, pp. 85–86) states the following: "In this connection, the cadres' manual notes: 'When carrying out military actions, it is not absolutely necessary to employ modern weapons; old-fashioned firearms, spears, knives, poles, axes, hoes, and stones can all kill enemy soldiers'."

Another indirect piece of evidence that suggests that Chinese communist guerillas inflicted heavy casualties on the Japanese troops is the "Three Alls Policy." This notorious policy was an order from Yasuji Okamura, the commander-in-chief of the Imperial Japanese Army in China. The policy resulted in a significant proportion of the deaths of 35 million Chinese people during the Sino–Japanese War. The Chinese population at the time was 517 million, indicating that the policy did not affect the potential number of Chinese soldiers fighting against Japanese troops. On the contrary, it only exacerbated the hatred and shame of the Chinese, and in turn enhanced the combative power of potential Chinese soldiers. Therefore, the policy could not have possibly helped Japan win the war. What was the rationale for the policy's implementation? The most plausible explanation is that Japanese troops were continuously suffering heavy causalities due to the attacks of communist guerillas. However, the "Three Alls Policy" and other Japanese atrocities did not weaken the Chinese communist troops. On the contrary, they created an infinite supply of soldiers for the Chinese communist guerilla forces.

The mass-scale rapes and lack of discipline on behalf of the Japanese troops might have substantially decreased their combative capacities, which may be an important reason why so many Japanese soldiers were killed by CCP guerillas with far inferior weapons and the Kuomintang troops. The point may be illustrated using the Battle of Hengyang as an example.

In 1944, the Imperial Japanese Army launched a series of attacks on at least a dozen Chinese cities. The Kuomintang army stationed in those cities fought the Japanese army only briefly and then deserted the cities. But there was one exception. In the city of Hengyang in Hunan Province, Lieutenant General Fang Xianjue of the Kuomintang army ordered his troops to fight to the last man and bullet to defend the city. Fang's troops were vastly outnumbered by the Japanese army, which possessed heavy artillery and an air force. However, the casualty ratio was unbelievable to almost everyone at the time. Fan's troops killed at least 19,000 Japanese troops while suffering only 4,700 military deaths. Wikipedia provides the following description of the Japanese-heavy casualties:[14] "In the middle of July, the Japanese troops no longer used ladders to climb up the cliffs. Instead, they used the piles of their corpses as ramps to scale the cliffs. According to (a KMT army) veteran, the bodies had piled up so much that he could not see through the firing port of his bunker. He had to shoot the corpses to pieces in order to see through."

Why did the Japanese troops perform so badly at the Battle of Hengyang? The most reasonable explanation may be that their Bushido spirit had largely disappeared after several years of increased sexual activity in China. The soldiers had taken every opportunity they had to rape Chinese women and enslaved "comfort women" from Korea, Japan, and China. They also enjoyed good food, and had robbed many Chinese farmers of their livestock. Having accustomed themselves to such extravagant lifestyles for years, most Japanese soldiers obviously wished to extend their lives. Consequently, they were much less willing to risk their lives on the battlefield. They came to prefer a situation in which other Japanese soldiers fought bravely while they avoided injury and death. When every Japanese soldier came to feel the same way, the combative power of the Japanese army decreased substantially, and its number of casualties rose enormously. This illustrates why Bushido required every samurai to lead a simple and frugal life.

Notes

1 http://www.yasukuni.or.jp/english/index.html
2 See, e.g., Breen (2008), and websites such as http://www.69shu.com/txt/8138/4986788 and http://en.wikipedia.org/wiki/Yasukuni_Shrine.
3 See, e.g., Frank (1999) and other references at http://pwencycl.kgbudge.com/C/a/Casualties.htm.
4 See, e.g., Zeiler (2004).
5 http://en.wikipedia.org/wiki/Battles_of_Khalkhin_Gol
6 http://en.wikipedia.org/wiki/Battles_of_Khalkhin_Gol
7 http://en.wikipedia.org/wiki/Japanese_prisoners_of_war_in_the_Soviet_Union
8 http://pwencycl.kgbudge.com/C/a/Casualties.htm
9 See, e.g., Cull (2004).
10 http://en.wikipedia.org/wiki/Second_Sino-Japanese_War#cite_note-ReferenceA-9
11 http://en.wikipedia.org/wiki/Second_Sino-Japanese_War
12 http://baike.baidu.com/view/2587.htm
13 http://www.secondworldwarhistory.com/world-war-2-statistics.asp
14 http://en.wikipedia.org/wiki/Defense_of_Hengyang

25 War rape and "comfort women"

Wikipedia provides the following description of war rape:[1] "During war and armed conflict, rape is frequently used as a means of psychological warfare in order to humiliate the enemy. War rape is often systematic and thorough, and military leaders may actually encourage their soldiers to rape civilians." Although I disagree with the statement that rape is frequently used as a means of psychological warfare by the perpetrators, I fully agree that war rape always has the consequence of deepest humiliation.

The previous three chapters demonstrate that the atrocities committed by Japanese troops and particularly rape fundamentally led to the defeat and surrender of Japan in the Second Sino–Japanese War. First, the horrendous atrocities encouraged the United States to participate in the war against Japan. Second, the war crimes of Japanese troops in China bred tremendous hatred from Chinese against the Japanese invaders, which in turn effectively fostered a formidable Chinese communist army that inflicted heavy casualties on the Imperial Japanese Army.

The effects of wartime rape cannot be exaggerated, which can be illustrated by the following two examples. (However, they were not taken from the period of the Second Sino–Japanese War, during which so many rapes took place so that the impact of any individual case is largely undocumented.)

The First Opium War began between Britain and China's Qing Dynasty in 1840. At that time, the Chinese people had little sense of nationalism, and most felt little about the war. In fact, some Chinese even helped the British invaders. However, a major revolt occurred in a place called Sanyuanli located in a northern suburb of Guangzhou over an incident in which a British soldier raped a Chinese woman.[2] A large group of Chinese peasants surrounded a group of British soldiers. A battle took place that killed 4 British soldiers and wounded more than 20.[3] Note that the British suffered only 69 military deaths in the First Opium War, which lasted for three years. Thus, this peasant revolt was one of the largest resistances that challenged the invasion of the British army during the war. A monument and a memorial hall have since been erected in Sanyuanli.

The second example, which is often referred to as "the Shen Chong case," took place on December 24, 1946. On this Christmas Eve, United States

Marines William Pierson and Warren Pritchard dragged Beijing University student Shen Chong to the adjacent Peiping Polo Field and raped her.[4] The event was witnessed by a Chinese mechanic who was working in a nearby repair shop. He reported it to police, and William Pierson was arrested later that night. Warren Pritchard was not arrested because he had already left when the police arrived at the scene. Pierson was soon brought to trial by the United States Marine Court and convicted. However, an American military doctor who examined Shen after the alleged rape stated that according to his observation the bruising on Shen's thighs and buttocks were significantly less than a typical rape case would present. Therefore, the United States Department of the Navy acquitted Pierson on the basis of insufficient evidence. The Shen Chong case triggered public anger and large-scale public demonstrations. In February 1946, the Kuomintang police arrested more than 1,000 people who were protesting the Shen Chong case.[5]

The sex crimes committed by Japanese troops in China were so horrendous as to make the two preceding examples appear somewhat trivial. The previous few chapters of this book demonstrate that these atrocities were the fundamental reason why Japan lost the war. Indeed, other war crimes such as the murder of innocent people were often consequences of rape. For example, Chen (2004) searched many old Chinese newspapers detailing the Japanese invasion, and found that most of the innocent people were killed while pleading with the Japanese soldiers not to rape their loved ones. Because the Japanese troops did not receive any hedonistic pleasure from taking innocent lives, the Japanese commanders would have found it easy to order their troops not to do so. However, Japanese soldiers were often tempted to feed their sexual desires through rape.

The Japanese troops committed rape on a unique scale, one much larger than that of the German soldiers or any other troops in WWII. This presents an important question that has rarely been addressed. Why did the Japanese generals allow their troops to rape and kill civilians? Indeed, the Japanese generals themselves usually neither raped women nor obtained any sexual pleasure from their soldiers' actions. Why did the Japanese generals allow their soldiers to do something so extremely harmful to Japan's interests?

Today, the Chinese media explains that the Japanese did so because they were bad people. Many articles found on Chinese websites often quote former United States President Franklin D. Roosevelt as saying "the Japanese are the most despicable and the most shameless people I've ever seen."[6] This argument very much fits the taste of many Chinese readers in the current social environment, in which anti-Japanese nationalism is very strong. However, from a social sciences perspective, it is highly unsatisfactory. Answering the question requires careful analysis, and economic theories can be usefully applied for this purpose. Indeed, if the Japanese were the worst people on earth, why were they the only force of foreign troops to not commit rape during the Boxer Rebellion? Furthermore, why is there no hard evidence that Japanese soldiers raped women in Manchuria on a massive scale?

These questions can be addressed by examining the history literature. Some of China's historical literature suggests that the Japanese troops' first mass-scale rape in China occurred immediately after the Battle of Shanghai, where the Japanese army suffered heavy casualties.[7] Among the 300,000 Japanese troops who participated in this battle, 70,000 (or 23 percent of the soldiers) were killed in action. The Battle of Shanghai ended on November 26, 1937, only two weeks before the start of the Battle of Nanjing on December 9, 1937.

Many Japanese soldiers were demoralized due to the heavy casualties. Although they managed to defeat the Kuomintang troops, they were disappointed at the outcome. For example, they had expected the Chinese troops to be as weak as their ancestors in the First Sino–Japanese War, in which the Japanese army suffered only minor casualties. After they experienced a real taste of death at the Battle of Shanghai, many Japanese soldiers felt that the war with China made them worse off. Although most of the Japanese soldiers were zealous nationalists, their emotions alone were not enough to fully compensate them for risking their lives. In response, the commanders of the Japanese army promised their troops that each soldier would receive a "flower girl" after the conquest of Nanjing,[8] a commitment that was indeed honored and allowed Japanese soldiers to commit rape.

Permitting soldiers to rape as a form of payment has a long history. For example, considering Europe during the late Middle Ages, Askin (1997, p. 27) observes that "opportunities to rape and loot were among the few advantages open to . . . soldiers, who were paid with great irregularity by their leaders . . . triumph over women by rape became a way to measure victory, part of a soldier's proof of masculinity and success, a tangible reward for services rendered . . . an actual reward of war."

This argument can also be explained by George Akerlof's (1982) social economics theory, which is briefly discussed in Chapter 6. Akerlof is a prolific economist who won the 2001 Nobel Memorial Prize in Economic Sciences. In an attempt to better understand employer-employee relationships and the issue of unemployment, Akerlof (1982) argues that the relationship between an employer and an employee is like a gift exchange. He posits that higher wages induce a high level of morale and gratitude from workers, which raises productivity. In other words, workers reciprocate with a high level of effort when they are paid with high wages, which they appreciate as a gift from their employer. As such, many firms pay their workers more than the wage that would lead to labor market equilibrium, resulting in unemployment at the aggregate level.

This theory can be applied to further explain war rape in general and the Rape of Nanjing in particular. From the perspective of Japanese generals, the Japanese emperor, and the senior officials of the Japanese central government, the further expansion of its territories was Japan's only reason for waging war against China. What were the benefits of such a war to the ordinary Japanese soldier? A victory in a battle would have brought national glory to Japan and made the soldiers happy. However, the soldiers might have thought this glory insufficient to compensate for the deaths and injuries sustained on the battlefield.

Indeed, almost any soldier who invades another country is largely mercenary in nature. Thus, to participate in an armed conflict with China, which might have led to serious injury or death, a Japanese soldier might have strongly demanded private gains. One may argue that all Japanese soldiers at the time considered their emperor as God, and were hence willing to die for him without receiving any material benefit in return. However, this statement may be more reflective of the Japanese propaganda used at the time rather than reality. Recall that the emperor had been a dummy figure in Japanese politics for centuries, during which he was dominated and bullied by military generals and local warlords. If the emperor was equated with God, this would not have been the case.

Indeed, although most of the Japanese generals were zealous militants and expansionists, most of the ordinary young Japanese men might not have shared their goals and ambitions. In 1937, Japan was in a golden age of economic development, and most Japanese were happy in their work, which enabled them to have increasingly better lives every year. Although the sense of nationalism was strong in Japan, the country's territory had already increased so much (even with the exclusion of Manchuria) over only a few decades that Japan needed time to "digest" the annexed new territory. In fact, in 1932, Japanese Prime Minister Inukai Tsuyoshi along with several other Japanese ministers was assassinated by several officers of the Japanese army for their strong resistance to the military expansion policy. Japan was a democratic country, and Inukai obviously spoke for many ordinary Japanese. Thus, fighting in China might have considerably decreased the wellbeing of many young Japanese men, who would have been risking their lives.

For example, about a quarter of Japanese troops who fought in the Battle of Shanghai were killed. The troops had a strong demand for "compensation." Therefore, the Japanese generals had to make sure that Japanese soldiers felt well compensated for serving in the army or risk a low morale among their troops. Some Japanese generals found that an effective, convenient, and cheap way of compensating soldiers for risking their lives in battles was to provide them with opportunities to have sex, including in the form of rape on a mass scale. This was an effective proposal for two reasons. First, sex represented one of the greatest pleasures in life for many men and particularly young men. Moreover, in many cultures, the pleasure of sex was vastly exaggerated to the point of becoming a status symbol. Thus, the Japanese soldiers considered the opportunity to have sex as a major form of payment. Second, the Japanese soldiers were not constrained by any religion that considered rape a sin, such as Christianity. After the conquest of a Chinese city, the Japanese troops immediately found a large pool of female flesh that could easily be obtained through violence or the threat of violence. Their rape sprees were often met with resistance from the victims and their family members, and the Japanese troops responded by mercilessly killing those Chinese civilians who stood in their way.

In fact, Japanese politicians echo these views even today. The following CNN report made in 2013 describes women forced into prostitution in the Imperial

Japanese Army rather than war rape, but the essential logic appears similar: "Japanese officials have distanced themselves from comments made by a prominent nationalist politician that suggested women forced to become prostitutes to entertain Japanese troops during World War II were 'necessary.' Toru Hashimoto, who serves as the Mayor of Osaka, told reporters at his weekly press conference Monday that 'anyone would understand' the role of 'comfort women' when soldiers were risking their lives and you wanted to give them 'a rest.' Though he acknowledged the issue was a 'tragic result of war,' Hashimoto, who is co-leader of the nationalist Japan Restoration Party, insisted the use of prostitutes by soldiers was not unique to Japan."[9]

However, once one group of Japanese soldiers committed rape without being punished, other Japanese troops made the same demand or considered it unfair. The economic theory of "fairness and work effort" can be applied here. George Akerlof and Janet Yellen developed the theory in an article entitled "The Fair Wage-Effort Hypothesis and Unemployment." Akerlof, a Nobel laureate, was introduced earlier. Yellen is his wife, and is currently the Chairman of the Board of Governors of the Federal Reserve System of the United States. Akerlof and Yellen (1990) argue that workers form a notion of a fair wage, and if the actual wage is lower they withdraw their effort proportionately.

Although Akerlof and Yellen (1990) focus on firms, their insights can be applied to the army. In this case, if the soldiers had withdrawn their effort due to their perception of unfairness, the army might have lost the war. Elliot Rodger, who carried out a shooting rampage in Santa Barbara, California, on May 25, 2014, did so out of "retribution" for having a life that was "unnatural and pathetic" and his enormous unhappiness over remaining a virgin at the age of 22.[10] He wrote a long story about his life that contained the following observations: "The boys in my grade talked about sex a lot. Some of them even told me that they had sex with their girlfriends. This was the most devastating and traumatizing thing I've ever heard in my life. . . How is it that they were able to have such intimate and pleasurable experiences with girls while I could only fanaticize about it?"[11] Although this case is extreme, it reflects the attitudes of many men toward sex, and particularly men with little moral constraint. In the words of the Bible, "jealousy is cruel as the grave." When Japanese soldiers began to adopt the mentality that it was fair for them to rape, preventing them from raping Chinese women became extremely difficult.

The historical documents related to the wartime rapes committed by the Japanese army in China exhibit a pattern: the extent of the rapes was often closely related to the military casualties.[12] In other words, the greater the casualties, the more serious the scale of rape. For example, after the Mukden Incident in September 1931, the Kuomintang's policy of non-resistance led to the Japanese army's "peaceful" occupation of Manchuria. As a result, hardly any reports confirmed that the Japanese troops were committing mass-scale rapes in northeast China. That the Japanese soldiers did not commit rape during the Boxer Rebellion might have also related to their low number of military casualties. In contrast, in the anti-Japanese areas in which the CCP guerillas were based, the

Japanese troops implemented the "Three Alls Policy" in response to the heavy casualties caused by CCP guerillas. The Japanese generals not only encouraged their troops to vent their anger and frustration by killing Chinese civilians, but also allowed them to freely rape Chinese women. Under the guidance of this policy, the rapes committed by Japanese troops were frequent and commonplace. In Hunan Province, the Japanese soldiers committed mass-scale rapes as possible compensation for the heavy casualties they suffered during battles fought in Changsha, the capital city of Hunan.

An early chapter of this book mentions Fang (1997), who interviewed some former soldiers of the Imperial Japanese Army in China. According to one of the interviewees, rape was committed frequently in areas where battles with CCP guerillas were frequent, and was considered the main payment to Japanese soldiers. The former Japanese soldier recalled the following: "We took raping Chinese women for granted. Our captain once said to us, 'Someone asked me why you were never paid a salary of 8.8 yen per month. I do not really know the answer. However, it is your freedom to rape Chinese women. We are the troop of occupation, and hence we are entitled to do so!' "[13]

Why were the Japanese soldiers the only troops to rape women on such a massive scale during World War II? (Soviet troops also raped women, but on a much smaller scale.) Two misjudgments made by some Japanese generals may answer this question. First, they did not understand Christianity and the Western culture well, and hence did not know that their actions would breed intolerance in the Americans and encourage the United States to join the war. Second, they misjudged the Chinese national character. For example, German soldiers did not rape French women on a massive scale because they expected that doing so would lead to substantial resistance from the French people. (By a similar logic, the Soviet troops justified raping German women on a massive scale in Berlin because they believed that the war had destroyed Germany's combative capacity.)

The economics concept of price elasticity of demand (PED) better explains this logic. It measures the responsiveness, or elasticity, of the quantity demanded of a good or a service to a change in its price.[14] The "law of demand" implies that when prices increase, the quantity demanded of a good decreases. However, the magnitude of such a response may differ between commodities. If the PED is small, a seller is tempted to increase prices. If it is large, the seller may lose revenue if he increases prices. German soldiers did not rape French women because they expected an enormous response from the French people (i.e., the responsiveness, or elasticity, would be high). However, Soviet troops raped German women because they expected that Germany had lost its capacity to retaliate (i.e., the responsiveness, or elasticity, would be low).

By a similar logic, Japanese generals allowed their soldiers to rape because they mistakenly thought that the Chinese people were so cowardly that they would not dare to fight back. They thought that the Chinese national personality remained as weak as it had been in ancient times. However, it had grown much tougher. In particular, the Japanese generals failed to recognize the growing fearlessness of the Chinese communists. Under the leadership of the CCP, many Chinese joined guerilla troops, and the ensuing brutal battles made their personalities increasingly tougher.

The Japanese generals ultimately learned that allowing their troops to rape Chinese women was a "bad deal." In particular, it was the fundamental reason behind the United States' decision to participate in the war against Japan and behind the growth of the Chinese communist troops, both of which dealt fatal blows to the Japanese army. In the middle of the war, some Japanese generals realized the mistake and tried to correct it. However, at this stage, it had become too difficult. After the Rape of Nanjing, the "culture of rape" prevailed in the Imperial Japanese Army. Under this new "culture," most Japanese soldiers did not take military discipline seriously and took every opportunity to rape Chinese women. The generals could not punish that many soldiers, on whom they were depending to fight in forthcoming battles. Hence, the only choice was to "forgive" their wrongdoings. To resolve this difficult problem, the Japanese army tried to decrease/stop the rapes by introducing the system of comfort women to the Japanese troops. According to Wikipedia, "comfort women were women and girls forced into sexual slavery by the Japanese Imperial Army during World War II."[15]

The "principal–agent problem" of economic theory, which is also known as the "moral hazard problem," can be applied to this situation. Such a problem often arises in a two-party relationship, such as that of an employer and a worker (e.g. Shapiro and Stiglitz, 1984). In this relationship, the principal delegates to the agent an action that influences the principal's welfare. For example, in the relationship between an employer and a worker, the employer is the principal and the worker is the agent, and the latter affects the former through the agent's production output. The moral hazard problem, which is interchangeable with the principal–agent problem, arises when the agent commits an action that maximizes his or her own interest at the expense of the principal. For example, a worker who is paid a fixed salary chooses to take it easy and has little incentive to work hard.

In a separate study (Fan, 2006), I adopt this "principal–agent framework" to study corruption. I analyze how a ruler implements anti-corruption measures, including both wage incentives and monitoring, to discourage opportunistic officials from seeking bribes. I show that the ruler pays an "efficiency wage" (i.e., a high salary) to his officials to eliminate corruption if and only if monitoring is relatively effective. The theoretical analysis I apply was empirically motivated by a number of observations, including that officials in ancient China were given an extra allowance known as "Yang-Lien."[16]

"Yang-Lien," which literally means "honesty silver," aims to nourish incorruptness. If a government official is already paid a high salary that enables him to live comfortably, why should he take the risk of corruption, which may lead to dismissal and imprisonment? "Honesty silver" was often very substantial. During the Qing Dynasty, an official often received "honesty silver" that totaled 10 to 100 times his basic salary. For example, although Taiwan Provincial

Governor Liu Ming-chuan received an annual salary of 155 taels of silver, his "honesty silver" amounted to 12,000 taels of silver.

Such a moral hazard problem might have also existed in the relationship between Japanese generals and their soldiers and junior officers. Indeed, from an abstract or theoretical perspective, "war rape" may be conceptualized as the worst type of "corruption." According to such a conceptualization, comfort women served as a type of "efficiency wage" to decrease or eliminate war rape.

During the Sino–Japanese War, the Japanese troops were spread across many areas of China's vast territories. Therefore, they could not perfectly monitor the behavior of Japanese soldiers and junior officers. From the perspective of a Japanese soldier, winning the war against China was important. However, because his own behavior was too trivial to affect the outcome of the entire war, he might also have been motivated to pursue his own interest. The early chapters of this book observe that the cavalries from nomadic tribes often engaged in looting in the border areas of China. However, looting was not so attractive for Japanese soldiers, as they could not go back to Japan in the near future and their officers might not have allowed them to carry heavy items on the move. Thus, rape was the greatest temptation for most Japanese soldiers.

Under most circumstances, the cost of allowing Japanese soldiers to rape the women of an enemy country was much higher than the benefit. However, Japanese generals (the principal) monitored the behavior of Japanese soldiers (the agent) imperfectly at best. Imposing penalties on the soldiers who were caught raping women was insufficient to deter the soldiers from doing so. Thus, the comfort women system was introduced as a complementary measure to impose discipline on the soldiers. For example, a circular of the War Ministry of Japan offers the following rationale for comfort women:[17]

> It is not necessary to emphasize how much the environment influences troops' psychology and therefore the promotion of discipline. Thus care must be taken in regard to suitable living conditions and comfort facilities. In particular the psychological influence received from sexual comfort stations is most direct and profound and it must be realised how greatly their appropriate direction and supervision affect the raising of morale, the maintenance of discipline and the prevention of crime and venereal disease.

A Japanese politician also advanced this view in 2013 in an effort to justify the comfort women system. The *Wall Street Journal* reported it as follows:[18]

> "Anyone can understand that the system of comfort women was necessary to provide respite for a group of high-strung, rough and tumble crowd of men braving their lives under a storm of bullets," Toru Hashimoto told reporters on Monday. Putting aside the moral question, "back then it was a necessary system to maintain military discipline," he said.

Therefore, Japanese generals found that the most cost-effective way to discipline their soldiers was through a combined carrot-and-stick measure, with the carrot being the comfort women and the stick being the military penalty. Although the senior generals of the Japanese troops might not have wanted the troops to engage in rape, the actions of the troops were not often known to the generals. The comfort women system was implemented for Japanese troops to mitigate this moral hazard problem.

Kim II Myon, a Korean writer, wrote a book entitled *The Emperor's Forces and Korean Comfort Women*. The book strongly criticizes Japanese militarism and describes the misery of the comfort women. However, it also describes a rationale for their existence, and more essentially the rationale for Japan compensating its soldiers with female flesh. Kim (1976, p. 33) states: "To soldiers in the frontline, ever surrounded by the sound of guns, wrapped in smoke stinking of death and not knowing when death would come . . . a visit to a comfort station was no doubt the only form of relief."

In another book about comfort women, Hicks (1995, p. 7) observes the following: "Some sources indicate that the practice of visiting comfort women was ritualised by the Japanese, especially before a unit was to leave for the front. The common rationale was that men without previous sexual experience should have intercourse at least once before death."

Although comfort women consisted of volunteers from Japan, most of the women were abducted or coerced to serve in the Japanese army. Historian Yoshiaki Yoshimi conducted the first academic study of comfort women. According to his estimation, their number totaled between 50,000 and 200,000. Yoshimi also inferred the countries of origin from the medical records of the Japanese army for venereal disease treatments from 1940. Assuming that the percentages of women treated reflected the general makeup of the total comfort women population, Yoshimi concluded that 51.8 percent of the comfort women were Korean, 36 percent were Chinese (including Taiwanese), and 12.2 percent were Japanese.[19]

To the extent that the introduction of comfort women significantly decreased the amount of war rape, it might have indeed decreased the misery of the Chinese people. Of course, such a "welfare improvement" came at the cost of those unfortunate comfort women. However, in comparison with the alternative, in which the Japanese soldiers would have tried to rape all of the women in the areas they occupied, the introduction of comfort women might have decreased the number of women who were ultimately raped.

However, even with the comfort women system in place, the Japanese generals might have only been able to discipline the Japanese soldiers in cities and towns. When a small group of Japanese troops went to a village in a remote area, they were often unobserved by their superiors, and rapes were committed frequently as a result. In study I coauthored with Lin and Treisman (2009), we show that political decentralization, particularly in the form of additional governance layers, usually increased corruption. The basic logic also applied here. When the Japanese troops became more decentralized in an effort to fight against guerilla warfare, they usually committed more atrocities and particularly war rape.[20]

Moreover, because comfort women were considered prostitutes, many Japanese soldiers were not content to have sex with them. Thus, when Japanese troops scored a major victory, suffered heavy causalities, or both, Japanese generals might have rewarded them with another way to satisfy their sexual appetites by allowing them to rape the women of the enemy country. The following is taken from a report related to the atrocities of Japanese troops after the Battle of Hong Kong in December 1941:[21]

> Hong Kong was a British colony before and after WWII . . . Japan started its invasion of Hong Kong on 12/8/1941 (or 12/7/1941 U.S. time, the same day Japan attacked Pearl Harbor). Great Britain surrendered Hong Kong to Japan on Christmas day, 12/25/1941 . . . a great deal of massacre and atrocities were committed by the Japanese soldiers against the Chinese, British, Canadians, and other people living in Hong Kong at that time. As many as 10,000 women were raped in the first few days. Tens of thousands, including women and children, were killed . . . The atrocities were not just against the Chinese, but also British, Canadians, and people of other nationalities. For example, at a hospital for injured British soldiers, the Japanese soldiers slaughtered 170 recuperating soldiers and a few hospital staff. The eyes, ears, noses, tongues, or limbs were cut off on many victims. Seventy of the soldiers were killed with swords while they were lying in bed. The hospital's seven nurses were raped, sometimes while lying on top of the bodies of murdered British soldiers.

Notes

 1 http://en.wikipedia.org/wiki/War_rape
 2 See, e.g., Lam and Zyu (2003). The woman's name was Li Xi, and her husband's name was Wei Shaoguang.
 3 See, e.g., Elleman (2005).
 4 See, e.g., Zhang (2002). Peiping Polo Field is currently the site of the Dongdan basketball courts.
 5 The Shen Chong case happened immediately after World War II. However, the Chinese never became accustomed to the humiliation of the rapes inflicted by Japanese troops on millions of Chinese women.
 6 See, e.g., http://bbs1.people.com.cn/post/2/1/1/139110520.html. A Google search of this "quotation" in English produces no matches.
 7 See, e.g., Chen (2006).
 8 See, e.g., Chen (2006).
 9 http://edition.cnn.com/2013/05/14/world/asia/japan-hashimoto-comfort-women/index.html
10 http://www.dailymail.co.uk/news/article-2638049/7-dead-drive-shooting-near-UC-Santa-Barbara.html#ixzz33FybSrg3
11 http://www.scribd.com/doc/225960813/Elliot-Rodger-Santa-Barbara-mass-shooting-suspect-My-Twisted-World-manifesto
12 See, e.g., Chen (2004) and Chen (2006).
13 Fang (1997, p. 235).
14 See, e.g., Mankiw (2007).
15 http://en.wikipedia.org/wiki/Comfort_women
16 Klitgaard (1987).
17 Hicks (1995, p. 7).

18 http://blogs.wsj.com/japanrealtime/2013/05/14/osaka-mayor-stirs-anger-by-calling-comfort-women-necessary-evil/
19 Yoshimi (2002).
20 In the economics literature, Fan, Lin, and Treisman (2010) and Shleifer and Vishny (1993) show that "centralized corruption" is better than "decentralized corruption" in terms of people's welfare. The argument of this paragraph, to some extent, shares this logic.
21 http://www.dontow.com/2007/04/massacre-and-atrocities-in-hong-kong-during-wwii/

26 Japanese atrocities and the transformation of the Chinese personality

An early chapter describing Japan's occupation of Manchuria mentions a leader of the anti-Japanese forces known as Yang Jingyu. Yang was a very tough soldier, and some interesting stories have been told about the events surrounding his death. The first story is that he was shot multiple times and killed by Japanese troops. After he fell to the ground, it took some time for the Japanese soldiers to approach his body because they remained afraid of Yang's marksmanship, made famous by his previous encounter with the Japanese army.

The second story is that the Japanese troops were suspicious that Yang Jingyu was a kind of superman, and they were curious about the kind of food he ate. When the Japanese conducted an autopsy on his body, they found only tree bark, cotton batting, and grass roots in his stomach, and not a single grain of rice. The Japanese commander at the scene, Ryuichiro Kishitani, was very much impressed. He ordered his soldiers to bury Yang's body with respect and called Yang "a true warrior." After Japan's defeat in 1945, Kishitani committed suicide via the ritual of seppuku. Before he did so, he wrote in his will that "His Majesty might be wrong in launching this war. China has steely soldiers like Yang Jingyu, and it would not fall."[1]

However, Kishitani was only partially correct. Before the Japanese troops committed their atrocities, heroic figures like Yang Jingyu were extremely rare in China, and they were mostly zealous communists. However, after Japan committed its horrendous atrocities against Chinese civilians, many Chinese people became fearless due to the anger, shame, and humiliation they had experienced at the hands of the Japanese invaders.

Of course, compared with the "national character" of the Chinese people at the time of the First Sino–Japanese War in 1894, the character in the 1930s was much tougher, largely due to the many years of bullying and oppression by foreign countries. For example, the media frequently reported that foreign countries such as Japan were extorting increasing amounts of political and commercial privilege from China, and that foreigners treated the Chinese as subhuman. Moreover, even the textbooks of elementary and secondary schools often stated that China was being bullied by foreigners and should seek revenge after it became a military power.

Before the end of the 19th century, the personality of the Chinese people was extremely weak. This was the best choice for the people, as it helped China remain a single large country that could credibly deter the harassment and invasion of war-like nomadic tribes. However, the humiliation imposed by the foreign powers made the personality of the Chinese people increasingly tougher.

For example, after the Japanese invasion of Manchuria in 1931, a large number of young Chinese men joined the AJUA. In fact, the AJUA soldiers quickly found that they were overwhelmed by the advanced weapons and combative power of the Japanese troops. Although the AJUA soldiers knew very well that they were fighting a war that they could not win, many of them continued the fight purely out of patriotism.

However, the Japanese occupation of Manchuria was very successful. Despite being the puppet state of Japan, Manchukuo was popular among many Chinese because their material wellbeing improved considerably during its rule, and there were almost no reports of the Japanese army raping women in Manchuria. Furthermore, the Japanese troops did not conduct other atrocities against civilians in public in Manchuria. The notorious Unit 731 of the Imperial Japanese Army undertook lethal human experimentation for its research on biological and chemical warfare in Harbin, Manchuria. However, it was highly confidential, and had no effect on the Chinese people of Manchuria at the time. The Kwangtung army used forced labor mainly to construct its military defense system against potential Soviet attacks. However, most of the slave labor was recruited in the Chinese provinces outside Manchuria, and the laborers were executed after the work was done. As cruel as it was, this war crime was largely unknown to the people in Manchuria, and hence did not affect their attitude toward the Japanese army.

Due to the lack of support from the populace, the AJUA was quickly annihilated by the Japanese army. In fact, Yang Jingyu sought help from several Chinese peasants, asking them to buy him food. Rather than treat Yang as their hero or savior, the peasants immediately betrayed Yang to the Japanese army, which led to his death. Although the Chinese personality would become tougher in the early 1930s, it was not strong enough. Thus, they could accept that they lived under the rule of Manchukuo, which was effectively a colony of Japan.

This kind of scenario changed fundamentally after Japan's invasion of China in 1937. The Japanese troops committed hideous atrocities including mass-scale rapes of Chinese women. These atrocities shamed most of the people in China, even if their family members were not the victims. The resulting humiliation and hatred toughened the personality of the Chinese people, and made many Chinese troops more determined to fight the Japanese invaders. In fact, this significant change in the national character was immediately reflected in two major battles only a few months after the Nanjing Massacre.

After the Battle of Shanghai, the Chinese central government panicked because most of its elite troops were sent to the battle and suffered heavy casualties. The government had no choice but to chiefly depend on the armies of local warlords, who might not have been loyal to the Kuomintang government. Moreover, Chiang Kai-shek worried that a "free rider" problem would emerge among the different warlords, and that each of them may want the other's forces to sacrifice themselves in the battles against the Japanese army. Such worries were natural. In fact, as early as 1930, the so-called Central Plains War broke out between Chiang Kai-shek and a coalition of three local warlords, including Yan Xishan, Feng Yuxiang, and Li Zongren. This civil war was very large in scale, and resulted in over 300,000 casualties for the two sides combined.[2]

Only four months after the Battle of Nanjing, the Battle of Taierzhuang broke out. The Chinese army consisted of the troops of several local warlords, and its commander-in-chief was Li Zongren, one of the three military strongmen who fought against the Chinese central army in 1930. Before the battle, Chiang Kai-shek was worried that the Chinese troops would not follow the order of Li Zongren. However, this turned out not to be the case. There was a strong solidarity within the Chinese army, and Li Zongren commanded the troops brilliantly. The warlords' hatred of the Japanese clearly dominated their concerns for personal gain or losses. As a result, the Chinese army scored a decisive victory over the Imperial Japanese Army at the Battle of Taierzhuang. Three months later, another major battle took place in the metropolitan city of Wuhan and its adjacent areas. Again depending mainly on the troops of different local warlords, the Chinese army fought bravely and killed about 100,000 Japanese troops. The casualty ratio between the Chinese and Japanese armies at the Battle of Wuhan was 2.1:1. This was a substantial improvement relative to the Battle of Shanghai, where the ratio was 3.6:1. The most reasonable explanation for these outcomes was that the horrendous atrocities of the Japanese troops significantly boosted the fighting spirit of the Chinese troops.

Because the weaponry of the Japanese army was far more advanced than that of the Chinese army, the troops of the Kuomintang and local warlords remained on the defensive side, and were driven to Sichuan Province and two other smaller provinces in the southwestern corner of China. Nevertheless, the hideous atrocities committed by the Japanese troops toughened the Chinese personality, and in fact might have narrowed the gap between the fighting spirit of the Chinese troops and the Bushido spirit of the Japanese soldiers. The toughened personality of the Chinese troops led to an impasse between the two sides. The Imperial Japanese Army made no more progress in defeating the Kuomintang troops, and the Kuomintang army did not launch any successful counter-offensives against the Japanese army.

As a result, although the vast areas of China were under the rule and occupation of the Japanese army and its puppet Chinese army, the Kuomintang army ultimately defended a major fraction of China. The Chinese communist troops operated mainly in the areas occupied by Japanese troops. The rule of the Japanese army in China was brutal and atrocious. The Chinese people felt extremely angry and unbearably shameful and humiliated, particularly due to the mass-scale rapes and murders frequently committed by the Japanese troops. As a result, the Chinese communists saw their support base begin to grow.

The horrendous atrocities committed by the Japanese troops caused the Chinese to form a deep hatred for the Japanese, and humiliated China as a nation. The Chinese people exhibited their weakest or most servile personality in ancient times. After the Second Sino–Japanese War, the war atrocities and fierce fighting against the Japanese troops turned the Chinese into possibly the toughest race in the world. This personality change and their hatred for the Japanese led the Chinese people to accept the communists, who had the greatest combative capacity, as their leaders. In fact, the toughening up of the Chinese national character might have been positively related to the popularity of the CCP among the Chinese populace. This point is discussed further as follows.

The Chinese national character had to be sufficiently tough so that some Chinese were willing to risk their lives to fight against the formidable Japanese army. The Chinese demanded the leadership of the Chinese communists, as it would substantially increase their chances of winning battles against the Japanese troops. However, after some small victories, the Japanese troops came back for revenge by committing more atrocities against the Chinese and their loved ones. These atrocities generated more hatred for the Japanese, making the Chinese people braver and convincing more young men to join the anti-Japanese gueril-las. A greater demand for CCP leadership arose, not only because of the increase in the guerilla forces but also because the Chinese people were expecting to fight additional stronger Japanese troops. Of course, the cycle continued, with the number of atrocities increasing and the Chinese national character growing tougher.

Douglass North received the 1993 Nobel Prize in Economics for his research related to institutional change. North's insight was that social institutions such as constitutions, laws, customs, and traditions are developed in a way conducive to economic growth and the improvement of social welfare. By this principle, social institutions tend to change along with economic fundamentals.

Before the Japanese invasion, most of the Chinese people had rejected com-munism. One need not study economics to know that one has no incentive to work hard under the economic system of communism, where one's payoff is independent of his work effort. In fact, even orthodox Marxism argues that socialism should be established on the basis of highly developed capitalism. A highly developed capitalist economy entails an extremely complicated form of industrial specialization, which Karl Marx thought could only be well coordinated by the central planning of the government. Marx also argued that the workers who engaged in complicated modern production had to coordinate well with other workers, which induced them to show concern for others and to be unselfish. When capitalism is developed to a sufficiently high level, it is replaced by socialism and communism, which is more conducive to economic develop-ment. Therefore, even according to orthodox Marxism, communism was not suitable for China at the time. This may explain the small size of the Chinese Red Army before 1937.

However, after the Sino–Japanese War, the hideous atrocities committed by the Japanese changed the Chinese people's mentality. The Chinese were no longer concerned about economic development. Instead, their main concern became defeating the Japanese invaders. For example, Zhao (2004, p. 100) observes the following: "A large portion of the Chinese population was brought to bear the brutal consequences of Japanese imperialism because victims of the Japanese policy included not only poor peasants but also landlords and rich peasants. The effect of this policy was to arouse even the most parochial villagers to the fact that there was no way to accommodate Japanese rule short of slavery; the only hope for a normal life lay in resistance."

The Chinese people quickly learned that the only force that could match and beat the Japanese army in terms of bravery and toughness was the Chinese Red Army under the CCP, which was renamed the Eighth Route Army of the National Revolutionary Army of the Republic of China after 1937. Although the Chinese communists were not good at managing the economy, they produced the toughest warriors and the best guerilla leaders in the late 1930s. In terms of economics, they were the best "military entrepreneurs," which were obviously in popular demand due to the cutthroat pressure from the Japanese invaders. In fact, even landlords and rich peasants joined forces with the CCP, and they often had weapons and private forces, whose original purpose was to protect their properties from bandits. Due to their hatred of the Japanese, they often provided the CCP-led guerillas with weapons and sometimes even the private guards of their homes.

The preceding argument is consistent with some of the history literature. For example, Johnson (1962, p. 69) states: "Japan's invasion and occupation of China decisively altered the political interests of the peasantry. Prior to 1937, the peasants were a passive element in politics; even the earlier Communist bid for power, based on an appeal to peasant economic interests, was a conspicuous failure. The pre-war peasant was absorbed in local matters and had only the dimmest sense of 'China.' Japan's invasion changed this condition by heightening the peasant's interest in such concepts as national defense, citizenship, treason, legitimacy of government, and the long-range betterment of the Chinese state. This came about as a result of certain specific new pressures on Chinese rural society that were contributed by the Japanese Army . . . Although the peasantry, on the eve of war, was no more opposed to the Japanese than it was to other authorities, it acquired anti-Japanese attitudes as a result of the behavior of Japanese troops and the failure of Japanese leaders to offer a better alternative than resistance or slavery. If anti-Japanese feelings were not created by the invasion itself, they were created by the 'mop-ups' – which were aimed directly at the peasantry. Japanese military activity in the rural areas compelled the Chinese peasant to join other activated peasants for the common defense . . . Japan made an overambitious estimate of the area it could safely occupy in China; the result was that the Imperial Army drove out the KMT and then, in effect, left the territory empty for the Communists to enter."

According to the analysis presented in this chapter and several of the previous chapters, the extent of the mass-scale rapes and other atrocities committed by the Japanese troops were often closely related to their casualties. In other words, the greater the casualties, the more serious the mass-scale rapes and killings.

A vicious cycle started in China, in which rape led to the Chinese resisting against the Japanese army, which led to more rape and then more resistance. During this process, the Chinese national character became increasingly tougher. The atrocities, which mostly occurred as a result of the Japanese troops oppressing China's guerilla warfare, usually happened in the areas where the fighting occurred.[3]

The toughness of the personality of the Chinese people who fought fiercely against the Japanese under the leadership of the CCP was well illustrated by the easy victory of the CCP in the civil war that ensured after the Second Sino–Japanese War. Japan's surrender in August 1945 set the stage for a resumed civil war between Chinese communists and the Kuomintang in China. The United States sided with the Kuomintang immediately. Although the Kuomintang was only nominally democratic and Chiang Kai-shek was really a dictator, the United States knew that its ideological differences with the Chinese communists were far greater than those with the Kuomintang.

The United States trained and armed the troops of the Kuomintang as if they were its own army. For example, a large proportion of Kuomintang troops were equipped with United States military supplies. The United States trained over 500,000 Kuomintang troops, and the American air force airlifted many KMT troops from central China to strategically important areas such as northeast China.

Thus, at the beginning of the civil war, it appeared that the Kuomintang had the upper hand. The Kuomintang had much better weapons, and its army numbered 4.3 million men. In comparison, the communist army had only 1.2 million soldiers. However, as soon as the full-scale war broke out in 1947, the Kuomintang army was simply no match for the communist army. At least 1.5 million Kuomintang troops were annihilated in the Liaoshen, Pingjin, and Huaihai Campaigns, and the communist troops often suffered only 10 percent of the casualties suffered by the Kuomintang troops.[4] In other words, the Kuomintang troops performed far worse against the Chinese communist troops than the Imperial Japanese Army.

In 1949, the Kuomintang troops were almost entirely annihilated by the People's Liberation Army (PLA). Fortunately for the Kuomintang, Taiwan was given back to China after World War II. In 1949, Chiang Kai-shek, the government of the Kuomintang, and a small fraction of the troops fled to this large island, which avoided complete annihilation.

The preceding historical facts have often been described in the literature. However, the reasons behind why the Chinese communist army defeated the Kuomintang army so easily and overwhelmingly remain unclear and unconvincing at best.

Wikipedia provides the following reasons:[5] "The Nationalists, who had an advantage in both numbers of men and weapons, controlled a much larger territory and population than their adversaries and enjoyed considerable world support including direct support from the United States, nevertheless suffered from a lack of morale and rampant corruption that greatly reduced their ability to fight, as well as their domestic civilian support. Crucially, during World War II, while Nationalists and Communists were in an alliance against fascist forces (chiefly Japanese troops and their Chinese supporters), the majority of the Nationalist troops had already been wounded or killed while the communists had suffered minimal losses."

This statement contains a number of deficiencies. First, as described earlier, when the Sino–Japanese War broke out in July 1937, the Chinese communist army had only 30,000 soldiers. By the time of the Japanese surrender in 1945, the communist army had 1.2 million soldiers and the CCP's membership comprised 2.7 million people. How could the CCP and its army have grown so rapidly if it had simply been hiding in the remote area of Yan'an? (There were only about 1.42 million people in Yan'an, including women, children, and the elderly.)

Second, it is true that 1.32 million troops of the Kuomintang army were killed in the Sino–Japanese War, and that many more were wounded. However, in 1946, the Kuomintang had an army of 4.3 million strong and healthy soldiers. Moreover, they acquired much better weaponry from the United States. (They also obtained the surrendered arms of most of the Japanese troops, although the Kuomintang troops did not often use them and preferred American weapons.)

Third, rampant corruption did exist in the Kuomintang army and government during the civil war period between 1947 and 1949. However, the level of corruption was also serious both before and during the Sino–Japanese War. Moreover, before 1937, the Chinese national government was composed of various warlords who often acted autonomously. After World War II, Chiang Kai-shek basically consolidated the control of various warlords, which greatly enhanced the combative effectiveness of the Kuomintang army. Thus, although corruption might have been an important factor in the CCP's defeat of the Kuomintang army, it was not the fundamental reason.

This chapter provides a new reason for why communists won the civil war, and it is based in human capital theory. In this case, "human capital" refers to the "quality" or combative capacities of the soldiers. In 1946, the Chinese communist army had far fewer soldiers than the Kuomintang army. However, the average "quality" of the CCP soldiers was much higher than that of the Kuomintang soldiers.

Most of the PLA soldiers were former CCP-led guerillas who had fought numerous bloody battles against the Japanese troops in an extremely difficult environment. The fighting skills of CCP soldiers were sharpened in their harsh battles against the brutal Japanese troops through "learning by doing." A large fraction of the Kuomintang soldiers also had the experience of fighting the Japanese army. However, since 1940, the Kuomintang and Japanese armies had waged relatively few battles, and the two sides had reached a confrontational stalemate. On the contrary, the CCP-led guerillas had been engaged in constant battles with the Japanese troops, who possessed far superior weapons. Indeed, the Japanese troops had implemented their "kill all" policy for both the Chinese communist troops and Chinese civilians. The guerillas who survived were trained to be superb warriors, and in terms of the evolutionary theory were the "fittest" survivors/fighters. In fact, some Kuomintang troops also tried to wage guerilla warfare in the Sino–Japanese War, but were quickly annihilated by the Japanese army. Indeed, only the fittest survived in such brutal and difficult environments.

Moreover, most of the CCP guerillas witnessed their loved ones being killed and raped by Japanese troops, which accounted for why they became guerillas in the first place. Their unbearable hatred and shame made them fearless fighters on the battlefield. However, most of the Kuomintang soldiers had not had such direct horrible personal experiences, and hence could not match the CCP guerillas in terms of personality toughness.

The combative skills of PLA soldiers improved substantially during the difficult guerilla battles. Because the communist guerilla soldiers had to fight efficiently to survive, they learned how to collaborate with other soldiers to fight like a team. In the words of Michael Kremer, they perfected their "O-ring production function" of combat in their frequent guerilla warfare with Japanese troops. One example of the bravery of the Chinese soldiers is Dong Cunrui, whom Wikipedia describes as follows:[6]

> Dong Cunrui (1929 – May 25, 1948) was a Chinese Communist soldier in the People's Liberation Army during the Chinese Civil War who blew himself up in order to destroy a Kuomintang bunker guarding to approach to an important bridge in Longhua County. Under heavy fire, he reached the bunker, but there was no place to effectively position the explosives. Reportedly shouting "For a new China!", he detonated the explosives he carried, killing himself and the defenders within the bunker.

Before the Chinese civil war started, the Kuomintang army had an obvious weaponry advantage. The Chinese communist troops obtained a large fraction of their weapons after killing or capturing the Japanese soldiers and puppet forces. In Manchuria, Chinese troops obtained some of the arms of former Japanese troops who surrendered to the Soviets. For example, the Fourth Division of the PLA led by Lin Biao was extremely formidable because it was equipped with the Japanese weapons. This might have been the only useful help the Chinese communists received from the Soviet Union.[7]

The combination of having the best-quality Chinese soldiers and Japanese weapons made Lin Biao's troops invincible. By way of an effective analogy, consider gifted professional swimmer Michael Phelps. Phelps won eight gold medals at the 2008 Beijing Olympic Games, a triumph that made him a household name in China and made him the popular subject of many stories. One story related to his training exercises. Phelps sometimes attached weights to his legs to create a handicap that helped him swim faster in competitions, when he was free of any handicaps. The soldiers in the communist army were "handicapped" in terms of the weapons they were using before the Japanese surrendered. When they acquired the Japanese weapons from the Soviet army, they became much better fighters.

However, the weaponry of the Kuomintang army, which was largely provided by the United States, was far more advanced than that of the PLA. In fact, the United States began to systematically arm the Kuomintang army with advanced weapons close to the end of the Sino–Japanese War for the purpose of defeating the Japanese army in China. However, the dropping of nuclear bombs on two Japanese cities and the Soviet invasion of Manchuria ended the war much earlier than expected. Because of this major advantage in military equipment, Chiang Kai-shek proclaimed in 1946 that it would take only three to six months to annihilate the Chinese communist army.[8] Many people at the time did not consider Chiang to be overly confident. Indeed, even with much poorer weapons, the Kuomintang army fought well against the Imperial Japanese Army, which was not only armed with a much more expansive artillery, but also motivated by the Bushido spirit.

However, the reality was quite different for Chiang and the Chinese national government. In most of their encounters with the PLA, the Kuomintang troops collapsed immediately. In the major battles against Lin Biao's PLA troops, who were armed with Japanese weapons, the casualty ratio between the Kuomintang army and PLA was about 10:1 (captives included). In fact, the Kuomintang troops were often commanded by the national heroes who made their names in the anti-Japanese war. The troops fought brilliantly against the Imperial Japanese Army, but often collapsed immediately after brief fights with the PLA. The PLA soldiers who survived the guerilla warfare against the Japanese army were simply too tough. Chiang and the Kuomintang army survived in Taiwan because the PLA did not have a navy, and the United States navy ultimately intervened in 1950.

In summary, the most important explanation for the devastating defeat of the Kuomintang army by the PLA is that the Chinese communist troops consisted of the soldiers with the toughest personalities and great combat skills. The Imperial Japanese Army was motivated by the spirit of Bushido, which proved to be formidable in the Russo–Japanese War and First Sino–Japanese War and at the beginning of the Second Sino–Japanese War. The fighting spirit of the Chinese communist troops appeared to be overwhelming, even when compared with the Bushido spirit. Indeed, the CCP guerillas who survived the numerous ruthless Japanese military campaigns in extreme harsh environments and witnessed their loved ones being killed and raped by Japanese soldiers developed a personality that was extremely tough, turning them into the best soldiers on the battlefields.

Notes

1　http://en.wikipedia.org/wiki/Yang_Jingyu
2　See, e.g., Forbes (1986).
3　See, e.g., Johnson (1962) and Zhao (2004).
4　http://en.wikipedia.org/wiki/Category:Battles_of_the_Chinese_Civil_War
5　http://en.wikipedia.org/wiki/Chinese_Civil_War
6　http://en.wikipedia.org/wiki/Dong_Cunrui

7 In fact, the Kuomintang and Soviet Union made a deal before the Chinese civil war that the Kuomintang would accept Mongolia's independence in exchange for the Soviet's agreement not to help the Chinese communists in China. This deal led the Kuomintang, the official central government of the Republic of China at the time, to announce its recognition of Mongolia's independence in January 1946. It signed a friendship treaty with the Mongolian government in February.

8 http://www.san.beck.org/21-5-ChinaatWar1937-49.html#a5

Part VII

The establishment of communist China and the Chinese national character

27 Korean War

The Korean War took place between 1950 and 1953, with the United States and China acting as the main forces. It ended in an armistice that restored the border between the two Korean nations near the 38th Parallel.

The Korean War has been China's most brilliant victory for nearly the last two centuries. With far inferior military equipment, the Chinese army went to Korea to fight the United States army, which had just defeated the almighty Imperial Japanese Army in the Pacific War. The weaponry of the United States army was far beyond that of the Chinese army. In particular, whereas the United States army enjoyed absolute air superiority, China barely had an air force to speak of. Moreover, still fresh in the memories of the people at the time, the United States army had just dropped two nuclear bombs on Japan five years earlier. The Chinese and United States armies fought fiercely for three years in Korea, a war that ultimately resulted in a tie between the two sides. The outcome of the Korean War and China's courageous participation are sources of enormous national pride for the Chinese people. In relation to the main theme of this book, they demonstrated that the "personality" of the Chinese people had become one of the toughest in the world.

Japan ruled Korea from 1910 to 1945. After the Japanese surrender, the Korean Peninsula was divided into two nations with the 38th Parallel acting as the national border. This division was a compromise made between the United States and Soviet Union at the Potsdam Conference in August 1945, rather than a decision made by the Korean people. North Korea became a communist regime, and South Korea was under the influence of the United States.

In 1950, Kim Il-sung, the leader of North Korea, decided to unite the Korean Peninsula by force. Kim received support from the Soviet Union and China. The Soviet Union supplied North Korea with tanks and artillery, and the Chinese army released ethnic Korean units who subsequently joined the army of North Korea. In June 1950, the army of North Korea launched its invasion and quickly captured Seoul. The United States army then stepped in to protect South Korea. After some fierce battles, the army of North Korea was completely defeated, and in October 1950 it retreated almost all the way back to the Yalu River, the border between Korea and China. MacArthur, the commander-in-chief of the United States army, demanded the unconditional surrender of the North Korean army.

The Chinese army, which was operating under the name of the "Chinese People's Volunteer Army" (PVA), entered Korea on October 19, 1950. The United Nations forces led by the United States were quickly repelled back to the 38th Parallel under the heavy assaults of the PVA. However, because China did not have a navy and had a much weaker air force than the United States, the PVA experienced increasing difficulties in receiving supplies of food, arms, and medicine when they got deeper into the Korean Peninsula. Beginning in late 1951, the Korean War fell into a stalemate. Although bloody battles continued, neither side was able to advance any farther.

Due in large part to the Americans' disappointment with the Korean War, United States President Harry S. Truman failed in his attempt at reelection in 1952. When Dwight D. Eisenhower took office as the new president, he immediately visited Korea and began to strongly and publicly hint that the United States may resort to the use of nuclear weapons. Perhaps due to Eisenhower's threats of nuclear attacks, an armistice agreement was reached in July 1953 between all of the parties involved in the Korean War. However, even today, many Chinese people consider Eisenhower's nuclear threat a great honor for China, as they believed it proved the combative power of the Chinese army in the Korean War. Indeed, Dwight D. Eisenhower was the supreme commander of the Allied Forces in World War II in Europe, and his extensive experience in the war made him a good judge of whether the United States would win the Korean War through the use of conventional weapons.

Although the American troops possessed far superior weapons and enjoyed absolute superiority in their air force and navy, the United States army failed to win the war against the PVA. The most reasonable explanation for this appears to be that the Chinese soldiers were much better fighters. The bravery of the PVA can be illustrated by the Battle of Triangle Hill, which took place between October 14 and November 25, 1952. Wikipedia describes part of the battle as follows:[1]

> Over the course of nearly a month, substantial American and South Korean forces made repeated attempts to capture Triangle Hill and the adjacent Sniper Ridge. Despite clear superiority in artillery and aircraft, escalating American and South Korean casualties resulted in the attack being halted after 42 days of fighting, with Chinese forces regaining their original positions.
>
> On October 14, 1952 at 4 am, following two days of preliminary air strikes, the ROK-American bombardment intensified across the 30 km (19 mi) front held by the Chinese 15th Corps. At 5 am, the 280 guns and howitzers of the IX Corps extended their firing range to allow for the ROK-American infantry to advance behind a rolling barrage. The concentrated bombardment succeeded in clearing the foliage on Triangle Hill and Sniper Ridge, destroying most of the above-ground fortifications on the two positions. The intense shelling also disrupted Chinese communication lines, eliminating all wired and wireless communications in the area.

As the American and South Korean forces approached the Chinese defenses, they were met with grenades, Bangalore torpedoes, shaped charges and rocks. Unable to safely advance, American and South Korean troops were forced to rely on close-support artillery to subdue Chinese resistance, but a complex network of bunkers and tunnels allowed the Chinese to bring up reinforcements as the above-ground troops were depleted. Although the 31st Infantry Regiment was equipped with ballistic vests in the first mass military deployment of modern personal armor; its 1st and 3rd battalions nevertheless suffered 96 fatalities, with an additional 337 men wounded in the first attack – the heaviest casualties the 31st Infantry Regiment had suffered in a single day during the war. . . .

To recover lost ground, the PVA 45th Division commander Cui Jiangong attempted a sneak attack with three infantry companies by 7 pm. When flares broke the night cover, the attackers launched bayonet charges and hand-to-hand fighting ensued. The UN forces responded with heavy artillery fire, but the determined Chinese assault troops marched through both Chinese and UN artillery screens to reach the UN positions – a strange sight that made some American observers believe that the attackers were under the influence of drugs. The intense fighting prevented UN forces from receiving any resupply, and the UN defenders were forced to give up all captured ground after running out of ammunition.

Running out of ammunition, the Chinese soldiers threw rocks at the American forces, who were equipped with the best military equipment (including ballistic vests) at the time. In fact, a rare photo of Chinese soldiers throwing rocks was taken and can be found on the website mentioned in the preceding article. This battle had a long-term effect that Wikipedia describes as follows:[2]

The Battle of Triangle Hill was the biggest and bloodiest contest of 1952. After 42 days of heavy fighting, the Eighth Army had failed to gain the two hill masses that were its original goal. For the Chinese, on the other hand, not only did the 15th Corps stop the UN attacks at Triangle Hill, the assaults conducted by the 44th Division on the Pyonggang front also resulted in Jackson Heights' capture on November 30. Although the Chinese had suffered 11,500 casualties with many units decimated during the battle, its ability to sustain such losses had slowly exhausted the US Eighth Army over two months of attrition. The PVA High Command viewed the victory as vindication that attrition was an effective strategy against the UN forces, while the Chinese became more aggressive in the armistice negotiations and on the battlefield. Meanwhile, the high UN casualties forced Clark to suspend any upcoming offensive operations involving more than one battalion, effectively preventing any major UN offensives for the rest of the war. Clark and US President Harry S. Truman later confided that the battle was a serious blow to the UN morale. . . Despite its impact and scale, the Battle of Triangle Hill is one of the least known episodes of the Korean War within the Western media. For the Chinese, this costly victory presented an opportunity to promote the value of endurance and sacrifice. The courage demonstrated by the Chinese soldiers at Triangle Hill was repeatedly glorified in various forms of media, including several major motion pictures.

The Chinese army faced serious logistical problems during the Korean War due to a lack of air support. In fact, a large fraction of Chinese casualties, and perhaps the major fraction according to some sources, resulted from starvation and a lack of clothing in cold weather. The little air force protection China received overextended the communication and supply lines in the narrow and long Korean Peninsula. As a result, the Chinese troops suffered severe logistical problems throughout the war. Peng Dehuai, the commander-in-chief of the Chinese army in Korea, once sent his deputy Hong Xuezhi to Beijing to meet Chinese Premier Zhou Enlai to discuss the matter, and Barnouin and Yu (2006, p. 149) describe their conversation as follows:

> (Hong said,) What his soldiers feared, he said, was not the enemy, but that they had nothing to eat, no bullets to shoot, and no trucks to transport them to the rear when they were wounded. Zhou replied the Soviet air force, despite Stalin's promises, has not arrived.

This logistical problem limited the number of Chinese soldiers that could be stationed on the frontline. For example, suppose that one soldier needed one unit of food to stay alive for a certain period. If there were 1,000 units of food that could have been supplied to the frontline, then only 1,000 soldiers or fewer should have been sent to the frontline. If 2,000 soldiers were sent to the front line, allocating the food would have been difficult. If the food was divided evenly, all of the soldiers would have starved. If not divided evenly, certain soldiers would have been assigned to die. This logic also applied to other valuable resources such as clothing and ammunition. The Chinese troops were often outnumbered by the joint forces of the United States and South Korea when they were pushed farther into the long and thin Korean Peninsula. A stalemate between the two sides was ultimately reached in the middle of Korea at the 38th Parallel.

Why did China participate in the Korean War in the first place? When Mao Zedong and other Chinese leaders were deciding whether to enter the war, they should have expected that it would be both costly and dangerous. The United States possessed powerful atomic bombs and demonstrated that it would use them in 1945, just five years before the Korean War. Even in conventional warfare, the United States army overwhelmingly defeated the formidable Imperial Japanese Army in the Pacific War, and the PLA had a far worse navy and air force than the Japanese army. On October 15, 1950, Douglas MacArthur, the commander-in-chief of the United Nations troops in Korea, met President Truman on an island in the mid-Pacific Ocean. General MacArthur assured Truman that it would be unwise for China to enter the war. Because Chinese ground troops had no air force protection, MacArthur stated that "if the Chinese tried to get down to Pyongyang, there would be the greatest slaughter."[3]

Moreover, when the United States had suffered severe casualties, General MacArthur seriously proposed using nuclear weapons against the inland areas of China. Fortunately for China, the American president rejected MacArthur's proposals. In sum, the potential expected cost for China to intervene in the Korean War was enormous, and should have been clear to Mao Zedong and other Chinese leaders. Therefore, China's entry into the war implied that it expected tremendous benefits from doing so.

What exactly were those benefits? The common answer to this question is that North Korea served as a "buffer zone" between the United States and China. At first sight, this argument appears plausible. If an American invasion into China had to go through the Korean Peninsula, then it might have made sense for China to help North Korea avoid being occupied by American forces. China's national security would have been enhanced by the hostility of the North Korean regime toward the United States.

However this argument has two major logical deficiencies. First, with their advanced military equipment, the United States army and navy would have been able to launch a lethal attack almost anywhere in China's coastal areas. Indeed, Japan engaged in the first major battle with China in Shanghai. In fact, going through Korea and then attacking Manchuria might not have been the best strategy for invading China if the United States had wanted to do so. Second, without a Chinese army stationed in Korea, which was the case shortly after the Korean War, the American army could have defeated the North Korean army within a few hours if it had concentrated its forces and launched a surprise attack. Thus, the cushion of North Korea would not have meant much during a large-scale American invasion into China.

This chapter offers some new explanations. First, Mao Zedong and other Chinese leaders must have expected that the United States would collude with the Kuomintang army to invade China.

In June 1950, when the news of North Korea's invasion of South Korea reached President Truman, he immediately rated it at the level of Adolf Hitler's aggressions in the 1930s. In his autobiography, President Truman observes the following: "Communism was acting in Korea, just as Hitler, Mussolini and the Japanese had ten, fifteen, and twenty years earlier. I felt certain that if South Korea was allowed to fall, Communist leaders would be emboldened to override nations closer to our own shores. If the Communists were permitted to force their way into the Republic of Korea without opposition from the free world, no small nation would have the courage to resist threat and aggression by stronger Communist neighbors."[4]

His reaction infers that the United States had already adopted a Cold War mentality. Because the United States entered the Korean War purely for ideological reasons rather than for the purposes of territory expansion or material benefit, it might have been reasonable for Mao Zedong to suspect that the United States was tempted to do the same thing in China with its support of the Kuomintang army. This suspicion was significantly reinforced when the Seventh Fleet of the United States navy was sent to the Taiwan Strait in June 1950, only two days after North Korea invaded South Korea. Due to the intervention of the Seventh Fleet, Chinese leaders knew immediately that a PLA invasion of Taiwan was out of the question. Chinese Premier Zhou Enlai angrily criticized the United States, calling its Seventh Fleet an "armed aggression on Chinese territory." On August 4, 1950, Mao Zedong decided to abort his plan to invade Taiwan.

Furthermore, the Chinese leaders might have feared that the United States generals were intoxicated by their would-be victory in Korea and thinking enthusiastically about helping the Kuomintang army in Taiwan invade Mainland China. This suspicion might have been further reinforced by Chiang Kai-shek's eager offer to send the Kuomintang troops to participate in the Korean War.

Under such an expectation, sending Chinese troops to fight the Korean War might have presented a huge potential benefit to China. Many United States generals such as Douglas MacArthur looked down on the Chinese army, judging the United States army as far superior due to its much more advanced military equipment. Therefore, there was an asymmetry of information between Mao Zedong and Douglas MacArthur. Mao knew that the Chinese soldiers were the best fighters in the world, and that this made up for their weak weaponry. However, Douglas MacArthur was unaware of this piece of information, and the only way to inform him was to send Chinese troops to fight against the United States forces in the Korean War. In recent years, there have been discussions over whether China showed ingratitude by fighting the United States army in Korea despite receiving its help in the Second Sino–Japanese War. However, this chapter would suggest that the fighting benefited both sides.

In fact, the preceding argument is line with the theory of signaling in economics, which Spence (1973, 1974) developed in his Nobel Prize–winning contribution. Spence analyzed a setting in which employees try to signal their productive skills to employers by acquiring a high degree of education. Because the cost of obtaining an education is usually lower for the individuals of higher abilities, they are more likely to obtain certificates. Spence then showed that there is a self-fulfilling equilibrium in which individuals who receive a high level of education signal their high abilities, and employers accept this signal by paying them high wages. According to this analysis, China used the Korean War to signal its military strength to the United States, potentially preventing a much more costly war between the two countries.

Notes

1 http://en.wikipedia.org/wiki/Battle_of_Triangle_Hill
2 http://en.wikipedia.org/wiki/Battle_of_Triangle_Hill
3 Donovan (1996, p. 285).
4 http://en.wikipedia.org/wiki/Korean_War

28 Cultural Revolution

On October 1, 1949, Mao Zedong announced the birth of the People's Republic of China at Tiananmen Square in Beijing, adding that "from now on, Chinese people will stand up." After over 100 years of humiliation, a proud China was born again. Indeed, it is not an exaggeration to say that the People's Republic of China was established on the bases of humiliation and pride.

The communist rule in China fundamentally changed Chinese culture and substantially reinforced the toughness and bellicose nature of the Chinese national character, which was largely created and fostered by the atrocities committed by Japanese troops. The term "Cultural Revolution" is usually used in reference to the political movement enacted in 1966 in China. However, this chapter argues that the whole period of communist rule in China, which lasted for several decades and may continue to exist today albeit under a lesser ideology, may be considered as a cultural revolution of the Chinese people. It has drastically changed the Chinese culture, and in particular almost eradicated the Confucian culture that had taken deep root in ancient China.

Why did the CCP want to destroy the Confucian culture? In the 1910s, many Chinese intellectuals wanted China to eliminate Confucianism. Back then, the purpose of the New Cultural Movement was to instill toughness in the Chinese national character and thereby improve the bravery of Chinese soldiers. However, in the "new China," Confucianism not only contradicted the ideology of communism in many ways, but also did not fit with how China's economy and politics were being managed. In contrast, cultivating people with a national character that emphasized valor and despised cowardice might have been only a minor purpose. Although the title of this chapter is "Cultural Revolution," it intends to show that the Chinese traditional culture was continuously attacked and seriously damaged during the entire period of communist rule in China. In particular, Mao Zedong observed that communist rule could be destroyed by corruption, which would be eliminated only when every CCP member subscribed to a strong communist ideology.

In the first few years after 1949, the Chinese economy developed quickly. The government was efficient at restoring war-damaged industrial installations and building new infrastructure. However, from the mid-1950s until the death of Mao Zedong in 1976, China's economic development was a total failure.

From an economics perspective, this failure was well expected. Most people have little incentive to work hard in an economic system in which one's payoff is little related to his or her work performance.

Moreover, Mao Zedong encountered another rarely noted difficulty in ruling China via communism: the corruption of government officials. Although corruption is a problem in all countries and societies, it is of greater concern in a communist country like China for two reasons. First, government officials have more power in a communist country. In a democratic country, an official's power is usually constrained by the "checks and balances" system applied in the country's political and legal institutions. However, in a communist country, an official, who is usually a member of the Communist Party, is assumed to be a person who is completely unselfish. Therefore, there are usually no "checks and balances" applied to his powers. Furthermore, a communist country like China operates in a planning economy, in which government officials are supposed to play key roles. Consequently, the cliché that "absolute power leads to absolute corruption" applies to China. Second, communism is based on the ideology of absolute equality. Therefore, the inequality resulting from officials' corruption bred bitterness and anger toward the CCP, which threatened to destabilize its rule in China.

Mao Zedong recognized the seriousness of this corruption at the birth of the People's Republic of China. For example, as early as December 1951, the CCP launched a major anti-corruption campaign in Manchuria known as the "Three-anti Campaign."[1] The campaign was mainly aimed at government officials within the CCP. Its targets included three areas: corruption, waste, and bureaucratism. Although the first category is clear, the latter two may require further explanation.

First, an official can gain from abusing his power in a number of ways. Taking bribes and embezzling public funds are usually the greatest temptations, and are placed in the category of "corruption." However, an official can also achieve personal gains from other channels. For example, he can buy a luxurious car using public money, or hold an expensive banquet. It is also easy for an official to find justifications or excuses for these kinds of expenditures. In fact, some public expenditures belonging to these categories can indeed be beneficial to a government and may enhance administrative efficiency. This explains why the Three-anti Campaign targeted "waste." It aimed to punish the officials who spent public money excessively for their personal gains.

The third target of the campaign was "bureaucratism," a word that might have been created in China and relates to an official who behaves like a bureaucrat. In the context of China at the time, this word had a number of meanings. First, in ancient China, a bureaucrat often behaved as if he were superior to ordinary people. Thus, if an official in the CPP government behaved with an attitude of superiority over others, the effect of his behavior was considered "bureaucratism." Second, for similar reasons, an official might have been reluctant to interact with ordinary workers and peasants. Although talking to peasants might have been beneficial to his work, he might have considered it a loss of social status. Third, an official might have found ways to demonstrate his powers, which often led to more inefficient administrations. Thus, the campaign targeted the officials who tried to satisfy themselves by demonstrating their power and status.

An official could also pursue personal gains through other channels. For example, through his powers and connections with other officials, he might have found good jobs for his relatives. In deciding to promote his subordinates, he might have chosen those with whom he had closer private connections, such as his relatives or family friends. Moreover, he might have sought sexual favors from his female subordinates with the promise of allocating them better jobs.

Since the 1990s, it has been an "unspoken rule" of the movie industry in China that many actresses are coerced explicitly or implicitly to have sex with movie directors or producers to obtain roles in movies. This pattern of corruption has found its way into many occupations in China, including the government. The downfall of a senior official is usually accompanied by reports that he had sex with his subordinates. Although this kind of corrupt behavior should have been much less serious and widespread in the early periods of the People's Republic of China, it is reasonable to suspect that it occurred. After all, the cliché "absolute power leads to absolute corruption" usually applies everywhere.

Evidence of corruption is relatively easy to obtain. However, it is usually harder to prove that an official engages in "waste" and "bureaucratism." The Three-anti Campaign allowed a large number of ordinary people to make judgments, and should have been an effective way of deterring officials from engaging in corruptive behavior. Of course, a side effect of the campaign was that many innocent officials were wrongly punished.

Another goal of the CCP was to promote the ideology of communism. A necessary condition for this promotion was that the government officials be relatively incorrupt. Thus, the goals of promoting communism and cracking down on corruption went hand in hand, and the campaigns against corruption and non-communist ideologies were often launched simultaneously. One such example is the Socialist Education Movement launched in 1963. This campaign was summarized in four government official "cleanups," including political, economic, organizational, and ideological cleanups. The economic cleanups were related to corruption. Mao Zedong aimed to clean up any capitalist elements related to the CCP government officials. However, the outcome of this campaign was disappointing to Mao Zedong, and was an important influence behind his launch of the Cultural Revolution in 1966.

Mao found that bourgeois elements in the government were undermining the ideology of communism, and that many government officials were taking a "capitalist road." In other words, he thought that many government officials were pursuing personal gains and losing their communism ideology. Many young people in China, mainly students, responded enthusiastically to Mao's call for the Cultural Revolution, and spontaneously formed groups of "Red Guards" across China. A large fraction of government officials were persecuted or even tortured by the corps of "Red Guards" and then purged from the government and CCP.

It may be human nature for an individual to try to pursue his self-interest and personal gains. China's communist government lacked a political and legal institution that could "check and balance" the powers of government officials. Therefore, Mao Zedong might have been correct in noticing that many government officials showed "bourgeois tendencies." A mass campaign may be an effective substitute for a political and legal institution in preventing government officials from abusing their power in the pursuit of personal gains. For example, if an official expected a cultural revolution to be launched every five years, he would be very unlikely to accept bribes or coerce his female subordinates to have sex with him based on the "unspoken rule." Of course, even if an official were to always behave decently, there would remain a non-trivial chance that he would be wrongly accused in a campaign. However, if an official coerced his female subordinates to have sex with him or even behaved rudely and arrogantly to others, he would definitely be persecuted and even tortured when a campaign such as a cultural revolution is launched. Perhaps based on this logic, Mao Zedong suggested that a cultural revolution be launched once every 10 years.

In addition to implementing the mass movement, Mao Zedong tried to instill the ideology of communism into people's minds. Indeed, Confucianism is supposed to operate in an economy of private ownership, and is not suitable as an ideology in a planning economy in which government officials often have unchecked absolute powers. Thus, if and only if the Chinese people and particularly government officials lived for the ideology of communism rather than Confucianism could selfishness and corruption be eliminated. How to achieve this purpose? The most effective ways of promoting communism were to create national heroes, who were usually those who sacrificed their lives on the battlefield.

Wikipedia provides the following description of the content of a famous essay written by War Wei Wei about Chinese heroes in the Korean War, entitled "Who Are the Most Beloved People?":[2]

> The essay revolves around the theme that the Chinese soldiers are the "most beloved people". To illustrate this point, Wei Wei lists three examples of the soldiers' sacrifices. The first example describes the battle between the Chinese 38th Corps and the US 2nd Infantry Division at the Battle of the Ch'ongch'on River and how a company of soldiers sacrificed themselves during combat. The second example shows an artilleryman rescued a child in the aftermath of an air strike and volunteers for rifleman duty in order to avenge the aggressions against the Korean people. The third example records a conversation from a soldier and his selfless commitment towards the liberation of Korea. The essay ends with a reminder that the peace at home is not possible without the sacrifices from the "most beloved people". . . . the essay succeed in elevating the soldiers' traditionally low social status within the Confucian culture, and it helped to boost the recruitment of soldiers for Korea. In the decades following the essay's publication, the phrase "most beloved people" has become synonymous

with the PVA, while the essay has become required reading in Chinese school curriculum.

This description indicates that the new Chinese culture promoted the extraordinary bravery of Chinese soldiers. Although the CCP's main purpose might not have been to promote the valor and fearlessness of the Chinese in military conflicts, it found it to be the best strategy for attracting the Chinese people's attention and transforming their mentality. If the Japanese invasion turned only a small fraction of Chinese into very tough soldiers, the decades of communist education in China changed the national character of the entire Chinese population as a whole. Indeed, giving one's own life is the biggest form of self-sacrifice and hence the best way of demonstrating unselfishness, which is a necessary condition of the ideology of communism.

For a long period during the CCP rule, the relationship between China and the Soviet Union was tense. Thus, turning people into potentially brave soldiers served a practical purpose, as they would have been of great value if war broke out between the two countries. This further motivated the CCP to promote Chinese figures who fought heroically on the battlefield and further toughened the Chinese personality.

Because Confucianism has many virtues that are valuable for all cultures including the culture of socialism, it did not come under attack before 1966, when the ideology of communism was relatively modest. In 1966, the real Cultural Revolution broke out, introducing the radical ideology of communism to China and tremendously changing the Chinese culture. Although communism had been a functioning ideology in China before 1966, traditional Confucian values were also prevalent in Chinese society. To fully promote the communist ideology and his own ideas, Mao Zedong sent out a call to purge the nation of the "Four Olds," including old customs, cultures, habits, and ideas. This movement culminated in the "Criticizing Confucius Campaign," which lasted from 1973 to 1976. In particular, Confucius himself was portrayed as an evil man and a clown. The vitriolic denunciations of Confucianism had a hand in permanently damaging the traditional Chinese values in Mainland China. Today, the Taiwanese obviously adhere to the Confucian tradition much more than the people in Mainland China.

However, the promotion of the communist ideology ultimately proved to be a failure in China. Millions of years of evolution have made human beings naturally selfish, and the CCP found this difficult to change. The Cultural Revolution also had very negative side effects. Many innocent people were persecuted, the economy collapsed, everyone became suspicious of one another, and factional struggles became widespread. The Cultural Revolution ultimately ended after Mao's death. China then engaged in economic reform by initially recognizing that people were selfishly driven in economic activities. Although the leadership in China continues to claim that it is pursuing communism, the communist ideology has largely disappeared from the populace.

Communism proved disastrous to the economic development of China and other former communist countries.[3] To accelerate its economic growth, China has implemented its "economic reform and open door" policy since 1978 under the leadership of Deng Xiaoping. To convince the Chinese people to changing their combative mentality, Deng argued that "peace and development was the major theme of the contemporary world despite that the international environments can sometimes be complicated."[4]

Looking back, one can see clearly that the Chinese economy has been transformed from a planning economy into a market economy over the past 35 years.[5] The deepening of capitalism in China has naturally been associated with the gradual vanishing of the Chinese people's Marxist and Maoist ideologies. For example, promoting capitalism entails the acceptance of pecuniary incentives and even greed, which completely contradicts the communist ideology. Furthermore, the post-reform period indeed witnessed a generally peaceful environment for China, and the belligerent propensity of most Chinese people has weakened substantially.

In fact, China implemented a development policy that considerably weakened the country's national character: the "single-child policy," which has been implemented in China since 1980. The policy emanated from a belief that China would not be able to achieve modernization and secure welfare gains without significantly curtailing the growth rate of its population.[6] However, an unintended consequence has been a change in the Chinese personality. The single-child generation has been generally spoiled by their parents and grandparents, which would make them bad soldiers on the battlefield. For example, Cameron, Erkal, Gangadharan, and Meng (2013) conducted an experimental study of 421 individuals who were born just before and just after the introduction of the single-child policy in 1979. In their study (p. 953), they find that this policy "has produced significantly less trusting, less trustworthy, more risk-averse, less competitive, more pessimistic, and less conscientious individuals." However, from another perspective, the implementation of the policy suggests that the current Chinese government has a much less bellicose mentality than Mao Zedong, and devotes most of its attention to economic development rather than international conflicts.

The success of China's economic policies introduced an "economic miracle" to China and led to immense changes in Chinese society. China's high-speed economic growth has increased the wealth of the country's population considerably and substantially enhanced its standard of living. Today, visitors to its major cities may well consider China a developed country.

However, a major issue currently facing the Chinese people and government is the lack of a national "core value" or national culture. The traditional culture of Confucianism was denounced and seriously damaged. Corruption among government officials is rampant, perhaps as a result of not only greed but also a lack of moral constraint in a "spiritual vacuum."

The above argument is empirically supported by a rigorous empirical study by three economists. Recently, Liu, Meng, and Wang (2014) designed a research experiment by comparing the reactions of the people in Taiwan and Mainland China toward Confucianism. They selected their subjects of study from the students of National Taiwan University in Taipei and Peking University in Beijing, and conducted their experiment with 195 Taiwanese students and 185 Mainland Chinese students from September 2012 to April 2013.

Liu, Meng, and Wang (2014) divided the students from both Taiwan and Mainland China into two groups: "treatment group" and "control group." Only students in the "treatment group" were given more Confucian education by analyzing six pieces of classic texts from the Analects of Confucius and Mencius, which aimed to increase their awareness of Confucianism. They then investigated how the students in Taiwan and Mainland China reacted to this experiment. They find that the students from Mainland China who were primed for Confucianism immediately afterwards exhibited behaviors that are not in accord with Confucian values, such as that they became more risk loving, less loss averse, and more impatient. In contrast, they find that the Taiwanese students who were primed for Confucianism demonstrated behaviors that are consistent with Confucian values, such as that they became more trustworthy.

Notes

1 See, e.g., Spence (1999).
2 http://en.wikipedia.org/wiki/Who_are_the_Most_Beloved_People%3F
3 See, e.g., Roland (2000), Weil (2009).
4 http://xsqks.ruc.edu.cn/Jweb_jxyyj/EN/abstract/abstract12949.shtml
5 See, e.g., Fan and Wei (2006), Fan, Li, and Wei (2006), and Fan, Wei, and Wu (forthcoming).
6 See, e.g., Bianco and Hua (1988).

29 Epilogue

This book conducts a comprehensive and rigorous analysis of the evolution of the Chinese personality, culture, political and legal institutions, and nationalism by examining numerous events throughout historical and contemporary China. By repeatedly applying the political Coase theorem, it investigates how a "national character" evolves endogenously along with an institutional environment. The book's basic tenet is that personality is determined by material fundamentals.

This book adds a new dimension to the economics literature. It contributes not only to "institutional economics," but also to the emerging literature related to the economics of personality traits (e.g., Borghans, Duckworth, Heckman, and Weel, 2008) and the economics of culture (e.g., Ginsburgh and Throsby (2006, 2014) and Throsby (2000, 2010)). Moreover, from an economics perspective, this book provides new explanations for a number of historical events and helps resolve many of the puzzles presented by historical and contemporary China. Using basic economic logic, it demonstrates that culture shapes history and vice versa.

I grew up in communist China, and went to the United States to pursue my graduate studies in economics. Immediately after obtaining my PhD at Brown University in 1994, I came to teach at Lingnan University in Hong Kong. One of my colleagues was a foreigner who had studied in Taiwan. I often chatted with him, and once told him that when I was in elementary school, my classmates and I all wanted to be soldiers when we grew up. He was very surprised, and replied that when he was in Taiwan, he heard an old Chinese proverb that "a high quality man will not be a soldier, just as a piece of good iron will not be made into nails." Because Taiwan has not experienced a brutal war, despite being colonized by Japan for 50 years, it has largely retained the Chinese Confucian culture. This simple example reflects the transformation of the national character of the Chinese people.

The atrocities committed by the Japanese in World War II fundamentally changed the Chinese national character, and the communist rule in China toughened it further. I was born in 1966, and began to study English in secondary school. Most of our lessons were colored by the communist ideology, but I recall one lesson about a Westerner named Nathan Hale. During the

American Revolutionary War against Britain, Hale, being an American soldier, was caught by the British troop during an intelligence-gathering mission. The lesson highlighted Hale's last words before his execution: "I only regret that I have but one life to give for my country."[1] My classmates and I were required to memorize this sentence. Indeed, the culture in communist China was almost the opposite of the Confucian culture in traditional China.

This book's basic tenet is that personality is determined by material fundamentals that may be reflected in social, political, and economic dimensions. When these material fundamentals change, a country's national character changes accordingly. In particular, the emphasis of valor in a national character is a double-edged sword. A strong social tendency to be violent creates more conflicts among people and increases the cost involved in maintaining a stable society. However, when a country faces an ongoing threat of foreign invasion, the toughness of its national character can be a major advantage that guarantees the combative capacity of its army. Thus, there is a tradeoff between these two aspects, and the best choice for a national character differs across the various economic and military environments. The people in ancient China faced severe threats from the nomadic tribes of the Mongolian steppe, which forced China to remain unified. A weak and submissive national character was the best choice for the ancient Chinese to decrease the cost of administering their country. In the 1930s, the hideous atrocities committed by Japanese soldiers prevented the Chinese from living like humans. To fight against the Japanese invaders, the Chinese people had no choice but to fight fearlessly. The enormous trauma caused by the horrendous atrocities of the Japanese troops, such as mass-scale rapes and murders, and the extremely difficult guerilla warfare conducted against the Japanese army made China's national character both brave and bellicose.

In contemporary times, there seem to be two opposing views related to the Chinese personality. First, many studies have praised the traditional Chinese culture of Confucianism. Chien's (1963) study is representative of this literature. Second, many studies have criticized or ridiculed the Confucian culture, such as those by Lu-Xun (1918, 1921) and others written during the New Cultural Movement in the early part of the last century.

Some books have severely criticized the Chinese culture in recent years, including *The Ugly Chinaman and the Crisis of Chinese Culture* by Bo-Yang (1985) and *I Don't Want to Be Chinese Again* by Joe Chung (2007). Although these authors are Chinese, the titles of their books alone might prevent them from being published in Western countries. However, these books are highly popular among Chinese readers. For example, Chung's book was first published in November 2007 and has already been printed in 55 editions. Bo-Yang's book was first published in 1985, and continues to rank among the top 10 bestselling books in Chinese communities.

One may be appalled by these facts and wonder how they could be true. Somewhat surprisingly, the political Coase theorem can be applied to find the answer. In the new social, political, and economic environment of the modern world, neither the traditional Confucian culture nor the communist ideology are the best choices for China's culture and national character. The Chinese people and particularly those on the mainland are virtually "culture-less" following the destruction of Confucianism after several decades of radical communist rule. They are searching for a new culture and welcome the criticisms of the old in doing so, which explains the popularity of Bo-Yang (1985) and Chung (2007) despite their offensiveness. The current book was written in a similar spirit to help the Chinese people better understand their cultures and search for the best new culture.

As the establishment of a new culture is difficult and costly, it would be best to base it on old cultures. For example, the ancient Chinese found a civilized and non-militaristic way to ensure their dignity and honor through the benevolence ("Ren") and etiquette ("Li") of Confucianism. Thus, the spirit of Confucianism may facilitate the establishment of the so-called Socialist Harmonious Society advocated by the current Chinese leaders. Indeed, in recent years, CCP leaders have tried hard to reinstall Confucian culture into China, and the culture may help China to maintain itself as a large and strong country with a stable social order. In contrast, a culture that implicitly or explicitly worships violence is no longer suitable in the modern world. In fact, as demonstrated by the wars between the United States and Iraq, military technologies determine the outcomes of modern warfare, and the bravery of soldiers plays almost no role. Thus, the political Coase theorem can be applied to predict that the Chinese national character will become increasingly less bellicose. However, it will take time for the toughness of the Chinese personality to disappear, and it has played a role in the formation and development of Chinese nationalism in recent years (Gries, 2003). Indeed, the essence of the political Coase theorem is not that people always choose the best policy or social custom at any point. Rather, it shows that people always tend to determine the best "institution" such as a culture from a long-run perspective, usually through an extensive trial-and-error process.

Moreover, globalization and economic integration may affect the formation of China's new culture. In my research on international economics (Fan, 2004, 2005), I show that one country's degree of international economic integration, which often greatly affects the country's economic growth, crucially depends on the difference in average human capital between that country and the rest of the world. In those studies, "human capital" mainly refers to education and industrial knowhow. However, by the same logic, it may be extended to include the culture and average "personality" of a country.[2] Therefore, the continuous development of China may require it to incorporate the Western culture and particularly the main spirit of Christianity into the formation of a new culture. This may explain the current rapid growth of Christianity in Chinese communities, including those in Mainland China. Finally, China's continuous economic development will ultimately lead to its full democratization,[3] which will in turn greatly influence the new Chinese culture and personality. Better still, with its further economic development, China may be entering the stage of a welfare state, such as many countries of the European Union, for which an altruistic culture and benevolent and non-violent attitudes of the people are its necessary social foundation (e.g., Pestieau, 2005).

Notes

1 See, e.g., Crocker (2006, p. 57).
2 In one study (Fan, 1998), I show that China was successful in attracting foreign investment in the 1980s and 1990s, mainly because there was a large Chinese community conducting international business overseas, which decreased the cost of business transactions.
3 For example, Treisman (2014) analyzes the strong impacts of economic development on democratization.

References

Acemoglu, Daron (1996), "A Microfoundation for Social Increasing Returns in Human Capital Accumulation," *Quarterly Journal of Economics*, 111(3): 779–804.

Acemoglu, Daron (2003), "Why Not a Political Coase Theorem? Social Conflict, Commitment, and Politics," *Journal of Comparative Economics*, 31(4): 620–652.

Acemoglu, Daron and James A. Robinson (2012), *Why Nations Fail: Origins of Power, Poverty and Prosperity*, New York: Crown Publishers.

Acemoglu, Daron, Simon Johnson, and James Robinson (2001), "The Colonial Origins of Comparative Development: An Empirical Investigation," *American Economic Review*, 91(5): 1369–1401.

Adorno, Theodor W., Else Frenkel-Brunswik, Daniel Levinson, and Nevitt Sanford (1950), *The Authoritarian Personality*, New York: Harper and Row.

Akerlof, George A. (1982), "Labor Contracts as Partial Gift Exchange," *Quarterly Journal of Economics*, 97(4): 543–569.

Akerlof, George A. and Janet Yellen (1990), "The Fair Wage-Effort Hypothesis and Unemployment," *Quarterly Journal of Economics*, 105(2): 255–283.

Alesina, Alberto and Enrico Spolaore (1997), "On the Number and Size of Nations," *Quarterly Journal of Economics*, 112(4): 1027–1056.

Alesina, Alberto and Enrico Spolaore (2005a), "War, Peace, and the Size of Countries," *Journal of Public Economics*, 89(7): 1333–1354.

Alesina, Alberto and Enrico Spolaore (2005b), *The Size of Nations*, Cambridge, MA: MIT Press.

Alesina, Alberto and Enrico Spolaore (2006), "Conflict, Defense Spending, and the Number of Nations," *European Economic Review*, 50(1): 91–120.

Allik, Jüri and Robert R. McCrae (2004), "Towards a Geography of Personality Traits: Patterns of Profiles across 36 Cultures," *Journal of Cross-Cultural Psychology*, 35(1): 13–28.

Arrow, Kenneth J. (1962), "The Economic Implications of Learning by Doing," *Review of Economic Studies*, 29(3): 155–173.

Asdrubali, Pierfederico, Bent E. Sorensen, and Oved Yosha (1996), "Channels of Interstate Risk Sharing: United States 1963–1990," *Quarterly Journal of Economics*, 111(4): 1081–1110.

Askin, Kelly Dawn (1997), *War Crimes Against Women: Prosecution in International War Crimes Tribunals*, The Hague: Martinus Nijhoff Publishers.

Bai, Ying and James Kai-sing Kung (2011), "Climate Shocks and Sino-nomadic Conflict," *Review of Economics and Statistics*, 93(3): 970–981.

Bai, Ying and James Kai-sing Kung (2014), "Diffusing Knowledge While Spreading God's Message: Protestantism and Economic Prosperity in China, 1840–1920," Hong Kong University of Science and Technology. *Journal of European Economic Association*, 13(4): 669–698.

Balazs, Etienne (1964), *Chinese Civilization and Bureaucracy: Variations on a Theme*, Hope M. Wright (trans.), Arthur F. Wright (ed.), New Haven and London: Yale University Press.

Barker, Sir Ernest (1979), *National Character and the Factors in Its Formation*, Westport, CT: Hyperion Press.

Barnouin, Barbara and Changgen Yu (2006), *Zhou Enlai: A Political Life*, Hong Kong: Chinese University Press.

Barro, Robert J. and David B. Gordon (1983), "A Positive Theory of Monetary Policy in a Natural Rate Model," *Journal of Political Economy*, 91(4): 589–610.

Baumol, William (1952), *Welfare Economics and the Theory of the State*, Cambridge, MA: Harvard University Press.

Baumol, William J. (1990), "Entrepreneurship: Productive, Unproductive, and Destructive," *Journal of Political Economy*, 98(5): 893–921.

Beasley, William G. (1972), *The Meiji Restoration*, Stanford, CA: Stanford University Press.

Beasley, William G. (1995), *The Rise of Modern Japan: Political, Economic and Social Change Since 1850*, New York: St. Martin's Press.

Becker, Gary S. (1991), *A Treatise on the Family*, Cambridge, MA: Harvard University Press.

Beckwith, Christopher I. (2009), *Empires of the Silk Road: A History of Central Eurasia from the Bronze Age to the Present*, Princeton, NJ: Princeton University Press.

Benedict, Ruth (1946), *The Chrysanthemum and the Sword: Patterns of Japanese Culture*, Boston, MA: Houghton Mifflin.

Bentley, Jerry H. (1993), *Old World Encounters: Cross-Cultural Contacts and Exchanges in Pre-Modern Times*, Cambridge, MA: Oxford University Press.

Berkowitz, Daniel and Karen B. Clay (2011), *The Evolution of a Nation: How Geography and Law Shaped the American States*, Princeton, NJ: Princeton University Press.

Bianco, Lucien and Chang-ming Hua (1988), "Implementation and Resistance: The Single-Child Family Policy," in *Transforming China's Economy in the Eighties: The Rural Sector, Welfare and Employment*, S. Feuchtwang, A. Hussain, and T. Pairault (ed.), Volume 1, London: Zed Books, pp. 147–168.

Bickers, Robert A. and Jeffrey N. Wasserstrom (1995), "Shanghai's 'Dogs and Chinese Not Admitted' Sign: Legend, History and Contemporary Symbol," *China Quarterly*, 142: 444–466.

Borghans, L., A.L. Duckworth, J.J. Heckman, and B. Ter Weel (2008), "The Economics and Psychology of Personality Traits," *Journal of Human Resources*, 43(4), 972–1059.

Boulger, Demetrius Charles (1893), *China*, New York: Kessinger Publishing.

Bo-Yang (1985), *The Ugly Chinaman and the Crisis of Chinese Culture* (丑陋的中国人), Taipei: Libai Press.

Breen, John (2008), *Yasukuni, the War Dead and the Struggle for Japan's Past*, New York: Columbia University Press.

Brook, Timothy (1998), *The Confusions of Pleasure: Commerce and Culture in Ming China*, Berkeley: University of California Press.

Cameron, L., N. Erkal, L. Gangadharan, and X. Meng (2013), "Little Emperors: Behavioral Impacts of China's One-Child Policy," *Science*, 339(6122): 953–957.

Chang, Jung and Jon Halliday (2005), *Mao: The Unknown Story*, London: Jonathan Cape.

Chen, Li Fei (2006), *The Japanese Comfort Women System: A Critique*, Beijing: Zhonghua Book Company. (in Chinese)

Chen, Qiang (2014), "Natural Disasters, Ethnic Diversity, and the Size of Nations: Two Thousand Years of Unification and Division in Historical China," mimeo, Shandong University.

Chen, Qiang (2015), "Climate Shocks, Dynastic Cycles and Nomadic Conquests: Evidence from Historical China," *Oxford Economic Papers*, 67(2): 185–204.

Chen, Xianchu (2004), *The Upside Down of Humanity: A Research on the Japanese Troops' Atrocities in Hunan Province*, Beijing: Social Sciences Academic Press.

Chen, Zhimin (2005), "Nationalism, Internationalism and Chinese Foreign Policy," *Journal of Contemporary China*, 14(42): 35–53.

Cheung, Steven N.S. (1972), "The Enforcement of Property Rights in Children and the Marriage Contract," *Economic Journal*, 82(326): 641–57.

Chien, Mu (1963), *The Spirit of Chinese History*, Taipei: Guomin Press. (in Chinese)

Ching, Frank (1974), *Ancestors: 900 Years in the Life of a Chinese Family*, New York: William Morrow and Company.

Chung, Joe (2007), *I Don't Want to Be Chinese Again in My Next Lifetime*, Taipei: Yun Chen Culture. (in Chinese)

Clark, Gregory (2007), *A Farewell to Alms: A Brief Economic History of the World*, Princeton, NJ: Princeton University Press.

Coase, Ronald (1937), "The Nature of the Firm," *Economica*, 4(16): 386–405.

Coase, Ronald H. (1960), "The Problem of Social Cost," *Journal of Law and Economics*, 3(1): 1–44.

Coleridge, Henry James (2011), *The Life and Letters of St. Francis Xavier*, Volumes I and II, Lexington, KY: Forgotten Books.

Covey, Stephen R. (1989), *The Seven Habits of Highly Effective People: Restoring the Character Ethic*, New York: Simon and Schuster.

Crocker, H. W. III (2006), *Don't Tread on Me*, New York: Crown Forum.

Cull, Brian (2004), *Hurricanes Over Singapore: RAF, RNZAF and NEI Fighters in Action Against the Japanese Over the Island and the Netherlands East Indies, 1942*, London: Grub Street Publishing.

Dang Nian Ming Yue (2006), *Those Stories in the Ming Dynasty*, www.tianya.cn/bbs/.

Dardess, John W. (2002), *Blood and History in China: The Donglin Faction and Its Repression*, Honolulu: University of Hawai'i Press.

Diamond, Jared (1997), *Guns, Germs, and Steel: The Fates of Human Societies*, New York: W. W. Norton & Company.

Di Cosmo, Nicola (1999), "The Northern Frontier in Pre-Imperial China," in *The Cambridge History of Ancient China*, Michael Loewe and Edward Shaughnessy (ed.), Cambridge and New York: Cambridge University Press.

Dixit, Avinash K. (2007), *Lawlessness and Economics: Alternative Modes of Governance*, Princeton, NJ: Princeton University Press.

Donovan, Robert J. (1996), *Tumultuous Years: The Presidency of Harry S. Truman 1949–1953*, Columbia: University of Missouri Press.

Dorn, Frank (1974), *The Sino–Japanese War, 1937–41: From Marco Polo Bridge to Pearl Harbor*, New York: MacMillan.

Drazen, Allan (2000), *Political Economy in Macroeconomics*, Princeton, NJ: Princeton University Press.

Dumas, Samuel and Knud Otto Vedel-Petersen (1923), *Losses of Life Caused by War*, Oxford: Clarendon Press.

Easterly, William and Ross Levine (1997), "Africa's Growth Tragedy: Policies and Ethnic Divisions," *Quarterly Journal of Economics*, 112(4): 1203–1250.

Ebrey, Patricia (1993), *Chinese Civilization: A Sourcebook*, New York: Simon and Schuster.

Ebrey, Patricia Buckley (1999), *The Cambridge Illustrated History of China*, Cambridge, UK: Cambridge University Press.

Ebrey, Patricia, Anne Walthall, and James Palais (2008), *East Asia: A Cultural, Social, and Political History*, Princeton, NJ: Cengage Learning.

Elleman, Bruce A. (2005), *Modern Chinese Warfare, 1795–1989*, New York: Taylor & Francis.

Elman, Benjamin A. (1991), "Political, Social, and Cultural Reproduction via Civil Service Examinations in Late Imperial China," *Journal of Asian Studies*, 50(1): 7–28.

Elman, Benjamin A. (2000), *A Cultural History of Civil Examinations in Late Imperial China*, Berkeley, Los Angeles, and London: University of California Press.

Fairbank, John King, Kwang-Ching Liu, and Denis Crispin Twitchett (1980), *Late Ch'ing, 1800–1911*, Volume 11, Part 2 of The Cambridge History of China Series (illustrated ed.), Cambridge, UK: Cambridge University Press.

Fairbank, John King and Merle Goldman (2006), *China: A New History*, Cambridge, MA: The Belknap Press of Harvard University Press.

Fan, C. Simon (1998), "Why Has China Been Successful in Attracting Foreign Investment: A Transaction Cost Approach," *Journal of Contemporary China*, 7(17): 21–32.

Fan, C. Simon (2004), "Quality, Trade, and Growth," *Journal of Economic Behavior and Organization*, 55(2): 271–291.

Fan, C. Simon (2005), "Increasing Returns, Product Quality, and International Trade," *Economica*, 72: 151–169.

Fan, C. Simon (2006), "Kleptocracy and Corruption," *Journal of Comparative Economics*, 34(1): 57–74.

Fan, C. Simon (2014), *Vanity Economics: An Economic Exploration of Sex, Marriage and Family*, Cheltenham, UK: Edward Elgar Publishing.

Fan, C. Simon, Na Li, and Xiangdong Wei (2006), "Market Integration between Hong Kong and Chinese Mainland," in *China, Hong Kong, and the World Economy: A Study of Globalization*, Robert Ash and Lok-sang Ho (ed.), Basingstoke, UK: Palgrave, pp. 170–185.

Fan, C. Simon, Chen Lin, and Daniel Treisman (2009), "Political Decentralization and Corruption: Evidence from Around the World," *Journal of Public Economics*, 93(1): 14–34.

Fan, C. Simon, Chen Lin, and Daniel Treisman (2010), "Embezzlement Versus Bribery," NBER Working Papers #16542.

Fan, C. Simon and Oded Stark (2007a), "International Migration and 'Educated Unemployment'," *Journal of Development Economics*, 83(1): 76–87.

Fan, C. Simon and Oded Stark (2007b), "The Brain Drain, 'Educated Unemployment,' Human Capital Formation, and Economic Betterment," *Economics of Transition*, 15(4): 629–660.

Fan, C. Simon and Oded Stark (2008), "Rural-to-Urban Migration, Human Capital, and Agglomeration," *Journal of Economic Behavior and Organization*, 68(1): 234–247.

Fan, C. Simon and Xiangdong Wei (2006), "The Law of One Price: Evidence from the Transitional Economy of China," *Review of Economics and Statistics*, 88(4): 682–697.

Fan, C. Simon, Xiangdong Wei, and Jia Wu (forthcoming), "The Border Effect between Hong Kong and Mainland China," *Pacific Economic Review*.

Fang, Jun (1997), *The Devil Soldiers I Know Of: Notes of a Student Studying in Japan*, Beijing: China Translation Press. (in Chinese)

Farnsworth, Robert M. (1996), *From Vagabond to Journalist: Edgar Snow in Asia, 1928–1941*, Columbia: University of Missouri Press.

Feng, Youlan (1985), Zhongguo zhexue jianshi [A Concise History of Chinese Philosophy], Beijing: Beijing University Press.

Feuerwerker, Albert (1958), *China's Early Industrialization: Sheng Hsuan-Huai (1844–1916) and Mandarin Enterprise*, Cambridge, MA: Harvard University Press.

Fischer, David Hackett (1989), *Albion's Seed: Four British Folkways in America*, New York: Oxford University Press.

Forbes, Andrew D. W. (1986), *Warlords and Muslims in Chinese Central Asia: A Political History of Republican Sinkiang 1911–1949*, Cambridge, UK: Cambridge University Press Archive.

Frank, Richard B. (1999), *Downfall: The End of the Imperial Japanese Empire*, New York: Random House.

Frank, Robert H. (1985), *Choosing the Right Pond: Human Behavior and the Quest for Status*, New York: Oxford University Press.

Frank, Robert H. (2011), *The Darwin Economy: Liberty, Competition and the Common Good*, Princeton, NJ: Princeton University Press.

Freedman, Maurice (1966), *Chinese Lineage and Society: Fukien and Kwangtung*, London: Athlone.

Fu, Zhengyuan (1996), *China's Legalists: The Earliest Totalitarians and Their Art of Ruling*, Armonk, NY: M. E. Sharpe.

Galiani, Sebastian, Gustavo Torrens, and Maria Lucia Yanguas (2014), "The Political Coase Theorem: Experimental Evidence," *Journal of Economic Behavior and Organization*, 103(C): 17–38.

Gallup, John Luke, Jeffrey D Sachs, and Andrew D Mellinger (1999), "Geography and Economic Development," *International Regional Science Review*, 22(2): 179–232.

Gardner, Daniel (1998), "Confucian Commentary and Chinese Intellectual History," *Journal of Asian Studies*, 57(2): 397–422.

Garfinkel, Michelle R. and Stergios Skaperdas (2007), "Economics of Conflict: An Overview," in *Handbook of Defense Economics*, Todd Sandler and Keith Hartley (eds.), Amsterdam: Elsevier, 2: 649–709.

Garfinkel, Michelle R. and Stergios Skaperdas (2012), *The Oxford Handbook of the Economics of Peace and Conflict*, New York: Oxford University Press.

Gifford, Rob (2007), *China Road: A Journey into the Future of a Rising Power*, New York: Random House.

Gilpin, Robert (2001), *Global Political Economy: Understanding the International Economic Order*, Princeton, NJ: Princeton University Press.

Ginsburgh, Victor A. and David Throsby (2006), *Handbook of the Economics of Art and Culture*, Volume 1, Oxford: North-Holland.

Ginsburgh, Victor A. and David Throsby (2014), *Handbook of the Economics of Art and Culture*, Volume 2, Oxford: North-Holland.

Glaeser, Edward L. and Andrei Shleifer (2002), "Legal Origins," *Quarterly Journal of Economics*, 117(4): 1193–1229.

Graff, David Andrew (2002), *Medieval Chinese Warfare, 300–900*, London: Routledge.

Greaves, Percy L. Jr. (2010), *Pearl Harbor: The Seeds and Fruits of Infamy*, Auburn, AL: Ludwig von Mises Institute.

Greenfeld, Liah (1992), *Nationalism: Five Roads to Modernity*, Cambridge, MA: Harvard University Press.

Greenfeld, Liah (2001), *The Spirit of Capitalism: Nationalism and Economic Growth*, Cambridge, MA: Harvard University Press.

Greif, Avner (1994), "Cultural Beliefs and the Organization of Society: A Historical and Theoretical Reflection on Collectivist and Individualist Societies," *Journal of Political Economy*, 102(5): 912–950.

Greif, Avner (2006), *Institutions and the Path to the Modern Economy: Lessons from Medieval Trade*, Cambridge, UK: Cambridge University Press.

Gries, Peter Hays (2003), *China's New Nationalism: Pride, Politics, and Diplomacy*, Berkeley: University of California Press.

Grossman, Herschel I. (1991), "A General Equilibrium Model of Insurrections," *American Economic Review*, 81(4): 912–921.

Grossman, Herschel I. (1999), "Kleptocracy and Revolutions," *Oxford Economic Papers*, 51(2): 267–283.

Grossman, Herschel I. and Suk Jae Noh (1990), "A Theory of Kleptocracy with Probabilistic Survival and Reputation," *Economics and Politics*, 2(2): 157–171.

Guiso, Luigi, Paola Sapienza, and Luigi Zingales (2006), "Does Culture Affect Economic Outcomes?" *Journal of Economic Perspectives*, 20(2): 23–48.

Gunther, John (1942), *Inside Asia – 1942 War Edition*, New York and London: Harper & Bros.

Guy, R. Kent (1987), *The Emperor's Four Treasuries: Scholars and the State in the Late Ch'ien-lung Era*, Cambridge, MA: Harvard University Press.

Hall, John A. (1985), *Power and Liberties*, London: Penguin Books.

Hamilton, John Maxwell (2003), *Edgar Snow: A Biography*, Baton Rouge: Louisiana State University Press.

Harrison, James (1969), *Modern Chinese Nationalism*, New York: Hunter College of the City of New York, Research Institute on Modern Asia.

Harrison, L.E., and S.P. Huntington, S. P. (2000), *Culture Matters: How Values Shape Human Progress*. Basic Books.

Hastings, M. (2007), *Nemesis: The Battle for Japan*, London: Harper Perennial.

Hicks, G.L. (1995), *The Comfort Women*, Australia: Allen & Unwin.

Hicks, John (1969), *A Theory of Economic History*, Oxford: Oxford University Press.

Hirshleifer, Jack (2001), *The Dark Side of the Force: Economic Foundations of Conflict Theory*, Cambridge, UK: Cambridge University Press.

Ho, Ping-ti (1962), *The Ladder of Success in Imperial China: Aspects of Social Mobility, 1368–1911*, New York: Columbia University Press.

Holmstrom, Bengt and Jean Tirole (1989), "The Theory of the Firm," in *Handbook of Industrial Organization*, R. Schmalensee and R. Willig (ed.), Amsterdam and New York: North-Holland; New York: Sole distributors for the U.S.A. and Canada, Elsevier Science Publishing Company, pp. 61–134.

Hsiung, James (1992), *China's Bitter Victory*, Armonk, NY: M. E. Sharpe.

Hsu, Long-hsuen and Ming-kai Chang (1972), *History of the Sino–Japanese War (1937–1945)*, Taipei: Chung Wu Publishing Company.

Hulsewé, A. F. P. (1985), *Remnants of Ch'in Law: An Annotated Translation of the Ch'in Legal and Administrative Rules of the 3rd Century BC* (Sinica Leidensia, No 17), Leiden: Brill.

Iyigun, Murat (2008), "Luther and Suleyman," *Quarterly Journal of Economics*, 123(4): 1465–1494.

Iyigun, Murat (2015), *War, Peace and Prosperity in the Name of God*, Chicago: University of Chicago Press.

Jiang, Yonglin (1997), *The Great Ming Code: A Cosmological Instrument for Transforming "All Under Heaven"*, Minneapolis: University of Minnesota.

Johnson, Chalmers A. (1962), *Peasant Nationalism and Communist Power: The Emergence of Revolutionary China*, Stanford, CA: Stanford University Press.

Karasulas, Antony (2004), *Mounted Archers of the Steppe, 600 BC–AD 1300*, Oxford: Osprey Publishing Company.

Keynes, John Maynard (1936), *General Theory of Employment, Interest and Money*, London: Macmillan.

Kim, Il Myon (1976), *The Emperor's Forces and Korean Comfort Women*, Tokyo: San-ichi Shobo.

Klein, Thoralf (2008), "The Boxer War – The Boxer Uprising," *Online Encyclopedia of Mass Violence*.

Klitgaard, Robert E. (1987), *Controlling Corruption*, Berkeley: University of California Press.

Koo, Telly H. (1920), "The Constitutional Development of the Western Han Dynasty," *Journal of the American Oriental Society*, 40: 170–193.

Kremer, Michael (1993), "The O-Ring Theory of Economic Development," *Quarterly Journal of Economics*, 108(3): 551–575.

Krugman, Paul R., Maurice Obstfeld, and Marc Melitz (2012), *International Economics: Theory and Policy*, Boston: Addison Wesley.

Kuiper, Kathleen (2011), *The Culture of China*, New York: Britannica Educational Publishing in association with Rosen Educational Services.

Kung, James Kai-sing and Chicheng Ma (2014), "Can Cultural Norms Reduce Conflicts? Confucianism and Peasant Rebellions in Qing China," *Journal of Development Economics*, 111: 132–149.

Kydland, Finn E. and Edward C. Prescott (1977), "Rules Rather Than Discretion: The Inconsistency of Optimal Plans," *Journal of Political Economy*, 85(3): 473–491.

Lam, Kai-jin and Jik-ji Zyu (2003), *A Reappraisal of the Opium War*, Hong Kong: Chinese University Press. (in Chinese)

Lazear, Edward (1995), *Personnel Economics*, Cambridge, MA: MIT Press.

Legge, James (1893), *Confucian Analects, the Great Learning, and the Doctrine of the Mean*, Oxford: Clarendon Press.

Levathes, Louise (1996), *When China Ruled the Seas: The Treasure Fleet of the Dragon Throne, 1405–1433*, Oxford: Oxford University Press.

Levitt, Steven D. and Stephen J. Dubner (2005), *Freakonomics: A Rogue Economist Explores the Hidden Side of Everything*, New York: William Morrow.

Levitt, Steven and Sudhir A. Venkatesh (2000), "An Economic Analysis of a Drug-Selling Gang's Finances," *Quarterly Journal of Economics*, 115(3): 755–789.

Li, Yu-ning (1977), *Shang Yang's Reforms*, New York: M. E. Sharpe.

Liang, Qichao (1984), *Collection of Articles by Liang Qichao of His Philosophical Thoughts*, (zhexue sixiang lunwen ji), Beijing: Beijing University Press.

Liang, Qichao (1989), " 'Aiguo lun' ['On Patriotism']," in Yinbingshi heji [Yinbingshi Collected Works], Volume III, Beijing: Zhonghua shuju, p. 66.

Liu, Elaine M., Meng, Juanjuan, and Wang, Joseph Tao-yi (2014), "Confucianism and Preferences: Evidence from Lab Experiments in Taiwan and China," *Journal of Economic Behavior and Organization*, 104(C): 106–122.

Liu, William G. (2006), *Wrestling for Power: The State and Economy in Later Imperial China, 1000–1770*, Ann Arbor, MI: UMI: ProQuest.

Loewe, Michael (2006), *The Government of the Qin and Han Empires: 221 BCE–220 CE*, Indianapolis, IN: Hackett Publishing Company.

Lu, Suping (2004), *They Were in Nanjing: The Nanjing Massacre Witnessed by American and British Nationals*, Hong Kong: Hong Kong University Press.

Lucas, Robert E. (1993), "Making a Miracle," *Econometrica*, 61(2): 251–272.

Lucas, Robert E. Jr. (2001), *Lectures on Economic Growth*, Cambridge, MA: Harvard University Press.

Lu-Xun (1918), *A Madman's Diary* (simplified Chinese: 狂人日记).

Lu-Xun (1921), *The True Story of Ah Q* (阿Q正传).

Ma, Dongyu (2012), Zhongguo zhi tan di yi di: yao kan Yongzheng zhi tan, Beijing: Tuanjie chubanshe.

MacKinnon, Stephen R. (2008), *Wuhan, 1938: War, Refugees, and the Making of Modern China*, Berkeley: University of California Press.

Man, John (2004), *Genghis Khan: Life, Death, and Resurrection*, New York: St. Martin's Press.

Mankiw, N. Gregory (2007), *Principle of Economics*, OH: South-Western Publishers.

McDonald, Ian M. and Robert M. Solow (1981), "Wage Bargaining and Employment," *American Economic Review*, 71(5): 896–908.

Miguel, Edward, Shanker Satyanath, and Ernest Sergenti (2004), "Economic Shocks and Civil Conflict: An Instrumental Variables Approach," *Journal of Political Economy*, 112(4): 725–753.

Mokyr, Joel (2007), "The Market for Ideas and the Origins of Economic Growth in Eighteenth Century Europe," *Tijdshrift voor Sociale en Economische Geschidenis*, 4(1): 3–38.

Montesquieu, Charles de (1989), *The Spirit of the Laws*, Anne M. Cohler, Basia C. Miller, and Harold S. Stone (trans.), Cambridge, UK: Cambridge University Press.

Mountford, Andrew (1997), "Can a Brain Drain Be Good for Growth in the Source Economy?" *Journal of Development Economics*, 53(2): 287–303.

Nash, John F. (1950), "Equilibrium Points in N-person Games," *Proceedings of the National Academy of Sciences*, 36(1), 48–49.

Ni, Shawn and Pham Hoang Van (2006), "High Corruption Income in Ming and Qing China," *Journal of Development Economics*, 81(2): 316–336.

Nisbett, Richard E. and Dov Cohen (1996), *Culture of Honor: The Psychology of Violence in the South*, Boulder, CO: Westview Press.

Nishijima, Sadao (1986), "The Economic and Social History of Former Han," in *Cambridge History of China: Volume I: The Ch'in and Han Empires, 221 B.C. – A.D. 220, 545–607*, Denis Twitchett and Michael Loewe (ed.), Cambridge, UK: Cambridge University Press.

Nitobe, Inazo (1900), *Bushido: The Soul of Japan*, Rutland, VT: Charles E. Tuttle Company. (1969 reprint)

North, Douglass C. (1990), *Institutions, Institutional Change and Economic Performance*, Cambridge, UK: Cambridge University Press.

North, Douglass C. (1991), "Institutions," *Journal of Economic Perspectives*, 5(1): 97–112.

North, Douglass C. and Robert Paul Thomas (1976), *The Rise of the Western World*, Cambridge, UK: Cambridge University Press.

North, Douglass C., John Joseph Wallis, and Barry R. Weingast (2009), *Violence and Social Orders*, Cambridge, UK: Cambridge University Press.

Nunn, Nathan and Diego Puga (2012), "Ruggedness: The Blessing of Bad Geography in Africa," *Review of Economics and Statistics*, 94(1): 20–36.

Olson, Mancur (1993), "Dictatorship, Democracy, and Development," *American Political Science Review*, 87(3): 567–576.

Olson, Mancur (2000), *Power and Prosperity: Outgrowing Communist and Capitalist Dictatorships*, New York: Oxford University Press.

Omata, Yukio (1988), *Memoirs of a Japanese Army Reporter: The Nanjing Massacre*, Beijing: World Knowledge Press. (in Chinese)

Ostrom, Elinor (1990), *Governing the Commons: The Evolution of Institutions for Collective Action*, Cambridge, UK: Cambridge University Press.

Ostrom, Elinor (2010), "Beyond Markets and States: Polycentric Governance of Complex Economic Systems," *American Economic Review*, 100(3): 641–672.

Oxnam, Robert B. (1975), *Ruling from Horseback: Manchu Politics in the Oboi Regency, 1661–1669*, Chicago and London: University of Chicago Press.

Paine, S. C. M. (2003), *The Sino–Japanese War of 1894–1895: Perceptions, Power, and Primacy*, Cambridge, UK: Cambridge University Press.

Parisi, Francesco (2003), "Political Coase Theorem," *Public Choice*, 115(1–2): 1–36.

Paul, T. V. (1994), *Asymmetric Conflicts: War Initiation by Weaker Powers*, New York: Cambridge University Press.

Pestieau, Pierre (2005), *The Welfare State in the European Union: Economic and Social Perspectives*, New York: Oxford University Press.

Pinker, Steven (2011), *The Better Angels of Our Nature*, New York: Viking.

Pirenne, Henri (1925), *Medieval Cities*, New York: Doubleday Anchor Books.

Pollak, Robert A. (1985), "A Transaction Cost Approach to Families and Households," *Journal of Economic Literature*, 23(2): 581–608.

Pomeranz, K. (2000), *The Great Divergence: China, Europe, and the Making of the Modern World Economy*, Princeton: Princeton University Press.

Preston, Diana (2000), *The Boxer Rebellion*, New York: Berkley Books.

Reischauer, Edwin Oldfather, John King Fairbank, and Albert M. Craig (1960), *A History of East Asian Civilization, Volume 1: East Asia: The Great Tradition*, Boston, MA: Houghton Mifflin.

Riker, William H. (1964), *Federalism: Origin, Operation, Significance*, New York: Little Brown.

Rodrik, Dani, Arvind Subramanian, and Francesco Trebbi (2004), "Institutions Rule: The Primacy of Institutions Over Geography and Integration in Economic Development," *Journal of Economic Growth*, 9(2): 131–165.

Roland, Gérard (2000), *Transition and Economics: Politics, Markets, and Firms*, Cambridge, MA: MIT Press.

Rosenberg, N., and L.E. Birdzell (1986), *How the West Grew Rich: The Economic Transformation of the Western World*, London: Basic.

Roy, Denny (2003), *Taiwan: A Political History*, Ithaca and London: Cornell University Press.

Salaff, Janet W. (1976), "Working Daughters in the Hong Kong Chinese Family: Female Filial Piety or a Transformation in the Family Power Structure?" *Journal of Social History*, 9(4): 439–465.

Schmitt, David P., Jüri Allik, Robert R. McCrae, and Verónica Benet-Martínez (2007), "The Geographic Distribution of Big Five Personality Traits Patterns and Profiles of Human Self-Description across 56 Nations," *Journal of Cross-Cultural Psychology*, 38(2): 173–212.

Shapiro, Carl and Joseph E. Stiglitz (1984), "Equilibrium Unemployment as a Worker Discipline Device," *American Economic Review*, 74(3): 433–444.

Shils, Edward A. and Morris Janowitz (1948), "Cohesion and Disintegration in the Wehrmacht in World War II," *Public Opinion Quarterly*, 12(2): 280–315.

Shleifer, Andrei and Robert W. Vishny (1993), "Corruption," *Quarterly Journal of Economics*, 108(3): 599–617.

Smith, Adam (1759), *The Theory of Moral Sentiment*, reprinted in D. D. Raphael and A. L. Macfie (ed.) (1976), Glasgow Edition of the Works and Correspondence of Adam Smith, Volume 7, Oxford: Oxford University Press.

Smith, Arthur Henderson (1894), *Chinese Characteristics*, New York: Revell.

Sniderman, Paul M. (1993), "Personality and Democratic Politics," in *Political Psychology: Classic and Contemporary Readings*, Neil J. Kressel (ed.), New York: Paragon House, pp. 154–166.

So, Kwan-wai (1975), *Japanese Piracy in Ming China during the 16th Century*, East Lansing: Michigan State University Press.

Sokoloff, Kenneth L. and Stanley L. Engerman (2000), "Institutions, Factor Endowments, and Paths of Development in the New World," *Journal of Economic Perspectives*, 14(3): 217–232.

Spence, A. Michael (1973), "Job Market Signaling," *Quarterly Journal of Economics*, 87(3): 355–374.

Spence, A. Michael (1974), *Market Signaling: Informational Transfer in Hiring and Related Screening Processes*, Cambridge, MA: Harvard University Press.

Spence, Jonathan D. (1999), *The Search for Modern China*, New York: W. W. Norton & Company.

Stark, Oded and C. Simon Fan (2007), "Losses and Gains to Developing Countries from the Migration of Educated Workers: An Overview of Recent Research, and New Reflections," *World Economics*, 8(2): 259–269.

Stark, Oded and C. Simon Fan (2011), "The Prospect of Migration, Sticky Wages, and 'Educated Unemployment'," *Review of International Economics*, 19(2): 277–287.

Stark, Oded, Christian Helmenstein, and Alexia Prskawetz (1997), "A Brain Gain with a Brain Drain," *Economics Letters*, 55(2): 227–234.

Stark, Oded, Christian Helmenstein, and Alexia Prskawetz (1998), "Human Capital Depletion, Human Capital Formation, and Migration: A Blessing or a 'Curse'?" *Economics Letters*, 60(3): 363–367.

Stark, Oded and Yong Wang (2002), "Inducing Human Capital Formation: Migration as a Substitute for Subsidies," *Journal of Public Economics*, 86(1): 29–46.

Steil, Benn (2013), *The Battle of Bretton Woods: John Maynard Keynes, Harry Dexter White, and the Making of a New World Order*, Princeton, NJ: Princeton University Press.

Suen, H. K. (2005), "The Hidden Cost of Education Fever: Consequences of the Kwago-Driven Education Fever in Ancient China," in *Education Fever in Korea,*

Education Fever in the World: Analyses and Policies, Jong-gak Lee (ed.), Seoul, Korea: Ha-woo Publishing Company, pp. 299–334.

Sweeny, Charles (1946), *Pearl Harbor*, Salt Lake City, UT: Arrow Press.

Syat, Yabu, Sekai Koh, and Chengfeng Shih (2001), Wu she shi jian: Tai wan ren de ji ti ji yi [Wushe Incident: Taiwanese Collective Memory], Taipei: Avanguard Publishing. (in Chinese)

Tada Corps, Chief of Staff (1941), Chugo kyosanto undo no kaisetsu [Explanation of the Chinese Communist Movement], Beijing, February 17, 1941.

Tapas, Kumu (2004), Bu luo ji yi: Wu she shi jian de kou shu li shi [Tribal Memory: Oral History of the Wushe Events], Taipei: Hanlu.

Taylor, Jay (2009), *The Generalissimo: Chiang Kai-Shek and the Struggle for Modern China*, Cambridge, MA: Harvard University Press.

Thomas, S. Bernard (1996), *Season of High Adventure: Edgar Snow in China*, Berkeley: University of California Press.

Thompson, Larry Clinton (2009), *William Scott Ament and the Boxer Rebellion: Heroism, Hubris and the "Ideal Missionary"*, Jefferson, NC: McFarland & Company.

Throsby, David (2000), *Economics and Culture*, New York: Cambridge University Press.

Throsby, David (2010), *The Economics of Cultural Policy*, New York: Cambridge University Press.

Treisman, Daniel (2007), *The Architecture of Government*, Cambridge, UK: Cambridge University Press.

Treisman, Daniel (2014), "Income, Democracy, and Leader Turnover," *American Journal of Political Science*, 59(4): 927–942.

Tsunoda, Ryusaku (1951), *Japan in the Chinese Dynastic Histories: Later Han through Ming Dynasties*, Ryūsaku Tsunoda (trans.), Carrington C. Goodrich (ed.), South Pasadena: P. D. and Ione Perkins.

Turchin, Peter (2003), *Historical Dynamics: Why States Rise and Fall*, Princeton, NJ: Princeton University Press.

Turchin, Peter (2009), "A Theory for Formation of Large Empires," *Journal of Global History*, 4(2): 191–217.

Turnbull, Stephen (2003), *Samurai: World of the Warrior*, Oxford: Osprey.

Van De Ven, Hans J. (2012), *War and Nationalism in China, 1925–1945*, London and New York: Routledge.

Veblen, Thorstein (1899), *The Theory of the Leisure Class*, New York: Macmillan.

Vira, Bhaskar (1997), "The Political Coase Theorem: Identifying Differences between Neoclassical and Critical Institutionalism," *Journal of Economic Issues*, 31(3): 761–779.

Wakeman, Frederic, Jr. (1972), "The Price of Autonomy: Intellectuals in Ming and Ch'ing Politics," *Daedalus: Journal of the American Academy of Arts and Sciences*, 101(2): 35–70.

Weil, David N. (2009), *Economic Growth*, Boston: Pearson Addison Wesley.

Weimer, D.L. (1995), *Institutional Design*, Boston: Kluwer Academic Publishers.

Weimer, D.L. (1997), *The Political Economy of Property Rights: Institutional Change and Credibility in the Reform of Centrally Planned Economies*, New York: Cambridge University Press.

Williamson, Oliver E. (1979), "Transaction-Cost Economics: The Governance of Contractual Relations," *Journal of Law and Economics*, 22(2): 233–261.

Williamson, Oliver E. (1981), "The Economics of Organization: The Transaction Cost Approach," *American Journal of Sociology*, 87(3): 548–577.

Williamson, Oliver E. (1985), *The Economic Institutions of Capitalism: Firms, Markets, Relational Contracting*, New York: Free Press.

Williamson, Oliver E. (1996), *The Mechanisms of Governance*, New York: Oxford University Press.

Williamson, Oliver E. (2000), "The New Institutional Economics: Taking Stock, Looking Ahead," *Journal of Economic Literature*, 38(3): 595–613.

Wills, John E. (1994), *Mountain of Fame: Portraits in Chinese History*, Princeton, NJ: Princeton University Press.

Wright, Richard N. J. (2001), *The Chinese Steam Navy, 1862–1945*, London: Conway Maritime Press.

Wu, K. C. (1982), *The Chinese Heritage*, New York: Crown Publishers.

Yamamuro, Shin'ichi (2006), *Manchuria under Japanese Dominion*, Philadelphia: University of Pennsylvania Press.

Yao, Xinzhong (2000), *An Introduction to Confucianism*, Cambridge, UK: Cambridge University Press.

Yap, Joseph P. (2009), *Wars with the Xiongnu: A Translation from Zizhi Tongjian*, Bloomington, IN: AuthorHouse.

Yoshimi, Yoshiaki (2002), *Comfort Women, Sexual Slavery in the Japanese Military during World War II*, New York: Columbia University Press.

Young, Crawford (1994), *The African Colonial State in Comparative Perspective*, New Haven, CT: Yale University Press.

Zeiler, Thomas W. (2004), *Unconditional Defeat: Japan, America, and the End of World War II*, Wilmington, DE: Scholarly Resources.

Zhang, Hong (2002), *America Perceived: The Making of Chinese Images of the United States, 1945–1953*, Westport, CT: Greenwood Publishing Group.

Zhao, Suisheng (2004), *A Nation-State by Construction: Dynamics of Modern Chinese Nationalism*, Stanford, CA: Stanford University Press.

Zou, Jiwan (1992), *Chinese History: History of the Wei, Jin, and Southern and Northern Dynasties (Zhongguo Tongshi – Weijin Nanbeichao Shi)*, Taipei: Chung Wen Book Company. (in Chinese)

Index